First World War
and Army of Occupation
War Diary
France, Belgium and Germany

51 DIVISION
Divisional Troops
Machine Gun Corps
51 Battalion
19 February 1918 - 28 February 1919

WO95/2857/2

The Naval & Military Press Ltd
www.nmarchive.com
Published in association with The National Archives

Published by

The Naval & Military Press Ltd

Unit 10 Ridgewood Industrial Park,
Uckfield, East Sussex,
TN22 5QE England
Tel: +44 (0) 1825 749494

www.naval-military-press.com
www.nmarchive.com

This diary has been reprinted in facsimile from the original. Any imperfections are inevitably reproduced and the quality may fall short of modern type and cartographic standards.

© **Crown Copyright**
Images reproduced by permission of The National Archives, London, England, 2015.

Contents

Document type	Place/Title	Date From	Date To
Heading	WO95/2857/2		
Heading	51 Division 51 Bn Machine Gun Corps 1918 Mar 1919 Feb		
Heading	War Diary 51st Battalion Machine Gun Corps March 1918		
Heading	War Diary Of 51st (Highland) Bn Machine Gun Corps From 1st March 1918 To 31st March 1918 Volume I		
War Diary	In The Field	19/02/1918	31/03/1918
Heading	51st Battalion Machine Gun Corps April 1918 Appendix- Account Of Operations 9th-12th		
Heading	51st Battalion Machine Gun Battalion		
Heading	War Diary Of 51st (H) Bn M.G Corps For April 1918		
War Diary	In The Field	01/04/1918	30/04/1918
Miscellaneous	51st (H) Battalion, M.G. Corps	09/04/1918	09/04/1918
Heading	War Diary Of 51st (H) Bn. M.G. Corps From 1st May 1918 To 31st May 1918		
War Diary	Field	01/05/1918	31/05/1918
Operation(al) Order(s)	51st (H) Battalion M.G. Corps Operation Order No. 10	03/05/1918	03/05/1918
Miscellaneous	51st (H) Battalion M.G. Corps Operation Order No. 16	16/05/1918	16/05/1918
Operation(al) Order(s)	51st (H) Battalion M.G. Corps Operation Order No. 17	26/05/1918	26/05/1918
Operation(al) Order(s)	51st (H) Battalion M.G. Corps Operation Order No. 18	21/05/1918	21/05/1918
Operation(al) Order(s)	51st (H) Battalion M.G. Corps Operation Order No. 19	27/05/1918	27/05/1918
Heading	War Diary Of 51st (H) Bn M.G. Corps For June 1918		
War Diary		01/06/1918	30/06/1918
Operation(al) Order(s)	51st (H) Battalion M.G. Corps Operation Order No. 20	02/06/1918	02/06/1918
Operation(al) Order(s)	51st (H) Battalion M.G. Corps Operation Order No. 22	03/08/1918	03/08/1918
Operation(al) Order(s)	51st (H) Battalion M.G. Corps Operation Order No. 21	05/06/1918	05/06/1918
Operation(al) Order(s)	51st (H) Battalion M.G. Corps Operation Order No. 23	13/08/1918	13/08/1918
Operation(al) Order(s)	51st (H) Battalion M.G. Corps Operation Order No. 24	14/06/1918	14/06/1918
Operation(al) Order(s)	51st (H) Battalion M.G. Corps Operation Order No. 25	16/06/1918	16/06/1918
Operation(al) Order(s)	51st (H) Battalion M.G. Corps Operation Order No. 26	19/06/1918	19/06/1918
Miscellaneous	51st (H) Battalion Machine Gun Corps.	19/06/1918	19/06/1918
Miscellaneous	Ref. Operation Order No. 26	19/06/1918	19/06/1918
Operation(al) Order(s)	51st (H) Battalion M.G. Corps Operation Order No. 27	20/06/1918	20/06/1918
Operation(al) Order(s)	51st (H) Battalion M.G. Corps Operation Order No. 28	21/06/1918	21/06/1918
Operation(al) Order(s)	51st (H) Battalion M.G. Corps Operation Order No. 29	26/06/1918	26/06/1918
Heading	51st Batt. Machine Gun Corps. July 1918.		
Heading	War Diary Of 51st (H) Bn. Machine Gun Corps for July 1918		
War Diary		01/07/1918	31/07/1918
Miscellaneous	The Undermentioned Operation Orders		
Operation(al) Order(s)	51st (H) Battalion M.G. Corps Operation Order No. 30	02/07/1918	02/07/1918
Operation(al) Order(s)	51st (H) Battalion M.G. Corps Operation Order No. 52	09/07/1918	09/07/1918
Operation(al) Order(s)	51st (H) Battalion M.G. Corps Operation Order No. 33	09/07/1918	09/07/1918
Operation(al) Order(s)	51st (H) Battalion M.G. Corps Operation Order No. 34	10/07/1918	10/07/1918
Operation(al) Order(s)	51st (H) Battalion M.G. Corps Operation Order No. 35	11/07/1918	11/07/1918
Miscellaneous	Reference Operation Order No. 37	14/07/1918	14/07/1918
Miscellaneous	Warning Order	15/07/1918	15/07/1918
Operation(al) Order(s)	Operation Order No. 38	19/07/1918	19/07/1918
Operation(al) Order(s)	51st (H) Battalion M.G. Corps Operation Order No. 39	19/07/1918	19/07/1918

Type	Description	Date From	Date To
Operation(al) Order(s)	51st (H) Battalion M.G. Corps Operation Order No. 40	21/07/1918	21/07/1918
Operation(al) Order(s)	51st (H) Battalion M.G. Corps Operation Order No. 41	22/07/1918	22/07/1918
Operation(al) Order(s)	51st (H) Battalion M.G. Corps Operation Order No. 42	26/07/1918	26/07/1918
Miscellaneous	Detailed Instructions To Accompany Operation Order No. 42	26/07/1918	26/07/1918
Operation(al) Order(s)	51st (H) Battalion M.G. Corps Operation Order No. 43	26/07/1918	26/07/1918
Operation(al) Order(s)	51st (H) Battalion M.G. Corps Operation Order No. 44		
Operation(al) Order(s)	51st (H) Battalion M.G. Corps Operation Order No. 45	28/07/1918	28/07/1918
Operation(al) Order(s)	51st (H) Battalion M.G. Corps Operation Order No. 46	31/07/1918	31/07/1918
Map	Map		
Miscellaneous	Combined Reims & Chalons 1/2000		
Map	Map		
Miscellaneous	Divisional Map 21-7-18	21/07/1918	21/07/1918
Miscellaneous	51st (H) Battalion, M.G. Corps.	19/07/1918	19/07/1918
Heading	War Diary Of 51st (H) Bn. M.G. Corps For Aug. 1918		
War Diary		01/08/1918	31/08/1918
Miscellaneous	Honours And Awards		
Operation(al) Order(s)	51st (H) Battalion M.G. Corps Operation Order No. 48	01/08/1918	01/08/1918
Operation(al) Order(s)	51st (H) Battalion M.G. Corps Operation Order No. 49	13/08/1918	13/08/1918
Miscellaneous	Amendment Of Operation Order No. 49	14/08/1918	14/08/1918
Operation(al) Order(s)	51st (H) Battalion M.G. Corps Operation Order No. 50		
Operation(al) Order(s)	51st (H) Battalion M.G. Corps Operation Order No. 50	13/08/1918	13/08/1918
Miscellaneous	A Form Messages And Signals		
Operation(al) Order(s)	51st (H) Battalion M.G. Corps Operation Order No. 51	17/08/1918	17/08/1918
Operation(al) Order(s)	51st (H) Battalion M.G. Corps Operation Order No. 52	12/08/1918	12/08/1918
Operation(al) Order(s)	51st (H) Battalion M.G. Corps Operation Order No. 54	20/08/1918	20/08/1918
Operation(al) Order(s)	51st (H) Battalion M.G. Corps Operation Order No. 55	20/08/1918	20/08/1918
Miscellaneous	51st (H) Battalion M.G.Corps Warning Order	21/08/1918	21/08/1918
Diagram etc	Diagram		
Operation(al) Order(s)	51st (H) Battalion M.G. Corps Operation Order No. 53	26/08/1918	26/08/1918
Operation(al) Order(s)	51st (H) Battalion M.G. Corps Operation Order No. 56	25/08/1918	25/08/1918
Operation(al) Order(s)	51st (H) Battalion M.G. Corps Operation Order No. 57	24/08/1918	24/08/1918
Miscellaneous	Addendum To Operation Order No. 57	25/08/1918	25/08/1918
Miscellaneous	51st (II) Battalion, C.Corps	24/08/1918	24/08/1918
Miscellaneous	51st (H) Battalion M.G. Corps Operation Order No. 58	24/08/1918	24/08/1918
Miscellaneous	A Form Messages And Signals		
Operation(al) Order(s)	51st (H) Battalion M.G. Corps Operation Order No. 59	25/08/1918	25/08/1918
Diagram etc	Diagram		
Map	Map		
Miscellaneous	51st (H) Bn MGC Fire Organisation Orders		
Miscellaneous	51st (H) Battalion, M.G. Corps.		
Operation(al) Order(s)	51st (H) Battalion M.G. Corps Operation Order No. 60	26/08/1918	26/08/1918
Map	Map		
Operation(al) Order(s)	Secret 0.0.57		
Miscellaneous	O.C. "A" Coy. 101st Bn. M.G. Corps.	27/08/1918	27/08/1918
Operation(al) Order(s)	51st (H) Battalion M.G. Corps Operation Order No. 61	27/08/1918	27/08/1918
Operation(al) Order(s)	51st (H) Battalion M.G. Corps Operation Order No. 62	23/09/1918	23/09/1918
Diagram etc	Diagram		
Map	Map		
Miscellaneous	A Coy 101st Bn. M.G.C.	29/08/1918	29/08/1918
Miscellaneous	51st (H) Battalion M.G.Corps Warning Order	29/08/1918	29/08/1918
Operation(al) Order(s)	51st (H) Battalion M.G. Corps Operation Order No. 63	30/08/1918	30/08/1918
Miscellaneous	O.G., "A" Coy.	25/08/1918	25/08/1918
Diagram etc	Diagram		
Map	Map		
Diagram etc	Tracing "A"		

Miscellaneous	Amendment To Operation Order No. 63	31/08/1918	31/08/1918
Miscellaneous	51st (H) Battalion, M.G. Corps.	30/08/1918	30/08/1918
Miscellaneous	Instruction For Statement Of 51st (H) Division	31/07/1918	31/07/1918
Miscellaneous Operation(al) Order(s)	51st (H) Battalion M.G. Corps Operation Order No. 47	31/07/1918	31/07/1918
War Diary	Field	01/09/1918	30/09/1918
Operation(al) Order(s)	51st (H) Battalion M.G. Corps Operation Order No. 64	01/09/1918	01/09/1918
Miscellaneous	Amendment No.2 At Operation Order No. 63	01/09/1918	01/09/1918
Miscellaneous	51st (H) Battalion, M.G. Corps.	03/09/1918	03/09/1918
Operation(al) Order(s)	51st (H) Battalion M.G. Corps Operation Order No. 65	05/09/1918	05/09/1918
Operation(al) Order(s)	51st (H) Battalion M.G. Corps Operation Order No. 66	04/09/1918	04/09/1918
Operation(al) Order(s)	51st (H) Battalion M.G. Corps Operation Order No. 67	09/09/1918	09/09/1918
Operation(al) Order(s)	51st (H) Battalion M.G. Corps Operation Order No. 68	10/09/1918	10/09/1918
Miscellaneous	Amendment To Operation Order No. 67	11/09/1918	11/09/1918
Operation(al) Order(s)	51st (H) Battalion M.G. Corps Operation Order No. 69	11/09/1918	11/09/1918
Miscellaneous	Table To Accompany Operation Order No. 69	11/09/1918	11/09/1918
Miscellaneous	51st (H) Battalion Machine Gun Corps	12/09/1918	12/09/1918
Miscellaneous	Amendment To Operation Order No. 69	12/09/1918	12/09/1918
Operation(al) Order(s)	51st (H) Battalion M.G. Corps Operation Order No. 70	21/09/1918	21/09/1918
Miscellaneous	Relief Chart To Accompany Operation Order No. 70	21/09/1918	21/09/1918
Miscellaneous	Amendment To Operation Order No. 70	21/09/1918	21/09/1918
Operation(al) Order(s)	51st (H) Battalion M.G. Corps Operation Order No. 71	22/09/1918	22/09/1918
Miscellaneous	51st (H) Battalion, M.G. Corps.	22/09/1918	22/09/1918
Operation(al) Order(s)	51st (H) Battalion M.G. Corps Operation Order No. 72	26/09/1918	26/09/1918
Miscellaneous	Addendum To 51st (H) Battalion M.G. Corps Operation Order No. 72	26/09/1918	26/09/1918
Miscellaneous	Instructions In Case Of Enemy Withdrawal	27/09/1918	27/09/1918
Heading	War Diary Of 51st (H) Bn. M.G. Corps For October 1918		
War Diary		01/10/1918	31/10/1918
Miscellaneous	51st (H) Battalion M.G.Corps Warning Order	01/10/1918	01/10/1918
Miscellaneous	Addendum To Operation Order No. 73		
Miscellaneous	51st (H) Battalion Machine Gun Corps Warning Order	05/10/1918	05/10/1918
Operation(al) Order(s)	51st (H) Battalion M.G. Corps Operation Order No. 74	05/10/1918	05/10/1918
Miscellaneous	Addendum No.2 To Operation Order No. 74	07/10/1918	07/10/1918
Miscellaneous	Administrative Instructions To Accompany Operation Order No. 75		
Operation(al) Order(s)	51st (H) Battalion M.G. Corps Operation Order No. 75	09/10/1918	09/10/1918
Miscellaneous	Amendment To Operation Order No. 75	09/10/1918	09/10/1918
Miscellaneous	Addendum No.2 To Operation Order No. 75	10/10/1918	10/10/1918
Miscellaneous	51st (H) Battalion Machine Gun Corps	12/10/1918	12/10/1918
Miscellaneous	O.C., "B" Company, 51st (H) Bn. M.G.O.	12/10/1918	12/10/1918
Operation(al) Order(s)	51st (H) Battalion M.G. Corps Operation Order No. 73	14/10/1918	14/10/1918
Operation(al) Order(s)	51st (H) Battalion Machine Gun Corps Operation Order No. 77	17/10/1918	17/10/1918
Miscellaneous	Instructions For Barrage Groups To Accompany		
Operation(al) Order(s)	51st (Highland) Battalion Machine Gun Corps Operation Order No. 78	18/10/1918	18/10/1918
Map	Map		
Miscellaneous	Instructions For Barrage Groups		
Miscellaneous	Fire Organisation Orders To Accompany Operation Order No. 78		
Miscellaneous	Orders For Assembly Of Barrage Group To Accompany O.O No.78		
Diagram etc	Diagram		
Map	Map		

Miscellaneous	Copy No.13	19/10/1918	19/10/1918
Miscellaneous	51st (H) Battalion, M.G. Corps.	19/10/1918	19/10/1918
Miscellaneous	51st (H) Battalion Machine Gun Corps.	21/10/1918	21/10/1918
Operation(al) Order(s)	51st (H) Battalion M.G. Corps Operation Order No. 79	22/10/1918	22/10/1918
Miscellaneous	O.O. "C" Coy.	22/10/1918	22/10/1918
Operation(al) Order(s)	51st (H) Battalion Machine Gun Corps Operation Order No. 80	23/10/1918	23/10/1918
Diagram etc	Diagram		
Map	Map		
Miscellaneous	Instructions For Barrage Groups To Accompany O.O. 80		
Miscellaneous	Fire Organisation Orders To Accompany Operation Order No. 80		
Miscellaneous	Addendum To Operation Order No. 80	23/10/1918	23/10/1918
Operation(al) Order(s)	51st (H) Battalion Machine Gun Corps Operation Order No. 81	24/10/1918	24/10/1918
Map	Map		
Miscellaneous	Instructions For The Assembly Of Guns	25/10/1918	25/10/1918
Map	Map		
Miscellaneous	Reference Map Maing, 1/20,000	25/10/1918	25/10/1918
Operation(al) Order(s)	51st (H) Battalion M.G. Corps Operation Order No. 82	25/10/1918	25/10/1918
Operation(al) Order(s)	51st (H) Battalion Machine Gun Corps Operation Order No. 83	26/10/1918	26/10/1918
Operation(al) Order(s)	51st (H) Battalion Machine Gun Corps Operation Order No. 84	26/10/1918	26/10/1918
Operation(al) Order(s)	51st (H) Battalion Machine Gun Corps Operation Order No. 85	27/10/1918	27/10/1918
Diagram etc	Diagram		
Map	Map		
Operation(al) Order(s)	51st (H) Battalion Machine Gun Corps Operation Order No. 86	28/10/1918	28/10/1918
Operation(al) Order(s)	51st (H) Battalion Machine Gun Corps Operation Order No. 87	30/10/1918	30/10/1918
Miscellaneous	Table To Accompany 51st (H) Bn.M.G.C. Operation Order No. 87		
Miscellaneous	Report On Operations, N.E. Of Cambrai	11/10/1918	11/10/1918
Miscellaneous	Lessons Learnt.		
Heading	War Diary Of 51st (H) Bn. M.G. Corps From 1st To 30th November 1918		
War Diary		01/11/1918	30/11/1918
Heading	War Diary Of 51st Bn. M.G. Corps For December 1918		
War Diary	Field	01/12/1918	31/12/1918
Heading	War Diary Of 51st (H) Bn M.G Corps For January 1919		
War Diary	Field	01/01/1919	31/01/1919
Operation(al) Order(s)	51st (H) Battalion M G Corps Operation Order No. 88	11/01/1919	11/01/1919
Miscellaneous	Amendment To Operation Order No. 88		
Miscellaneous	Amendment No.2 To Operation Order No. 88	12/01/1919	12/01/1919
War Diary	Field	01/02/1919	28/02/1919
Miscellaneous	D.A.D.S. 51st (4) Division	03/04/1919	03/04/1919

W095/28572

51 DIVISION

51 BN MACHINE GUN CORPS

1918 MAR — 1919 FEB

51st Divisional M.G.C.

WAR DIARY

51st BATTALION

MACHINE GUN CORPS

MARCH 1918

51st Divisional M.G.C.

CONFIDENTIAL.

WAR DIARY.

of

51st (Highland) Bn. Machine Gun Corps.

from 1st March 1918 to 31st March 1918

Volume. I

Army Form C. 2118.

WAR DIARY
or
INTELLIGENCE SUMMARY.

(Erase heading not required.)

Instructions regarding War Diaries and Intelligence Summaries are contained in F. S. Regs., Par II. and the Staff Manual respectively. Title pages will be prepared in manuscript.

Place	Date	Hour	Summary of Events and Information	Remarks and references to Appendices

A6945 Wt.W14927/M1160 35,000 12/16 D.D. & L. Forms/C/2118/14.

WAR DIARY
INTELLIGENCE SUMMARY.
(Erase heading not required.)

Army Form C. 2118.

Place	Date	Hour	Summary of Events and Information	Remarks and references to Appendices
In the field	1918 19.3.18		Formation of 51st (Highland) Battn. M.G.C. FREMICOURT.	See
	22.3.18		Arrival of 2nd in command and Adjutant at 51 (H) Divisional H.Q. from ENGLAND. Companies still under their own organisation. 152nd M.G. Coy. in rest billets at ARTILLERY CAMP. FREMICOURT. 153rd M.G. Coy., 154th M.G. Coy., & 133rd M.G. Coy. in the line.	
	2 M'ch		Battalion H.Q. established at LINDOP CAMP. FREMICOURT. 152nd M.G. Coy. becomes "A" Coy. 51st (H) Battn. M.G.C. 153rd " " "B" Coy " " " 154th " " "C" Coy " " " 133rd " " "D" Coy " " " Reorganisation of the positions on the front - 3 Coys in the line each holding its own front, organised in depth and finding its own reliefs. This demanded 2 sections of each coy in the line, echelond in depth, and one section of each coy in reserve billets, but relief the four reserve sections form a	

WAR DIARY
INTELLIGENCE SUMMARY.
(Erase heading not required.)

Army Form C. 2118.

Place	Date	Hour	Summary of Events and Information	Remarks and references to Appendices
			Divisional Reserve of 16 guns. Order on the Divisional front from the right: "C" Coy, "A" Coy, "D" Coy, "B" Coy.	9ac.
	11 Mch		Two reserve guns of "C" Coy move into the reserve positions in the line. Guns in reserve – 14.	9ac.
	12 Mch		Has two reserve guns of "C" Coy move into the line. No reserve guns each of "D" Coy, "D" Coy, and "B" Coy move into the line – Guns in Divisional Reserve – 6.	9ac.
	19 Mch		Preparation for enemy offensive. 58 guns of the 51(H) Batt: M.G.C. 8 guns of the 25th Batt. M.G.C. in all 66 guns were distributed on the Divisional front in a depth of over 4000 yards from our front line.	9ac.
	21 Mch 5pm		6 guns of 51(H) Bath: M.G.C. were in Reserve in vicinity of LEBUCQUIÈRE. During the German offensive with intense bombardment left flank of Division threatened to be heavily engaged. 600 guns in Divisional Reserve were moved to numerously return shooting on left flank to reinforce in attack the BEAUMETZ-MORCHIES Line. During the day a Brigade of the 25th Division reinforced the left flank of the Division along with a Machine Gun Coy of the 25th Bn M.G.C. Battn: transport concentrated during the afternoon between PAPRUME and FREMICOURT. At the end of the day 41 guns of the 51(H) Bn M.G.C. were still in action; the right flank of the Division was withdrawn during the night to a line running from the intermediate line north of HERMIES thence	9ac.
	21/22			

Army Form C. 2118.

WAR DIARY
INTELLIGENCE SUMMARY.
(Erase heading not required.)

Place	Date	Hour	Summary of Events and Information	Remarks and references to Appendices
			Through the month of Douignies to the Beaumetz-Morchies line E. of Beaumetz.	
			13 guns which were holding out on the Right flank its front of this	
			were successfully withdrawn and were echeloned from the intermediate	
			line to a depth of 1500 yards behind the Beaumetz-Morchies line	9a.c.
			During the day the night of the line were forced back on the Beaumetz-	
	22 mch		Morchies line running into Target 76. N.W. of Hermies and during the enemy	
			a heavy enveloping attack on the left flank, the direction of Morchies forced	
			the Bn. front on to the line Morchies-Beetroot-Factory Road during the month	
			line (Beaumetz-Morchies) was worked even where the rest of Beaumetz. fighting out	
			with the Beetroot Factory on the Cambrai Road	
			At the end of the day 27 guns were still in action	
			Batn. H.Q. moved to Grevillers in the afternoon and handed to	
			Grevillers - Irles Road	
			During the night two guns complete 20,000 rounds in belts and 8,000 in	9a.c.
			belts were sent up to "A" & "C" Coy. H.Q. in I.26.L and 1 obtained.	

WAR DIARY
or
INTELLIGENCE SUMMARY.
(Erase heading not required.)

Army Form C. 2118.

Place	Date	Hour	Summary of Events and Information	Remarks and references to Appendices
	23 Mch		Continuous fighting took place all along the line. The 19th Division had taken over the Green Line behind the Division. The left flank of the Division was heavily engaged and driven in. The Division on the right retired in accordance with a pre-arranged scheme, and the right flank of the Division fought a rear-guard action passing through the 19th Division line and concentrating round BARCOURT. Major HESCOURT OC C Coy 51(4) Batn. M.G.C. in command at his 4 Gun held the position for 5 hours enabling the right flank of the Division to retire. During the day a complete muddle to guns were sent up to FREMICOURT. These took up positions in the new Divisional Line (GREEN LINE) BARCOURT — RIENCOURT — outskirts of VILLERS-AU-FLOS.	
	24 Mch		During the morning the enemy attacked the green line on the right of the Divisional Front and breaking it turned the right flank of the BARCOURT — VILLERS-AU-FLOS line. The right flank of this line	9 a.e.

WAR DIARY or INTELLIGENCE SUMMARY

Army Form C. 2118.

Place	Date	Hour	Summary of Events and Information	Remarks and references to Appendices
			fell back to positions about BEAULENCOURT. The 19th Division passed through the Division's line to positions N. of BAPAUME and towards evening the RIENCOURT- BEAULENCOURT LINE was withdrawn. The Division having through the 19th Division assembled in the LOUPART WOOD - WARLENCOURT LINE taking such on a composite battalion holding the line with this composite battalion one a M.G. Coy of 16 having which had been formed during the afternoon at GREVILLERS, of various details of various parties which had been sent over from the new dump, the guns of this Bn. were in position from LOUPART WOOD to the ALBERT-BAPAUME ROAD near the BUTTE de WARLENCOURT. Battn. H.Q. moved during afternoon to ACHIET-LE-PETIT. Transport moved to MIRAUMONT.	9a.c.
	26 M.L		LOUPART WOOD - WARLENCOURT LINE continued to be going from RIENCOURT LINE held Battn. the day, but towards evening was passed back as there was no both banks away. Battn. H.Q. moved to PUISIEUX-AU-MONT, during the morning to CLINCAMPS and at night to FONQUEVILLERS	9a.c.

WAR DIARY

INTELLIGENCE SUMMARY.

(Erase heading not required.)

Army Form C. 2118.

Instructions regarding War Diaries and Intelligence Summaries are contained in F. S. Regs., Part II. and the Staff Manual respectively. Title pages will be prepared in manuscript.

Place	Date	Hour	Summary of Events and Information	Remarks and references to Appendices
	25/III/18	2 am	Transport moved to near FORCEVILLE	
			During night transport moved to near FORCEVILLERS	9 a.c
	25/3/18		During night the Division was withdrawn and concentrating at COLINCAMPS and SAILLY-AU-BOIS, the M.G. Coy. concentrating near SAILLY-AU-BOIS.	9 a.c
	26 Mch		At dawn a Divisional outpost line with 2 guns was put out E of SAILLY-AU-BOIS. This line was withdrawn about 9 am to positions E. of SOUASTRE.	
			then B.Q. moved to SOUASTRE.	
			At 4 p.m. a firm line had been established around SOUASTRE.	
			At a later hour we were relieved by a M.G. Coy. of the 3rd Australian Division.	
			We casualties during the two days of fighting by the 2 coys. were as follows:— Major D.N. HIMBERLEY Wounded. Lieut D.N. MENZIES Missing.
			" H.C. HARCOURT " " J.M. HENDRY "
			" W.J. LOYE " " E.V. CULLY "
			Lieut D.G. POTTER " S.E. CHARLTON "
			" R.K. FLETCHER " 2nd Lieut W.R. SAVAGE "
			2nd Lieut A.E. MILLER " " J.R.M. MITCHELL "
			" H.C. BERRETT " H. BIRCHWOOD "
				" W. SIMPSON "
				" J. McGARRIE "
			O.R. killed Wounded Missing R.A. BARKER "
			17 95 168 T.G. MANNERS "
				G.E. ROSS "
				C.M. APPERLEY "

WAR DIARY
INTELLIGENCE SUMMARY.
(Erase heading not required.)

Army Form C. 2118.

Instructions regarding War Diaries and Intelligence Summaries are contained in F. S. Regs., Part II. and the Staff Manual respectively. Title pages will be prepared in manuscript.

Place	Date	Hour	Summary of Events and Information	Remarks and references to Appendices
			In the evening Battn. HQ moved to PAS (BOIS de CHATELET) Transport concentrated near MONTICOURT and moved to BAVINCOURT at 9pm arriving 6pm	
		10pm	Transport arrive back from BAVINCOURT to near PAS arriving 12am	9a.e.
	27th A		Battn moved to RANSART near PAS. arriving at POMMERA HUT. Battn & RANSART at	9a.e.
		2.30pm	Transport marching via POMMERA. Transport arrived RANSART 3:30pm	9a.e.
	28th		Battn moved to BOURGUEMAISON via hills.	9a.e.
	29th		Battn marched to between SS ESCART and 1st LAPUGNOY in new Hospital Areas & Army	
				9a.e.
			The Battn was moving all next forenoon when it was ordered to his vicinity The King. The battalion was drawn up beside the road & marched to the position which 46 were of the officers and men who to gathered around the Back. Battn continued PREVENT Sham and cut March to K B was relieved & arrived & Jae	Jae
	30th		Battn arrive & LAPUGNOY 2am and was to turn in at Hamy.	
			Marched from BYAS to HEIVEN	9a.e.
	31st		Battn is being training at LAPUGNOY an effective strength 10 officers and 1528 rank &	9a.e.

Jas A. Clarke
Lt Col Comdg 6th Highld L.I.

A6945 Wt. W14427/M160 35,000 12/16 D. D. & I.— Forms/C./2118/14.

Army Form C. 2118.

WAR DIARY
or
INTELLIGENCE SUMMARY.
(Erase heading not required.)

Instructions regarding War Diaries and Intelligence Summaries are contained in F. S. Regs., Part II. and the Staff Manual respectively. Title pages will be prepared in manuscript.

Place	Date	Hour	Summary of Events and Information	Remarks and references to Appendices

51st Divisional M.G.C.

WAR DIARY

51st BATTALION

MACHINE GUN CORPS

APRIL 1 9 1 8

Appendix - Account of Operations 9th-12th

51st Divisional M.G.Corps.

51st BATTALION

MACHINE GUN BATTALION

51st Divisional M.G.Corps.

Confidential.   Vol 2

War Diary

of

51st (H) Bn M.G. Corps

April, 1918.

WAR DIARY
INTELLIGENCE SUMMARY.
(Erase heading not required.)

Army Form C. 2118.

Place	Date	Hour	Summary of Events and Information	Remarks and references to Appendices
In the field	July 1918 1-2		HOUCHIN – Refitting and Resting	
	3		Draft – 181 O.R.	
	4		Moved to ANNEZIN to billets – Draft 8 officers 113 O.R.	
	6		ANNEZIN – Draft 20 O.R. Reorganizing Coys & Refitting	
	8		Moved to GODDENHEM to billets	
	9		Line attacked NORTH of BETHUNE. "A" Coy moved to 152 Bde. H.Q. near PACAUT. "B" Coy to 153 Bde. H.Q. near PACAUT. "C" Coy to 154 Bde. H.Q. at LOCON. Bat. H.Q. & "D" Coy moved to ROBECQ. During the night 9/10, the guns of the three Coys in the line were distributed along the line of the Rivers LAWE from near LESTREM thence along the Canal de la LAWE to 1000 yards S of LOCON. Thence from the right of the Divisional front were "C" Coy, "A" Coy, "B" Coy.	
	10	1 a.m.	ROBECQ – 1 section of "D" Coy moved to 153 Bde. H.Q.	
		9 a.m.	A second section of "D" Coy moved to 153 Bde. H.Q. In the afternoon remainder of "D" Coy moved to 153 Bde. H.Q. The line of the LAWE was held throughout the day.	

WAR DIARY
INTELLIGENCE SUMMARY

Army Form C. 2118.

Place	Date	Hour	Summary of Events and Information	Remarks and references to Appendices
	11		The line of the LAWE was broken on the left and during the day the guns of the battalion fell back in conformity with the Division on to a line roughly PACAUT - LA TOMBE - WIULOT - LOCON. Much fighting took place all day and the guns were constantly in action. Transport marched to LA MIQUELLERIE.	
	12		The line fell back towards the canal fighting on the right Bn - right of line relieved by 3rd Division. Battalion H.Q. moved to BUSNES [acualteu 9th Bn Hofeneer 2050R] A composite company of the battalion was formed and went into position with Flemings force in ROBECQ DEFENCES.	[rae]
	13		Transport moved to BERGUETTE. H.Q. in BUSNES. Concentration of remainder of battalion from line in BUSNES.	
	17		Action (1 MGH guns) reinforced positions in ROBECQ as a relieved 39th Bn. M.G.C. making 20 guns in ROBECQ DEFENCES.	1.30p
	18		Draft of 48 O.R.	
			Draft of 80 O.R.	

Army Form C. 2118.

WAR DIARY
of
INTELLIGENCE SUMMARY.
(Erase heading not required.)

Instructions regarding War Diaries and Intelligence Summaries are contained in F.S. Regs., Part II. and the Staff Manual respectively. Title pages will be prepared in manuscript.

Place	Date	Hour	Summary of Events and Information	Remarks and references to Appendices
	19		"A" Coy & 1 Section "C" Coy relieved "B" & "D" Coys in the line	
	20		Battalion moved to billets at FONTES with the exception of "A" Coy in the line	
			Section of "C" Coy in the line with "A" Coy withdrawn leaving baws with "A"	
	21		Batt. less "A" Coy resting	
	22		Bathing & Equipping	
	23		"C" Coy relieved "A" Coy in the line. Relief complete 6.30pm	
	24		Training at FONTES	
	25		Training. Commanding Officers inspection of "A" "B" "D" Coys	
	26		Training. The 10 guns of "C" Coy relieved by 39th Batt. M.G.C.	
			& 2 guns by the 61st Batt. M.G.C. the remaining 4 guns of "C" Coy	
			being withdrawn without relief. After relief "C" Coy moved to billets	
			in FONTES.	
	27		Equipping	
	28		Training at FONTES. 2nd Lieut (A/Major) H.G. HARCOURT awarded a D.S.O. for	
			gallantry displayed between 21st and 26th March 1918	
	29.30		Training	

W. Howlr Lt. Col.
Comdg 51(H) Bn. M.G.C.

SECRET.

51st (H) BATTALION, M.G. CORPS.

ACCOUNT of OPERATIONS,
9/12th April, 1918.

Map Reference:-
LACOUTURE, 1/20,000.

On the afternoon of 9th April, 1918, while the 51st (H) Battalion M.G. Corps was resting at GONNEHEM, orders were received to send one Machine Gun Company to report to each of the 152nd, 153rd and 154th Infantry Brigades and these Companies marched upwards of nine miles before reaching their battle positions. Later, the remaining Company together with Battalion Headquarters was ordered to ROBECQ.

Instructions received from Brigade:-

"A" Company to take up position on Brigade Front (X.2.d.6.6. to R.5.d.3. covering Bridge etc. over RIVER LAWE.

"B" Company to send TWO Sections under the 7th GORDON HIGHLANDERS, these guns being sited close to RIVER LAWE (R.15.central to R.21.central) and to send other TWO Sections, less 1 Sub-section in Reserve at PACAUT, under the 6th BLACK WATCH, which had taken up a position in front of LESTREM.

"C" Company to place 2 guns at LA TOMBE WILLOT (R.31.d.) and 8 guns in LOCON DEFENCES (X.2.c. and X.7.b.) with further instructions to press forward if possible to CANAL de la LAWE and later 4 additional guns were ordered to positions in LOCON DEFENCE

During the night of the 9th/10th, there was little activity, except for occasional heavy shelling on VIEILLE CHAPELLE, whereby "A" Company had one gun in R.33.a. put out of action.

"B" Company having temporarily placed their guns in position during hours of darkness, made a further reconnaissance at dawn and adjusted the disposition of their guns.

"C" Company during the night distributed their guns according to instructions.

At 3-30 a.m. on the 10th, a Section of "D" Company was sent to come under the orders of B.G.C., 153rd Infantry Brigade.

During the morning of the 10th, the Infantry and Machine Gun positions along the front were shelled heavily, causing the Infantry to vacate their positions, until the activity ceased, when they were again occupied.

"A" Company had another gun put out of action at this time, having the officer and Section Sergeant both killed, (X.2.b.30.25.)

In the forenoon, owing to further casualties and new dispositions, 2nd Lt. STEPHENS was sent from "A" Company Headquarters to obtain definite information, reorganise the detachments under 2nd Lt. MORRISON who had been killed, and report dispositions to O.C., 6th SEAFORTH HRS.

The guns of "C" Company during the morning came into action, covering the footbridge over the Canal (X.3.a.2-2-) which had not been destroyed when our Infantry retired to the West side, and several enemy formations were dispersed. persistent attempts were made by the enemy to reach the Bridge and eventually he managed to cross, one man at a time, by crawling, and so formed a body of men in the Farm in X.3.a. This was done regardless of the heavy losses he sustained.

2nd Lt. STEPHENS was ordered by O.C., 6th SEAFORTH HIGHLANDERS to command a mixed force of Infantry and Machine Gunners and to attack the Farm, X.3.a. The attack was only partially successful and although many of the enemy retired over the Bridge, some still remained on the West of the Canal.

The 2 guns at X.2.b. had both been destroyed by shell fire and 2 of the four guns in R.33.a. were moved to R.32.d. to fill the gap so caused.

2.

Between 7 and 8 a.m. on the same morning, the Section of "D" Coy. which had previously reported at 153rd Infantry Brigade Headquarters, was sent forward to occupy positions between LESTREM and L'EPINETTE (R.7.central), but two of these guns after getting into position were immediately ordered forward into LESTREM.

The reserve of 2 guns of "B" Company at PACAUT were ordered to report to the 6th BLACK WATCH and were placed in position on the RIVER LAWE.

A further Section of "D" Company proceeded from ROBECQ at 10-30 a.m. to report to the 153rd Infantry Brigade at PACAUT, followed at 1-30 p.m. by the remaining two Sections.

On the left, during the afternoon of the 10th, enemy snipers and Machine Guns occupied a position in a haystack at R.9.d.1.5. with snipers in other positions causing many casualties. No organised enemy attack, however, developed.

Later, "C" Company received instructions from 154th Infantry Brigade to move the two guns covering the bridge at X.3.a. to a position at about X.2.4., and this move was carried out during the following night. Further orders were received by "C" Guns in Reserve at Company Headquarters to a position in X.1.b. where the Left Company of the 4th GORION was lying. These guns were in position by 8 p.m.

By arrangement between B.G.Cs. 153rd and 152nd Infantry Brigades at 7 p.m., a Section of "D" Company from PACAUT was sent to replace casualti in "A" Company.

The front of the 152nd Infantry Brigade at 11 p.m. on the 10th was from FOSSE (Left) West side of RIVER LAWE to R.33.d.2.2. to R.32.d.7.4. to X.2.b.3-5. to X.2.d.3.0.

Orders were received by "C" Company at midnight 10th/11th to move th two guns at X.1.b. and the two guns at LA TOMBE WILLOT to positions right and left of houses in R.31.central. About this time it was reported that VIEILLE CHAPELLE and LESTREM were œoccupied by the enemy and further that they were pushing down the LOCON ROAD. Along the line occupied by these guns, two Companies of the 4th GORIONS dug themselves i

At 1 a.m. on 11th, one Section of "D" Company under orders of 153rd Infantry Brigade was sent to report to the 8th ROYAL SCOTS followed at 7-30 a.m. by the remaining section.

Dur-ing the night and at dawn of the 11th, the enemy attacked, preceded by heavy shelling and succeeded in penetrating the line from LESTREM to the SOUTH of VIEILLE CHAPPELLE, although heavy casualties were inflicted during his attacks and at places he was held up for some considerable time. In some cases, the enemy came quite close dressed in the kilt and apron.

Many targets were engaged, including Infantry, Cavalry, and Cyclist Machine Gunners. 2nd Lt. SIDDALL at LA TOMBE WILLOT, with one man and one gun, succeeded in driving back many determined attacks of the enemy but he was finally killed.

A defensive flank was formed from LA TOMBE WILLOT along the Road to PARADIS.

On the North, after the Infantry had been forced back, they consolidated a line in front of the Road running North and South through PARADIS.

During the afternoon, the enemy continued to advance forcing us back to a prepared line along the GRID, Q.17.central to Q.23.central.

At 3 p.m., the remaining guns and teams, together with the 6th and 7th BLACK WATCH and other details, also took up a prepared line behind QUENTIN.

During the day, the 39th Battalion, M.G.C. was placed under the orders of the B.G.sC. 152nd and 153rd Infantry Brigades, and reinforced in depth the Left flank.

At 6 a.m. on the 12th, the enemy again attacked, advancing rapidly by LE CORNET MALO (Q.28.) thus compelling the Infantry to make a series of withdrawals towards LE VERTBOIS FARM. The enemy also attacked towards LOCON at 6 a.m. and the 8 guns in squares X.8.a.; X.8.c., X.2.c., and X.1.b., successfully held up the enemy until mid-day, and orders were received at 6-30 p.m. to withdraw the guns, the relieving guns of the 3rd Battalion being then in position.

The line at LE VERTBOIS FARM was held until 6 p.m. before which time the enemy were seen moving along the Road in Q.34.b.; fire was opened with good effect, but the Infantry having been outflanked on the Left, were compelled to retire to a prepared line on the LA BASSEE CANAL. This withdrawal was covered by the three remaining Machine Guns, resulting in the loss of one gun and several members of the teams.

On the 12th, a Composite Company of 16 guns was formed and on the afternoon moved up to positions in defence of ROBECQ for support of FLEMING'S FORCE.

On the night of 12th, the Division concentrated in BUSNES area.

On the 13th, an additional section of 4 guns reinforced the ROBECQ DEFENCES and relieved the 39th Battalion M.G.C.

4th May, 1918.

Lt.Col.,
Cmdg., 51st (H) Battalion, M.G.Corps.

Confidential

War Diary Vol 3

51st (H) Bn. M. G. Corps

from 1st May 1918
to 31st May 1918

WAR DIARY
INTELLIGENCE SUMMARY

Army Form C. 2118.

Place	Date	Hour	Summary of Events and Information	Remarks and references to Appendices
Field	May 1		Training at FOSSEUX - Reinforcements - Capt. A.Y. Pearson M.C.	
	2		Training	
	3		Training - Reinforcements - 10 O.R.s	
	4		"A" "C" Coys left FOSSEUX - 4.15 p.m. - Entrained AIRE 7.08 p.m. detrained ACQ 10 p.m. and proceeded to billets at ECOIVRES	
		8.30 a.m.	Transport left FOSSEUX for ECOIVRES - Route - BELLERY - CHATELAIN - CAMBLAIN - DIVION - HOUDAIN - ESTREE - COCHY - MONT ST ELOY	
	4/5		Transport stayed at DIVION - Estafe 8 officers	
	5		Transport left DIVION - Route - HOUDAIN - ESTREE - COCHY - MONT ST ELOY - ECOIVRES, arriving ECOIVRES 3 p.m. - "B" "D" Battn H.Q. moved from FONTES at 3 p.m. - Entrained KILLERS 6.27 p.m. detraining MAROEUIL 11.30 p.m. & proceeded to billets at ECOIVRES, arriving midnight.	
		5.30 p.m.	"A" & "C" Coys moved from ECOIVRES. 18 guns of "C" Coy and 16 guns of "A" Coy relieving no.1 Coy of the 11th Canadian Divisional M.G. Battn covering 10th Canadian Infantry Brigade.	
	6		2 guns of "A" Coy in Canadian Divisional Reserve at NEUVILLE ST VAAST. 10 guns of "D" Coy & 12 guns of "B" Coy relieved No.2 Coy of the 11th Canadian	

Army Form C. 2118.

WAR DIARY
INTELLIGENCE SUMMARY.
(Erase heading not required.)

Place	Date	Hour	Summary of Events and Information	Remarks and references to Appendices
	May 6		Divisional M.G. Battn. covering 152rd Infantry Brigade. Remaining 6 guns of "D" boy, & remaining 2 guns of "B" boy in Divl. Reserve.	AW
	7	6am	Battalion took over command of the line	AW
		11.30am	80t Echelons moved from Ecouvres to FLANDERS CAMP ECURIE, taking over billets from the 152h Battn. M.G.C. 2hrs.	AW
	8th		4 gns & Echelon B at ECURIE. Six guns of "D" boy were relieved by 4 guns of "B" boy and 2 guns of "A" boy. Detachments returned to billets at FLANDERS CAMP ECURIE.	AW
	9th		At night the 52nd Battn. M.G.C. relieved 12 guns of "B" boy & Hist remaining guns of "D" boy. These detachments returned to billets at FLANDERS CAMP ECURIE.	AW
	10th		During the night "D" boy relieved one boy of the 15th Battn. M.G.C.	AW
	11th		Owing to the alteration to the Divisional Sector Daily bathing commenced from 5 pm – 6 pm.	AW
	12th		Casualties – 1 O.R. wounded	AW
	13th		Draft – 1 O.R.	AW

WAR DIARY
INTELLIGENCE SUMMARY.
(Erase heading not required.)

Army Form C. 2118.

Place	Date	Hour	Summary of Events and Information	Remarks and references to Appendices
Field	May 14th		At night A & C boys moved their bombing H.Qs + guns with the exception of the guns at ROME to new dispositions	AW
	15th		During the morning B boy moved their Coy H.Q. to B.25.b.4.5	AW
	16th		"B" boy relieved "C" boy in the line. "C" boy withdrawn to Killets in ECURIE	AW
	17th		"C" boy in Divisional Reserve - Casualties - 1 O.R. wounded	AW
	18th		Casualties 3 O.R. wounded	AW
	19th			
	20th			
	21st		Two guns of D boy in Reserve relieved 2 guns of D boy at the Railway Embankment. B.26.c.5.1. The two guns of "D" boy which were relieved moved to D boy H.Q. in Reserve for the night Brigade	AW
	23rd		Reserve for the night Brigade. "C" boy relieved "A" boy in the line. "A" boy withdrawn to Killets at FLANDERS Camp ECURIE, + formed the with 4 guns Anti-Aircraft Defence of the Battalion at ECURIE	AW

WAR DIARY
INTELLIGENCE SUMMARY.
(Erase heading not required.)

Army Form C. 2118.

Place	Date	Hour	Summary of Events and Information	Remarks and references to Appendices
Field	May 23		Draft 20 O.Rs. – Major C.H. Rose rejoined Battalion from hospital.	AW
	24		Casualties – 1 O.R. Killed 1 O.R. wounded	AW
	25			
	26			
	27			
	28		"A" Coy. relieved "D" Coy. in the line – D Coy. withdrawn to Killus at Flanders Camp Ecurie & formed the Anti-Aircraft defence of the Battalion at Ecurie	AW
	29			
	30		Casualties 1 O.R. Killed 1 O.R. wounded	AW
	31		Honours. "For gallantry displayed in the field". 2nd Lieut. W.J. Goddard awarded Military Cross. 2nd Lieut. H.A. Enanton awarded Military Cross	

Army Form C. 2118.

WAR DIARY
or
INTELLIGENCE SUMMARY.
(Erase heading not required.)

Instructions regarding War Diaries and Intelligence Summaries are contained in F. S. Regs., Part II. and the Staff Manual respectively. Title pages will be prepared in manuscript.

Place	Date	Hour	Summary of Events and Information	Remarks and references to Appendices
			20192 Corpl. W. Brodie. M.M. awarded Distinguished Conduct Medal.	
			60025 Private J. Synnis " " " "	
			141200 " J. Graham " " " "	
			20122 Sgt. W. Brodie. M.M. – Bar to Military Medal.	
			50606 Corpl. D. Benson " " " "	
			23061 Cpl. J. Valentine " Military Medal.	
			90310 Pte. W. Watts " "	
			141001 Corpl. J. Tierney " "	
			10098 " J. Bramley " "	
			19124 Sgt. T. McCarran " "	
			125108 Pte. W. Kirkwood " "	
			251408 " B. Corio " "	
			236024 Corpl. Godfrey " "	
			20133 Pte. W. McKinnon " "	
			102971 Corpl. L.G. McQueen " "	
			66340 Pte. W. Ruddy " "	
			68025 Pte. B. Buck " "	
			53631 Corpl. G. Thompson " "	
			106287 " J.G. Davies " "	
			93932 Pte. N. Watson " "	
			Mentioned in Despatches.	
			In accordance with His Majesty's Birthday Honours Gazette dated June 3/18	
			Lt. Col. S.J.L. HARDIE. D.S.O. Major A.S. Vernon	
			Lieut. B. Well.	
			Capt. C.H. Rossi.	
			" B. Hampshire.	
			2242 Sergt. G. Norton.	

M.A. Vernon
Lt. Col.
Comdg. 57(H) Batt. M.G.C.

SECRET-   51st (H) BATTALION, M.G. CORPS.
              OPERATION ORDER No. 10.   3-5-18.

1. The 51s (H) Division will be transferred to XVIIth Corps and take over part of front held by 4th CANADIAN DIVISION.

2. The 51st (H) Battalion M.G.C. will relieve the 4th Canadian Div. Battalion M.G.C. on the front taken over as follows:-

   (a) On the night of 5th/6th May, 1918:-
       "C" Company will relieve 16 guns,
       "A" Company will relieve 14 guns,
of No.1 Company of the 4th Canadian Divisional Battalion covering 10th Canadian Infantry Brigade and on relief will come under the orders of the 4th Canadian Divisional M.G. Battalion.

   (b) The remaining 2 guns of "A" Company will be Divisional Reserve at Battalion Headquarters.

   (c) On the night 6th/7th May, 1918:-

       "D" Company will relieve 10 guns,
       "B" Company will relieve 12 guns,
of No.2 Company of 4th Canadian Divisional M.G. Batn covering 153rd Inf. Brigade and on relief will come under the orders of the 4th Canadian Divisional M.G. Battalion.

   (d) The remaining 6 guns of "D" Company and
       the remaining 4 guns of "B" Company will be Divisional Reserve at Battalion Headquarters.

   (e) The 51st (H) Battalion M.G.C. will take over command at 6 a.m. on 7th May, 1918.

3. Details of relief of Companies as above will be arranged by M.G. Company Commanders concerned.

4. The dismounted personnel of "A" and "C" Companies will move by tactical trains to the area MONT ST. ELOY - NEUVILLE ST. VAAST on May 4th under orders to be issued by 153rd Infantry Brigade. Details of entraining will be notified later.

5. Battalion H.Q. and "B" and "D" Companies will proceed to same area by tactical trains on May 5th, 1918. Details of entraining will be notified later.

6. The transport of the Battalion will move at 8-30 a.m. under the orders of the B.T.O. by road to same area on 4th May, 1918, and will stage at DIVION night 4th/5th May, 1918.
   ROUTE: Road JUNCTION B.4.d.9.7. - BELLERY - CHATELAIN - CAMBLAIN - HOUDAIN - ESTREE-COCHY. - MONT ST. ELOY.
   Hour of passing Starting Point (B.4.d.9.7.) 10 a.m., 4-5-18.
   Order of March, Next after 154th Inf.Bde.Group, followed by 8th
       Royal Scots. The usual intervals will be observed.

7. Rations will be issued to "A" and "C" Companies and Transport for the 5th May, 1918.

8. One lorry will report for baggage of "A" and "C" Companies at 8-30 a.m. on 4th May, 1918.

9. ACKNOWLEDGE.

                                             Capt. Adjt.,
Copy No.1-4 - Coys.   51st (H) Battalion M.G.Corps.
         5 - Division "G"
         6 - 4th Can.M.G.Bn.
         7 - War Diary.
         8 - File.

Copy No: 6
Wauchan(?)

51ST (H) BATTALION M.G. CORPS.

Reference map Operation Order No. 14. 16/5/18.
MAROEUIL 1/20000.

1. One the night 16/17th May, 1918, the following Inter-Company relief will take place:-

    "B" Company will relieve "C" Company.

2. The necessary arrangements will be made between Company Commanders.

3. Tripods, Belt Boxes and Trench Stores will be handed over and receipts taken of latter, copy of which will be handed into Battn. H.Q. by 8 p.m. 17/5/18.

4. On completion of relief "C" Coy. will withdraw to Billets in ECURIE.

5. Completion of relief to be notified Battn. H.Q. by Code word "MAC."

6. "C" Coy. will become Divisional Reserve and all officers will reconnoitre machine gun positions in the ST. CATHERINE'S SWITCH and POINT DU JOUR - THELUS RIDGE LINE in accordance with Divisional Defence Scheme, Para. 8(c).

7. ACKNOWLEDGE.

Issued at 10 am.

Copy No. 1. "B" Coy.
"   " 2. "C" "
"   " 3. 51st Div. "G."
"   " 4. 152nd Inf. Bde.
"   " 5. 154th Inf. Bde.
"   " 6. War Diary.
"   " 7. File.

Capt. & Adjt.
51st (H) Bn. M.G.C.

SECRET.   Copy No..........

                    51st (H) BATTALION, M.G.CORPS.
                    OPERATION ORDER No.17.   21-5-18.

Ref.Map:
HAMBURG, 1/20,000.

1. The TWO Guns of "D" Coy. 51st (H) Battalion, M.G.Corps. in RESERVE
    will relieve TWO Guns of "B" Coy. 51st (H) Battalion M.G.C.
    at the MEILLERIE EMBANKMENT, S.26.c.9.1. on the night of the
    21st/22nd May, 1918.

2. The TWO Guns of "B" Coy. which will be relieved will go back
    to "B" Company's Headquarters and will be in RESERVE for the
    RIGHT Brigade.

3. This will make FOUR Guns in RESERVE for the RIGHT Brigade.

4. Details of Relief will be arranged between Coy.Commanders and
    notification of completion will be reported in the usual way to
    Battalion Headquarters.

5. Trench Stores will be handed over and receipt obtained, copy of
    which will be forwarded to Battalion H.Q. not later than 6 p.m.
    on the 22nd May, 1918.

6. ACKNOWLEDGE.

                    Issued at ... 5-30 p.m.
                                                    [signature]
                                                    Capt.& Adjt.,
                                                    51st (H) Battalion, M.G.Corps.
Copy No.1 - "B" Coy.
       2 - "D" Coy.
       3 - 153rd Inf.Bde.
       4 - 154th Inf.Bde.
       5 - 51st (H) Div. "G".
       6 - War Diary.
       7 - File.

SECRET.   51ST (H) BATTALION, M. G. CORPS.

Operation Order No. 18.

21/5/18.

Reference map
MAROEUIL, 1/20,000.

1. On the night 22/23rd May, 1918, the following Inter-Company relief will take place.

   "C" Company will relieve "A" Company.

2. The necessary detail of arrangements/made between Company Commanders concerned.
   (will be)

3. Tripods, Belt Boxes, Trench Stores and work in hand will be handed over and receipts obtained for Trench Stores and Note of work will be handed into Battn. H.Q. by 5 p.m. 23rd May, 1918.

4. On completion of relief, "A" Company will withdraw to Billets in ECURIE.

5. Completion of relief to be notified to Battn. H.Q. by Code Word "FAIL."

6. "A" Company will become Divisional Reserve and Officers and as many N. C. Os. as possible will reconnoitre positions in the Second System, before relief.

7. Trench Stores of Reserve Company ("C") will be handed over to "A" Company, receipt obtained and copy forwarded to Battn. H.Q.

8. "A" Company will form the Anti-Aircraft Defence of the Battalion at ECURIE with 4 guns.

9. ACKNOWLEDGE.

Issued at 2.0 p.m.

Capt. & Adjt.,
51st (H) Bn. M.G.C.

Copy No. 1 - "A" Coy.
    2 - "B" "
    3 - "C" "
    4 - "D" "
    5 - T. O.
    6 - 51st (H) Div. "G."
    7 - 152nd Inf. Bde.
    8 - 153rd   "   "
    9 - 154th   "   "
    10 - War Diary.
    11 - File.
    12 - QM
    13 - Rem

SECRET.   51ST (H) BATTALION, M. G. CORPS.   Copy No. 10

Operation Order No. 19.

27/5/18.

Reference map
MAROEUIL 1/20,000.

1. On the night 28/29th May, 1918, the following Inter-Company relief will take place.

    "A" Coy. will relieve "D" Coy.

2. The necessary detail of arrangements will be made between Company Commanders concerned.

3. Tripods, Belt Boxes, Trench Stores and work in hand will be handed over and receipts obtained for Trench Stores and Note of Work will be handed into Battn. H.Q. by 5 p.m. 29th May, 1918.

4. On completion of relief "D" Company will withdraw to Billets in ECURIE.

5. Completion of relief to be notified to Battn. H.Q. by Code Word "PYLE."

6. "D" Company will become Divsional Reserve and Officers and as many N. C. Os. as possible will reconnoitre positions in the Second System before relief.

7. Trench Stores of Reserve Company ("A") will be handed over to "D" Coy., receipt obtained and copy forwarded to Battn. H.Q.

8. "D" Company will form the Anti-Aircraft Defence of the Battalion at ECURIE with 4 guns.

9. ACKNOWLEDGE.

Issued at 11.0 a.m.

Capt. & Adjt.,
51st (H) Bn. M.G.C.

Copy No. 1 - "A" Coy.
         2 - "B" "
         3 - "C" "
         4 - "D" "
         5 - T.O.
         6 - 51st (H) Div. "G."
         7 - 152nd Inf. Bde.
         8 - 153rd Inf. Bde.
         9 - 154th Inf. Bde.
        10 - War Diary.
        11 - File.
        12 - Q.M.
        13 - R.S.M.

Vol 4

Confidential

War Diary
of
51st (N) Bn. M.G. Corps.
for June 1918

WAR DIARY
INTELLIGENCE SUMMARY
(Erase heading not required.)

Army Form C. 2118.

Place	Date	Hour	Summary of Events and Information	Remarks and references to Appendices
	June			
	1		Batn. HQ. "D" Coy & Echelon B at Maroeuil Camp, ECURIE	
			Transport at BRAY.	
	2		Casualties - 1 O.R. wounded	
	3		"D" Coy relieved "B" Coy in the line on completion of relief. "B" Coy were withdrawn to billets in ECURIE, & became Divisional Reserve.	
			"B" Coy formed the Anti-Aircraft defence of the Battalion at ECURIE with H guns. Casualties - 1 O.R. wounded.	
	4		Casualties - 1 O.R. wounded.	
	5		Lewis W.S. Lorrie T.R.A.S. Henderson joined Battalion, the latter from hospital.	
	6		Reinforcements - 5 O.Rs. - Casualties - 1 O.R. wounded.	
	7		do - 38 O.Rs. - do - 2 O.Rs. do	
			Honours & Awards. Lt. Gallant (Highland Division) 1st and 2nd Marathon	
			Lieut. D.G. Millar }	216117 L/Cpl J Bach to
			Lieut. R.G. Millar }	135122 Gunner M.R. Hyde
			Lieut. A.E. Millar } Military Cross	23217 L/Cpl A.D. Ferguson M.M.
			Lieut. Cam Murchie }	23916 Sgt A.D. Gire
			Lieut. W. Bradie }	44447 Sgt J Semmons
			Lieut. P.H. Strahan }	23715 Pte J Rundell

WAR DIARY / INTELLIGENCE SUMMARY

Army Form C. 2118.

Place	Date	Hour	Summary of Events and Information	Remarks and references to Appendices
	June 8			
	9		"B" Coy relieved "C" Coy in the line. On completion of relief "C" Coy were withdrawn to Willis in Lourie, and became Divisional Reserve.	
			"C" Coy turned the Anti-Aircraft Defence of the Battalion at Lourie with 4 guns	All
	10	1.15 am	Gas Bean attack on Divisional front between Lynx Lane and Arleux Road. Machine gun harrassing fire carried out. Lieut D.A. MacRae joined Battalion + 2nd Lieut E.F. Reay returned from hospital	
	11			
	12		2 Reserve guns of "A" Coy at H.1.c.9.8. moved to position at H.30.3.3. 2 guns of "A" Coy at H.2.45.4. moved to position at B.27.a.10.90. 2 guns of "B" Coy at B.25.a.10.05. moved to position at B.21.c.30.45.	
			Reinforcements – 20 ORs – Casualties – 1 OR wounded – 2nd Lieut E.G. Holding evacuated sick.	All
	14			

WAR DIARY
INTELLIGENCE SUMMARY.
(Erase heading not required.)

Army Form C. 2118.

Place	Date	Hour	Summary of Events and Information	Remarks and references to Appendices
	June 15		"C" Coy relieved "A" Coy in the line. On completion of relief "A" Coy went withdrawn to billets in ECURIE & became Divisional Reserve	
	16		"A" Coy formed the Anti Aircraft Defence of the battalion at ECURIE with it guns. 2 guns of "D" Coy at Vic (B.21.c.75.40) moved to position at GERTIE (B.21.a.60.30.)	MW
	17			
	18		Billets & vicinity of camp shelled by long range enemy howitzer 1.30am - Casualties 3 O.R. wounded. Reinforcements - 1 O.R.	MW MW
	19			
	20			
	21	2am	2 guns of "A" Coy & 4 guns of "C" Coy cooperated in raid on enemy trenches by 12th Royal Scots on right Divisional front. "A" Coy relieved "D" Coy in the line. On completion of relief "D" Coy were withdrawn to billets in ECURIE and became Divisional Reserve. "D" Coy formed the Anti Aircraft Defence of the battalion	MW

WAR DIARY
INTELLIGENCE SUMMARY

(Erase heading not required.)

Army Form C. 2118.

Place	Date	Hour	Summary of Events and Information	Remarks and references to Appendices
	22		at ECURIE with 4 guns	
			2 guns of "B" bty at H.W.C. 9.8 (PET) moved into new positions	M
			completed at B.28.c.5.9. 2nd Lieut G.F. Beaumont-Orchard with	M
	23		Reinforcements - 2 ORs	M
	24		Casualties - 1 OR missing	M
	25		do. 1 OR wounded	M
	26		Reinforcements - 1 OR	M
	27		"B" bty relieved "D" bty in the line. On completion of relief "D" bty were withdrawn to billets in ECURIE, and became Divisional Reserve. "B" bty formed the Anti-Aircraft defence of the Battalion	M
	28		at ECURIE with 4 guns	
	29		Honours & Awards - The Meritorious Service Medal. 22920 R.Q.M.S. Black J.M. 6794th Regt Airways.og.	M
	30			

[signature] Major
Comdg. 51 (V) Bat. M.G. Corps

SECRET. Copy No. 10

51ST (H) BATTALION, M. G. CORPS.

Reference Map
MAROEUIL 1/20,000.   Operation Order No. 20.

2/6/18.

1. On the night 3/4th June, 1918, the following Inter-Company relief will take place.

    "D" Coy. will relieve "B" Coy.

2. The necessary detail of arrangements will be made between Company Commanders concerned.

3. Tripods, Belt Boxes, Trench Stores and work in hand will be handed over and receipts obtained for Trench Stores and Note of Work will be handed into Battn. H.Q. by 5 p.m. 4th June, 1918.

4. All Harassing Fire Schemes will be handed over by "B" Coy. to "D" Coy. as a going concern; there will be no intermission due to relief.

5. On completion of relief "B" Coy. will withdraw to Billets in ECURIE.

6. Completion of relief will be notified to Battn. H.Q. by Code Word "PEAR."

7. "B" Company will become Divisional Reserve and Officers and as many N. C. Os. as possible will reconnoitre positions in the Second System before relief.

8. Trench Stores of Reserve Company ("D") will be handed over to "B" Coy., receipt obtained and copy forwarded to Battn. H.Q.

9. "B" Company will form the Anti-Aircraft Defence of the Battalion at ECURIE with 4 guns.

10. ACKNOWLEDGE.

Capt. & Adjt.,
51st (H) Bn. M.G.C.

Issued at 10.30 a.m.

Copy No. 1 - "A" Coy.
    2 - "B" "
    3 - "C" "
    4 - "D" "
    5 - T.O.
    6 - 51st (H) Div. "G."
    7 - 152nd Inf. Bde.
    8 - 153rd Inf. Bde.
    9 - 154th Inf. Bde.
    10 - War Diary.
    11 - File.
    12 - Q.M.
    13 - R.S.M.

SECRET   COPY NO. 12

51st (H) BATTALION, M. G. CORPS.

Reference Map
HAROEUIL 1/20,000.   Operation Order No. 22.   8/6/18.

1. On the night 9/10th June, 1918, the following Inter-Company relief will take place.

    "B" Coy. will relieve "C" Coy.

2. The necessary detail of arrangements will be made between Company Commanders concerned.

3. Tripods, Bolt Boxes, Trench Stores and Work in Hand will be handed over and receipts obtained for Trench Stores and Note of Work will be handed into Battn. H.Q. by 5 p.m. 10th June, 1918.

4. All Harassing Fire Schemes will be handed over by "C" Coy. to "B" Coy. as a going concern; there will be no intermission due to relief.

5. On completion of relief "C" Company will withdraw to billets in ECURIE.

6. Completion of relief will be notified to Battn. H.Q. by Code Word "ROSE."

7. "C" Company will become Divisional Reserve and Officers and as many N. C. Os. as possible will reconnoitre positions in the Second System before relief.

8. Trench Stores of Reserve Company ("B") will be handed over to "C" Coy., receipt obtained and copy forwarded to Battn. H.Q.

9. "C" Company will form the Anti-Aircraft Defence of the Battalion at ECURIE with 4 guns.

10. ACKNOWLEDGE.

                                                              Capt. & Adjt.,
                                                              51st (H) Bn. M.G.C.

Issued at 10.30 a.m.

Copy No. 1 - "A" Coy.
         2 - "B" "
         3 - "C" "
         4 - "D" "
         5.- T.O.
         6 - 51st (H) Div. "G."
         7 - 152nd Inf. Bde.
         8 - 153rd Inf. Bde.
         9 - 154th Inf. Bde.
        10 - Q.M.
        11 - R.S.M.
        12 - War Diary.
        13 - File.

SECRET. 51ST (H) BATTALION, M. G. CORPS.

Reference Map Operation Order No. 21. 5/6/18.
BAILLEUL Sheet:
1/20,000.

1. A Gas Beam attack will be carried out on the front of the 51st Division between TYNE ALLEY and the ARLEUX Road on the night June 7th/8th, or on the first subsequent night upon which the wind is favourable. O.C. "B" Special Company R.E. will be in charge of the operation and will have at his disposal "B" and "O" Special Companies R.E. His position during the operation will be at the Left Brigade Headquarters.

2. The wind limits for the operation will be S.W. through W. to W.N.W.; velocity between 6 and 15 m.p.h.

3. The gas will be discharged simultaneously from two tramway heads on the TYNE LINE (CEMETERY SPUR) and the ARLEUX LINE respectively. The forward limits of the discharging points will be approximately B.22.b.8.5. and B.16.b.0.7.

4. Each line will be allotted 80 trucks, each containing 21 cylinders. Trucks will be loaded and made up into trains of 10 trucks each at ANZIN; they will be sent forward to Power Heads under arrangements to be made by O.C. "B" Special Company R.E. direct with the Corps Light Railway Officer and the O.C. No. 7 Foreways Company. Traffic control ahead of ROCLINCOURT will be entirely in the hands of the O.C. Foreways.

5. On the TYNE LINE trucks will be pushed from Power Head at B.16.c.1.1. by infantry pushing parties.

   (a). Rendezvous.

      To reach Power Head at 10 p.m. to be disposed under cover and to be so distributed that each party can come out simultaneously and form up rapidly on the half train it has to push.

   (b). Action.

      Parties will in succession push out their half trains to the discharging point, whence they will withdraw to the nearest suitable trench and be reorganised at once ready for the return journey.

      On completion of the discharge, and on the order of the Special Company Officer in charge, parties will pull back with drag ropes to Power Head the same half trains as they pushed up.

   (c). Precautions.

      (i). In the event of a cylinder being hit by hostile fire, all ranks will adjust respirators but will not ring bells nor sound Strombos Horns.

      (ii). After discharge, parties will keep to windward of the trucks when pulling them back, and will wear box respirators while waiting to move off.

6. On the ARLEUX LINE trucks will be pushed up to the discharging point by tractors.

7. The G.O.C. 153rd Infantry Brigade will detail the pushing parties, and will make all arrangements involved, in consultation with the O.C. "B" Special Company R.E.

- 2 -

The G.O.C. 154th Infantry Brigade will grant any facilities in his Brigade area which may be required by the G.O.C. 153rd Infantry Brigade.

8. The following precautions will be observed :-

(a). The firing line and support line will be completely evacuated by 12 midnight on the night of the operation between B.23.c.7.6. and the SUGAR FACTORY - ANNEXE ROAD (exclusive).

(b). All troops within the area, which will be laid down by the B.G.C. 153rd Infantry Brigade, will wear box respirators from 12 midnight until orders for their removal are given by an officer. The order will in no case be given until Zero plus 30 minutes. Company Commanders will obtain full particulars of this area from B.G.C. 153rd Infantry Brigade.

9. The gas personnel of the three Infantry Brigades will be at the disposal of the Divisional Gas Officer and will work under his orders. In order that they may be recognised and may not be impeded in their duties, they will wear white arm bands on each arm.

The Divisional Gas Officer will be responsible for giving to the troops referred to in para. 8(b) permission to remove their Box Respirators.

He will also be responsible for ascertaining that the evacuated area is free from gas, and troops will not re-occupy this area until they have received the permission of the Divisional Gas Officer, which will be conveyed personally by Brigade Gas Officers.

10. Artillery action which might draw retaliation on to squares B.22. and 16, or on to the tram lines leading there will be avoided. Machine Gun Fire between above areas will be avoided.

11. M.G. Harassing Fire will be increased on night 6/7th and same programme for night 7/8th.

12. Zero hour will be at 12 midnight or as soon after as the trucks are reported to be in position. The actual order for the discharge will be given by the O.C. "B" Special Company R.E. and will be repeated to the G.O.C. 153rd Infantry Brigade, who will pass it on by 'priority' telephone call to 51st Divisional Headquarters and to the Brigades on either flank.

13. The decision as to whether the operation will take place or not will be given at 1 p.m. on June 7th and on subsequent dates as and if necessary, the following code words being employed:-

"Operation will take place to-night" ... JOY.

"Operation Postponed" ... ... SORROW.

"Cancel Operation previously ordered" ... ANGER.

14. On the day that it is decided to carry out the operation the tramways will be closed to supply and engineer material traffic from 6 p.m. onwards. Two days' supplies will be carried up to the units affected on June 6th and the extra days' supply will be kept in hand for consumption on the day following the operation.

15. ACKNOWLEDGE.

Copy No. 1 - "A" Coy.   - 5 - 51st (H)
  "   " 2 - "B" "   Div. "G."
       3 - "C" "   - 6 - Q.M.   Capt. & Adjt.,
  "   " 4 - "D" "   - 7 - File.   51st (H) Bn. M.G.C.
                                            8 - War Diary.

SECRET.   Copy No. 14

                    51st (H) BATTALION, M. G. CORPS.
Reference Map   ---------------------------------
MAROEUIL 1/20,000.
                      Operation Order No. 23.   13/6/18.
                      ※※※※※※※※※※※※※※※※※※

1. The following moves will take place to-day, 13th June, 1918 :-

    "A" Company.

        2 Reserve Guns at H.1.c.9.8. to position at H.3.c.3.5.

        2 Guns at H.2.b.5.4. to position at B.27.c.20.90.

    "D" Company.

        2 Guns at B.25.a.10.05. to position at B.31.c.30.45.

2. Companies concerned will telegraph, on completion, to Battalion

        H.Q. by word "ADJUSTED."

3. ACKNOWLEDGE.

                                                    Capt. & Adjt.,
Issued at 10 a.m.   51st (H) Bn. M.G.C.

Copy No. 1 - "A" Coy.
        2 - "B" "
        3 - "C" "
        4 - "D" "
        5 - T. O.
        6 - Q. M.
        7 - 152nd Inf. Bde.
        8 - 153rd Inf. Bde.
        9 - 154th Inf. Bde.
       10 - 51st (H) Div.
       11 - 15th Bn. M.G.C.
       12 - 52nd Bn. M.G.C.
       13 - XVII C.M.G.O.
       14 - War Diary.
       15 - File.

S E C R E T.   Copy No. 12

51st (H) BATTALION, M. G. CORPS.

Reference Map
HAREBUIL 1/20,000.   Operation Order No. 24.   14/6/18.

1. On the night 15/16th June, 1918, the following Inter-Company relief will take place :-

    "C" Coy. will relieve "A" Coy.

2. The necessary detail of arrangements will be made between Company Commanders concerned.

3. Tripods, Bolt Boxes, Trench Stores and Work in Hand will be handed over and receipts obtained for Trench Stores and Note of Work will be handed into Battn. H.Q. by 5 p.m. 16th June, 1918.

4. All Harassing Fire Schemes will be handed over by "A" Coy. to "C" Coy. as a going concern; there will be no intermission due to relief.

5. On completion of relief "A" Company will withdraw to billets in ECURIE.

6. Completion of relief will be notified to Battn. H.Q. by Code Word "IAN."

7. "A" Company will become Divisional Reserve and Officers and as many N. C. Os. as possible will reconnoitre positions in the Second System before relief.

8. Trench Stores of Reserve Company ("C") will be handed over to "A" Coy., receipt obtained and copy forwarded to Battn. H.Q.

9. "A" Company will form the Anti-Aircraft Defence of the Battalion at ECURIE with 4 guns.

10. ACKNOWLEDGE.

Issued at 10.0 a.m.

Capt. & Adjt.,
51st (H) Bn. M.G.C.

Copy No. 1 - "A" Coy.
    2 - "B" "
    3 - "C" "
    4 - "D" "
    5 - T.O.
    6 - 51st (H) Div. "G."
    7 - 152nd Inf. Bde.
    8 - 153rd Inf. Bde.
    9 - 154th Inf. Bde.
    10 - Q.M.
    11 - R.S.M.
    12 - War Diary.
    13 - File.

SECRET. Copy No. 10

51st (H) BATTALION, M. G. CORPS.

Reference Map
MAROEUIL 1/20,000. Operation Order No. 25.

1. The following move will take place to-day, 16th June, 1918:-

    "D" Company.

    2 Guns at VIC (B.21.c.75.40.) to position at GERTIE (B.21.d.60.30.)

2. "D" Company will wire completion to Battalion H.Q. by word "STRAP".

3. ACKNOWLEDGE.

                                    [signature]
                                    Capt. & Adjt.,
                                    51st (H) BN. M.G.C.

Issued at 10 a.m.

Copy No. 1 - "A" Coy.
        2 - "B" "
        3 - "C" "
        4 - "D" "
        5 - 152nd Inf. Bde.
        6 - 153rd Inf. Bde.
        7 - 154th Inf. Bde.
        8 - 51st (H) Div. "G."
        9 - XVII C. M.G.O.
       10.- War Diary.
       11 - File.

SECRET.   Copy No. 8.

51st (H) BATTALION, M. G. CORPS.

Reference Map
CHANTECLER –   Operation Order No. 23.
GREENLAND HILL   19/2/18.
1/20,000.

1. At a date and time to be notified later the 15th Royal Scots will carry out a raid on enemy trenches in H.5.b. & d., H.6.a. & c., H.11.b. and H.12.a.

   (a). Right Boundary, Hudson Alley to point of SNOUT, thence EAST. Left Boundary, Light Railway through H.5.b. for 400 yards to junction of FENTON and new C.T. (H.5.b.97.50.) to NAVAL and along CIVIL.
   (b). The furthest objective HOARY and HAGGARD between CHILI and CIVIL, blocks being made in CHILI, CALEDONIAN and CIVIL, 50 yards East of HOARY and HAGGARD.

2. The 15th Bn. M.G.C. will co-operate as follows :-

   2 guns at about H.9.b.15.45. (guns to be used 21 & 21a.)
   Target H.11.b.77.59. to H.11.b. 80.03.
   2 guns at about H.9.b.15.45. (guns to be used 22 & 22a.)
   Target H.11.b.93.40. to H.12.a.01.03.

   4 guns at about H.10.c.35.98. (guns to be used S9.10.11.12.)
   Target H.6.d.44.75. to H.6.d.36.80.
   4 guns about H.10.c.50.35. (guns to be used S5.6.7.8.)
   Target H.6.d.36.20. to H.12.b.56.68.

3. The 51st (H) Bn. M.G.C. will co-operate as follows :-

   (a). "D" Company.
        2 guns - Target H.6.b.40.40. to H.6.b.45.10.
        2 guns -   "   H.6.a.12.93. to H.6.a.21.66.

   (b). "C" Company.
        2 guns - Target H.6.b.45.10. to H.6.d.45.78.
        2 guns -   "   H.6.a.56.93. to H.6.a.50.04.

4. Rate of fire :-

   Z to Z plus 10.   -   -   5 bolts.
   Z plus 10 to Z plus 40. -   8   "
   Z plus 40 to Z plus 65. - 10   "

5. Machine Guns will not open fire until the Artillery barrage commences.

6. An Officer from "C" Company, 51st (H) Bn. M.G.C. will synchronize watches at 45th Inf. Bde. Hqrs. (G.12.b.85.50.) at 10 p.m. on the night of the raid.

7. ACKNOWLEDGE.

Issued at 11 a.m.

                                                    Capt. & Adjt.,
Copy No. 1 - "C" Coy.   51st (H) Bn. M.G.C.
        2 - "D" "
        3 - "B" "
        4 - 51st (H) Div. "G."
        5 - 45th Inf. Bde.
        6 - 152nd Inf. Bde.
        7 - 154th Inf. Bde.
        8 - War Diary.
        9 - File.
       10 - 15th Bn. M.G.C.

SECRET.

War Diary.

> 51ST
> (H) BATTALION,
> MACHINE GUN CORPS.
> No. O.O.26/1.
> Date 19/6/18.

H.

Reference Operation Order No. 26 of to-day's date, the raid by the 13th Royal Scots will take place on the night 20/21st inst.

ACKNOWLEDGE.

Bagnelyll
Capt. & Adjt.,
51st (H) Bn. M.G.C.

19/6/18.

SECRET

> 51st
> (H) BATTALION.
> MACHINE GUN CORPS.
> OO 26/2

Ref. OPERATION ORDER No, 26, dated 19/6/1918

1. Zero day will be 21st June 1918.
2. Zero hour will be 3 a.m.
3. ACKNOWLEDGE by wire.

Capt. & Adjt.
51st (H) Bn. M.G.Corps.

20th June 1918

Distribution
Copy No. 1 - "C" Coy.
2 - "D" "
3 - "B" "
4 - 152nd Inf. Bde.
5 - 154th " "
6 - War Diary.
7 - File.

SECRET. Copy No. 12

51st (H) BATTALION, M.G. CORPS.

Reference Map
MAROEUIL 1/20,000. Operation Order No. 27.
****
20/6/18.

1. On the night 21/22nd June, 1918, the following Inter-Company relief will take place :-

    "A" Coy. will relieve "D" Coy.

2. The necessary detail of arrangements will be made between Company Commanders concerned.

3. Tripods, Belt Boxes, Trench Stores and Work in Hand will be handed over and receipts obtained for Trench Stores and Note of Work will be handed into Battn. H.Q. by 5 p.m. 22nd June, 1918.

4. All Harassing Fire Schemes will be handed over by "D" Coy. to "A" Coy. as a going concern; there will be no intermission due to relief.

5. On completion of relief "D" Coy. will withdraw to billets in ECURIE.

6. Completion of relief will be notified to Battn. H.Q. by Code Word "BENT."

7. "D" Company will become Divisional Reserve and Officers and as many N.C.O's. as possible will reconnoitre positions in the Second System before relief.

8. Trench Stores of Reserve Company ("A") will be handed over to "D" Coy., receipt obtained and copy forwarded to Battn. H.Q.

9. "D" Company will take over the Anti-Aircraft Defence of the Battalion at ECURIE.

10. ACKNOWLEDGE.

Issued at 10.30 a.m.

Capt. & Adjt.,
51st (H) Bn. M.G.C.

Copy No. 1 - "A" Coy.
2 - "B" "
3 - "C" "
4 - "D" "
5 - "T.O."
6 - 51st (H) Div. "G."
7 - 152nd Inf. Bde.
8 - 153rd Inf. Bde.
9 - 154th Inf. Bde.
10 - Q.M.
11 - R.S.M.
12 - War Diary.
13 - File.

SECRET.   Copy No. .....
                                                                              11
                    51st (H) BATTALION, M. G. CORPS.

Reference map   21/6/18.
MAROEUIL 1/20,000. Operation Order No. 28.

1.   The two guns at H.4.c.9.8. (PET) will move into new positions

completed at B.28.c.5.9. to-morrow night, 22/6/18.

2.   Completion of move to be reported to Battalion H.Q. by word "PET."

3.   ACKNOWLEDGE.

                                                        [signature]
                                                        Capt. & Adjt.,
Issued at 6.30 p.m.   51st (H) Bn. M.G.C.

Copy No. 1 - "C" Coy.
          2 - "B" "
          3 - "A" "
          4 - "D" "
          5 - 51st (H) Div. "G."
          6 - 152nd Inf. Bde.
          7 - 153rd Inf. Bde.
          8 - 154th Inf. Bde.
          9 - 15th Bn. M.G.C.
         10 - C.H.G.O.
         11 - War Diary. ✓
         12 - File.

SECRET. Copy No. 12

51st (H) BATTALION, M.G. CORPS.

Reference Map
MAROEUIL, 1/20,000. Operation Order No. 29. 26/6/18.

1. On the night 27/28th June, 1918, the following Inter-Company relief will take place :-

    "D" Coy. will relieve "B" Coy.

2. The necessary detail of arrangements will be made between Company Commanders concerned.

3. Tripods, 10 Belt Boxes per gun, Trench Stores and Work in Hand will be handed over and receipts obtained for Trench Stores and Note of Work will be handed into Battn. H.Q. by 5 p.m. 28th June, 1918.

4. All Harassing Fire Schemes and Intelligence Reports will be handed over by "B" Coy. to "D" Coy. as a going concern; there will be no intermission due to relief.

5. On completion of relief "B" Coy. will withdraw to billets in ECURIE.

6. Completion of relief will be notified to Battn. H.Q. by Code Word "SON."

7. "B" Coy. will become Divisional Reserve and Officers and as many N.C.Os. as possible will reconnoitre positions in the Second System before relief.

8. Trench Stores of Reserve Company ("D") will be handed over to "B" Coy., receipt obtained and copy forwarded to Battn. H.Q.

9. "B" Coy. will take over the Anti-Aircraft Defence of the Battalion at ECURIE.

10. ACKNOWLEDGE.

Issued at 12.30 a.m.

Capt. & Adjt.,
51st (H) Bn. M.G.C.

Copy No. 1 - "A" Coy.
2 - "B" "
3 - "C" "
4 - "D" "
5 - T.O.
6 - 51st (H) Div. "G."
7 - 152nd Inf. Bde.
8 - 153rd Inf. Bde.
9 - 154th Inf. Bde.
10 - Q.M.
11 - R.S.M.
12 - War Diary.
13 - File.

51st (Highland) Div. Troops.

51st. BATT. MACHINE GUN CORPS.

JULY, 1918.

"Confidential"

War Diary

of

51st (H.) Bn. Machine Gun Corps.

for July, 1918

Army Form C. 2118.

WAR DIARY
or
INTELLIGENCE SUMMARY.

(Erase heading not required.)

Instructions regarding War Diaries and Intelligence Summaries are contained in F. S. Regs., Part II. and the Staff Manual respectively. Title pages will be prepared in manuscript.

Place	Date	Hour	Summary of Events and Information	Remarks and references to Appendices
	July 1.		References Maps:- MOREUIL 1/20,000, AMIENS 1/40,000, CHAULNES 1/40,000, ALBERT III - E/100,000. Division holding G.H.Q. LINE COPY ATTACHED. 1st & Lancs Gun Coy. in the Line. B.H.Q. and "B" Company at Fluxicourt Camp, ECUIRE. Transport at BRAY.	Appy
	2.			Appy
	3.		"B" Company relief of "C" Company in the line, on completion of relief "C" Company were billeted to billet in ECUIRE and with are Divisional Reserve.	Appy
	4-7.			Appy
	8.		Camp broken up after the dec by bn - 2 O.Rs (2nd Lt Campbell, 2nd Lt Gingles-Rev-2nd Lt Major L.T. Gow - camped - Capt. Mr. J.K. BRADLEY - wounded - 7 O.Rs Wdd. - 2 O.Rs gas	Appy
			1 wounded at Bray	
	9-10.			Appy
	11.10 a.m.		"B" Company H.Q. moved to billets at BRAY	Appy
			No. 1 Company 4th Bn. Gundilon C.C. relieved 16 men of "B" Company and 10 men of "A" Co.	
			On completion of relief Company moved to Brd.	
	12.		No. 4 Company 4th Bn. Canadian M.G. relieved 16 men of "B" Company and 8 men of "A" Co.	Appy
			On completion of relief Coy. moved from 5 B.H.Q. to the 25th Bn. Canadian G.O.	
	1 p.m.		B.H.Q. moved from MOURT to BRAY to billets in MARICOURT. Transport moved by Rail.	
	13.	5 p.m.	B.H.Q. moved from MOURT to BRAY to billets in MARICOURT. Transport moved by Rail.	Appy
			Warning orders received to move to MAICOURT, at an unknown area, & all ranks to be ready.	
	14.	5 p.m.	"A" Company - small at BRAY. (Coys standing by.) moved to Bn lines.	Appy
		6 p.m.	"B" Company called out orders for BRAY.	
	15.	2 p.m.	"B" Company left for Bn. lines.	Appy
	16.	10.30 p.m.	B. H.Q. "C" Co. and "D" Co. - arrived at match route, assembled here 12/14/18	Appy
	17.		Remainder of coys arrived in H.... lots via small lane 13th.	Appy
			"A" "B", "C" Companies and H.Q. companies over. Battle Group 2 were billeted at CHUIGNES to MENTs to join KEIT O.R.	
			"D" Coy and "D" Company as Brigade reserve. Brigade Group 1 were billeted as MIT - CH. All I.H.... to join KEIT O.R.	
			Corps reserve. MRI, CHUILLEY to MORLANCOURT.	

WAR DIARY
or
INTELLIGENCE SUMMARY

Army Form C. 2118.

Place	Date	Hour	Summary of Events and Information	Remarks and references to Appendices
	18.			
	19.	3 a.m.	H.Q. and "D" Company and Transport moved by march route - HUMRY - BLEE PAGETE, arriving at noon. "A", "B" and "C" Companies move to CH PELON, HUMRY - BLEE PAGETE - BELLEVUE respectively.	Lay
		5 p.m.	Orders issued by Divi'ion for attack the following morning. "A", "B" and "C" Companies move at 8.30 a.m. to 152, 155 and 154 Brigades respectively for Battn. "B" and "D" Companies move to assembly positions. "D" Company move to assembly position in BOIS de St. QUENTIN. 152 Infantry Brigade being in Divisional Reserve. "D" Company move to BOIS de St. QUENTIN.	Lay
	20.	8 a.m.	Adv. H.Q. opened at Pt. TINQUE.	Lay
		8 a.m.	4th Corps attack on whole position with TT Corps attack on right - attached left. 51st (H) Division - attack with 62nd Division on right 4th French Division on left.	
			Disposition of Brigades - 154 Infantry Brigade on right.	
			153 " "	
			152 " " in Divisional Reserve.	
	21.	9 a.m.	Attack continued by 152 and 153 Brigades, also 62nd Division. 154 Brigade in support. "D" Company moved to position South of MARTFUIL as being HQ/4-AGS/4. R Formass Map -	Lay
			ENEMY.	
			Advance pushed as far as outskirts of HAPLAY and BULLIN Pts.	
			Advance continued by peaceful penetration.	
	22.		IV CORPS renew attack with a view to gaining ground in valley of R. Somme. Attached on 51st Divisional front carried out by 152 Brigade. Troops of 154 Brigade on left flank advanced in line with 152 Brigade and extended line turning E.W. from TTIENCY putting off the flank to which settled at that point. Later operation without Success. Mobb "D" Company severe shrapnel fire. Infantry by two bat-ries of 8 guns each.	Lay
	23.		Advanced B.H.Q. close up to Pt. TINQUE and "D" Company 3.15 - .30 in HUMHY H.S. area hour. 153 Infantry Brigade and "B" Company billeted in B18 de St. QUENTIN.	Lay
			Brett 5 officers and 20 O.R. Brett 4 Officers and 149 O.R.	
	24.		154 Infantry Brigade and "B" Company relieved by 153 Infantry Bde. and "D" Company; preparatory to attack.	Lay
	25.			

WAR DIARY
or
INTELLIGENCE SUMMARY

Army Form C. 2118.

Place	Date	Hour	Summary of Events and Information	Remarks and references to Appendices
	27.		Attack carried out by 153 and 154 Bri..des in conjunction with 6th D Div'l.... "B" & "C" "C" Company under of capt. P. ...a. 152. B..... 154 Brigade took..... "D"Company and "A" Company on a line of the of "A" Company in barrage and the advance. guns, co-operated with Bd'n. of "A" Company continued... CHIPILLY All object.. ..ta..ed....... continued... "D" Company comme..ced in ..set 200 yards C... 1/D' RE.. "D" Company...to have at strength about... 154 Infantry Brigade and "C" Company moved forward of H.WL.YLL. Battalion H.Q. moved to MERULL vis- Divisional 1 H.q. 154 Brigade 171 and Brigades on flanks ..CLIT.... on BOIS d'en ECLIT.... "C" Company "D" Company under "B" C...mer. coll. the O Companies in line. Line – P.I.Ks. .... n a.ag.. BOISES MARISSEL –	See See See See
	29.	6 p.m.	1/G' GM DE BLIGNY. "C" Company Cave Inter Division R....r, fording ....orward "C" Company as carried by "D" Company t "D' RDE. " " " " " " ac.. MANT UEL. "B" " " " " " " D'ARMS. " " " " " " " WELLEY. "B" Company a../l "C" Company moved t YOLE UYL 'AD... "C" " " " " " bo... " D D "D" " " " " " " .a... de L..x ....t.. i... LNT VE.. "B" Company moved to HAUTVILLERS CASUALTIES for period 20/7/.. - 7 O..VI/.re.	
	30.			

```
                                1 Other Ranks killed.
                              5 Other R..ks Died of Wounds.
                            157 Wounds.
                              3 Missing.
                              1 Gassed, 25 Ord..
                 HORSES:-   13 Killed.
                              4 ..uncled and Evac..uated.
```

SIGNATURE T/C... Lieut. D. A. ACR.. – 2/Lieut. J.AUSTIN. – 2/Lieut. C.ANTHUR. –
O/C .. B..   O.C.

N O T E :   The undermentioned OPERATION ORDERS

would appear to be missing :-

No. 31
36
37

SECRET.   Copy No. 12.

51st (H) BATTALION, M. G. CORPS.

Ref: map
MAROEUIL,
1/20,000.   Operation Order No. 30.
                        ************************   2/7/18.

1. On the night 3/4th July, 1918, the following Inter-Company relief will take place:-

    "B" Coy. will relieve "C" Coy.

2. The necessary detail of arrangements will be made between Company Commanders concerned.

3. Tripods, 10 Belt Boxes per gun, Trench Stores and Work in Hand will be handed over and receipts obtained for Trench Stores and Note of Work will be handed into Battn. H.Q. by 5 p.m. 4th July, 1918.

4. All Harassing Fire Schemes and Intelligence Reports will be handed over by "C" Coy. to "B" Coy. as a going concern; There will be no intermission due to relief.

5. On completion of relief "C" Coy. will withdraw to billets in ECURIE.

6. Completion of relief will be notified to Battn. H.Q. by Code Word "GON."

7. "C" Coy. will become Divisional Reserve and Officers and as many N.C.Os. as possible will reconnoitre positions in the Second System before relief.

8. Trench Stores of Reserve Company ("B") will be handed over to "C" Coy., receipt obtained and copy forwarded to Battn. H.Q.

9. "C" Coy. will take over the Anti-Aircraft Defence of the Battalion at ECURIE.

10. ACKNOWLEDGE.

Issued at 12.30 p.m.

                                        Capt. & Adjt.,
                                        51st (H) Bn. M.G.C.

Copy No. 1 - "A" Coy.
        2 - "B" "
        3 - "C" "
        4 - "D" "
        5 - T.O.
        6 - 51st (H) Div. "G."
        7 - 152nd Inf. Bde.
        8 - 153rd Inf. Bde.
        9 - 154th Inf. Bde.
       10 - Q.M.
       11 - R.S.M.
       12 - War Diary.
       13.- File.

SECRET.   Copy No. 10

                    51st (H) BATTALION, M.G. CORPS.
                    ───────────────────────────────

Ref. Map   Operation Order No. 52.   9/7/18.
HAZEBROUCK 1/20,000.

1. The following moves will take place to-night 9/10th July, 1918:-

    "A" Company.

        2 guns at IAN (B.27.b.55.45.) to position at GOT (B.20.b.15.15

    "B" Company.

        2 guns at GOT (B.20.b.15.15.) to position at LILY ELSIE
        (B.14.b.70.35.)

2. The time of the relief of guns at GOT position by "A" Company

        will be arranged by Companies concerned.

3. Companies concerned will wire completion to Battalion H.Q.

        by word "PARIS."

4. ACKNOWLEDGE.

                                           [signature]

                                             2/Lieut. & Adjt.,
    Issued at 11 a.m.   51st (H) Bn. M.G.C.

    Copy No. 1 - "A" Coy.
             2 - "B" "
             3 - "C" "
             4 - "D" "
             5 - 152nd Inf. Bde.
             6 - 153rd Inf. Bde.
             7 - 154th Inf. Bde.
             8 - 51st (H) Div. "G."
             9 - XVII C.M.G.O.
            10 - War Diary.
            11 - File.

S E C R E T.   Copy No. 12.

51st (H) BATTALION, M. G. CORPS.

9/7/18.

Operation Order No. 33.

Ref: map
MAROEUIL 1/20,000.

1. The 51st (H) Division will be relieved in the line by the 4th Canadian Division on the night 10/11th and 11/12th July, 1918.

2. The 51st (H) Bn. M. G. C. will be relieved by the 4th Battn. Canadian M. G. C. as follows :-

(a). Night 11/12th July. - (Left Sector).

No. 1 Coy. 4th Bn. Canadian M. G. C. will relieve :-
   (i).   16 Guns of "D" Coy., 51st (H) Bn. M. G. C.
   (ii). 10 " " "A" "   "   " " "   "

at the following positions :-

   2 Guns at CONEY.   B.21.b.20.20.
   2 " " GERTIE.   B.21.d.50.30.
   2 " " VERNON.   B.21.c.30.40.
   2 " " COT.   B.20.b.15.15.
   2 " " CRY.   B.20.a.10.20.

(b). Night 12/13th July. - (Right Sector).

No. 2 Coy. 4th Bn. Canadian M. G. C. will relieve :-
   (i).   16 Guns of "B" Coy., 51st (H) Bn. M. G. C.
   (ii). 6 " " "A" "   "   " " "   "

at the following positions :-

   2 Guns at PILL.   B.28.a.50.90.
   2 " " VEX.   B.27.b.35.40.
   2 " " TONY.   B.26.c.50.20.

3. Details of relief will be arranged between Officers Commanding Companies concerned.

4. Lists of Trench Stores handed over and Receipts for same will be forwarded to Battn. H.Q. when relief is completed.

5. On completion of relief Companies will move to Divisional School, BRAY.

6. Completion of relief will be reported to Battn. H.Q.

7. 51st (H) Bn. M. G. C. Headquarters will close at ECURIE 12 noon 12th July and re-open at Divisional School, BRAY, 2 p.m.

8. A C K N O W L E D G E.

Issued at 6.30 p.m.

Copy No. 1 - "A" Coy.
       2 - "B" "
       3 - "C" "
       4 - "D" "
       5 - 51st (H) Div. "G."
       6 - 152nd Inf. Bde.
       7 - 154th Inf. Bde.
       8 - 4th Bn. Canadian M. G. C.
       9 - T.O.
     10 - S.O.
     11 - Q.M.
     12 - War Diary.
     13 - File.

Capt. & Adjt.,
51st (H) Bn. M. G. C.

SECRET.   Copy No. 10

51st (H) BATTALION, M.G. CORPS.

Operation Order No. 34.   10/7/18.

Ref. map
MAROEUIL 1/20,000.

1. Under 51st (H) Division A.I. No. 54, "C" Coy. and Echelon "B" details at FLANDERS CAMP will move to Billets at BRAY, 11th July, 1918.

2. Company details will parade under orders of Officers Commanding Coy. Rear H.Q., who will report to Battn. H.Q. before moving off.

3. Transport will move independently under Company arrangements.

4. All huts will be left scrupulously clean and the Orderly Officer will render a certificate that this has been done. Attention must be paid to the trenches under the huts.

5. Huts will be vacated not later than 10 a.m.

6. An interval of 100 yards will be maintained between Sections on the march.

7. On arrival at BRAY, Companies will report to Capt. Eadie by whom guides will be provided.

8. "C" Company will become Reserve Company and will be ready to move at 4 hours notice to support the VIII Corps.

9. A C K N O W L E D G E.

Issued at 12 noon.

for Capt. & Adjt.,
51st (H) Bn. M.G.C.

Copies 1 to 4 - Coys.
      5 - 51st (H) Div. "G."
      6 - T.O.
      7 - S.O.
      8 - Q.M.
      9 - R.S.M.
    10 - War Diary.
    11 - File.

S E C R E T.   Copy No. 10

                    51st (H) BATTALION, M. G. CORPS.

Ref: Map   Operation Order No. 35.
FRANCE, SHEETS 11,   11.7.18
1/100000.

1.   The Battalion will move by train from BRAY to billets in
MAGNICOURT 15th July, 1918.

2.   The train will leave BRAY at 6 p.m. on 15th instant.

3.   Exact entraining point and time of parade will be notified later.
Dress - Full Marching Order.

4.   Transport will move independently by road under orders of
Battalion Transport Officer, via ACQ - AUBIGNY - FREVILLERS.

5.   Limbers will be packed by 9 a.m. 15th instant.

6.   Brakesmen will be provided by Companies for their own Transports.
Cooks will move with Company Cookers.

7.   During the march 100 yards distances will be maintained between
Company Transports.

8.   O's. C. Companies will arrange for dixies to be kept behind for
meals on 15th instant.

9.   Blankets will be stacked in bundles of 10 at the BILLET WARDEN'S
HUT, BRAY, by 6.30 a.m. 15th instant under Company arrangements.
The loading of the blankets will be supervised by the R.Q.M.S.

10.   A C K N O W L E D G E.

                                                        [signature]
Issued at 5 p.m.   for Capt. & Adjt.,
                                                        51st (H) Bn. M. G. C.

Copy No. 1 - "A" Coy.
         2 - "B" "
         3 - "C" "
         4 - "D" "
         5 - 51st (H) Div. "G."
         6 - T.O.
         7 - S.O.
         8 - Q.M.
         9 - R.S.M.
        10 - War Diary.
        11 - File.

O.

51ST
(H) BATTALION,
MACHINE GUN CORPS.

No. O.O.37/1
Date.

Reference Operation Order No. 37 :-

1) Battalion H. Q. personnel will parade outside the Battalion Orderly Room at 3 a.m. tomorrow morning - Dress, full Marching Order, - and will move off at 3-15 a.m.

2) Headquarter's Transport will parade and move off under the orders of the Transport Officer.

Capt. & Adjt.
51st (H) Bn. M.G.Corps,

14th July 1918

S E C R E T.   C O P Y.

81st Bn. M. G. Corps.

WARNING ORDER.

1. 51st (Highland) Division will move by rail to-morrow, 14th July. It is believed that units will not entrain before noon.

2. All baggage/~~will be~~ which cannot be carried on units' Transport will be ready for removal to AUBIGNY at 5 a.m. to-morrow at the units' Q.M. Stores. Baggage wagons will be sent to units to-morrow, 14th.

3. Battalions will take Lewis guns on train and 20 magazines per gun - remainder on Transport.

4. Detailed orders will follow.

5. ACKNOWLEDGE.

6.30 p.m.   Sgd. E.D.C. HUNT, Captain,
13th July, 1918.   Brigade Major, 154th Infantry Brigade.

"Operation" Order. No 38.

Refce. Map. CHALONS.
Sheet.

19. 7. 18

(1) The 51(H) Bn. M.G. Corps (less 2 companies marching in Brigade Groups) will march to HAUTVILLERS to-day, via EPERNAY and DIZY MAGENTA from PIERRY.

(2) "D" Coy will march by sections complete with transport, with 100 yards interval between sections, followed by Battn. H.Q. at 100 yards interval, with remaining transport.

(3) Battn. will parade at 8 a.m. in road facing "D" Coy billet, ready to move off.

(4) All packs and surplus stores will be dumped at a Battalion Dump at "D" Coy. H.Q. and a guard detailed by ~~O.C. "D" Coy.~~ from B.H.Qrs

(5) Acknowledge.

[signature]
Lt Col
~~Lieut + Adjt.~~
51(H) Bn. M.G. Corps.

19. 7. 18.

Issued at 4.30 a.m.

SECRET. 51st (H) BATTALION, M.G.CORPS,   Copy No..........
         OPERATION ORDER No. 39.
                                          19/7/18.

Ref. Map:-
REIMS No.54 &
Attd. Map.

1. The enemy on our front appears to be retiring covered by Rear Guards.

2. In order to follow him up and to hold him on this front, the XXII Corps is to attack tomorrow 20/7/18, supported on the right by the I French Colonial Corps and on the Left by the V French Corps.

3. The 51st (H) Division will attack with the 62nd Division on its Right and the 9th French Division on its Left.

4. Objectives and boundaries are shown on the attached Map.

5. Action of Artillery:-
(a) French Artillery will form the barrage as far as their Range permits which will be to a short distance West of the GREEN Line. Before ZERO, there will be only the normal harassing fire.
At ZERO the barrage will open in advance of the front line held by the French and will creep forward at the rate of 100 metres every 4 minutes.
(b) Beyond the range of the French guns, the advance will be covered by the 51st (H) Divisional Artillery who will be in positions of readiness before ZERO with a view to carrying out this role.
(c) On completion of the barrage programme, the French and Italian Field and Heavy Artillery covering the Divisional front may be moved forward under the orders of the G.O.C., 51st (H) Division to cover the further advance of the Infantry.

6. Action of Infantry:-
(a) The 154th Infantry Brigade will attack on the RIGHT.
The 153rd Infantry Brigade will attack on the LEFT.
The 152nd Infantry Brigade will be in Divisional Reserve.
By 12 midnight, 19th/20th July, the 154th and 153rd Infantry Brigades will be formed up on the Line shown on the attached Map and at ZERO hour will pass through the leading FRENCH line closely following the barrage.
Each Brigade will attack on a front of one Battalion and will leap-frog on the GREEN Line and first Objective.
(b) The 152nd Infantry Brigade will move South of ST. IMOGES to a position SOUTH of the first "M" in B. de ST. QUENTIN; to be in position by 12 midnight 19th/20th instant. not to march before 9 p.m. 19th instant.
(c) First objective will be consolidated as the main line of resistance.

7. Touch with Flanks:-
In order to keep touch with the 62nd Division liaison posts will be established at each Bridge across the River ARDRE, which River is said to be unfordable.
Special care will be taken by the 153rd Infantry Brigade to maintain touch with the 9th French Division.

8. The general compass bearing of the attack is 352 degrees.
8a. A.B.& C. Coys will come under orders of 152, 153 & 154 Inf Bdes respectively
9. "D" Coy. will move to the same place as the Reserve Brigade in accordance with para. 6 (b) and will arrange to arrive in position at 12 midnight, 19th/20th instant, and will report arrival in position to Battalion H.Q.
"D" Coy. will be in Divisional Reserve and may be employed to reinforce either of the Brigade fronts.

10. T.M. Communication will be established by "D" Coy. to Battalion H.Q. through Reserve Brigade H.Q.

11. An aeroplane dropping station is being established at ST. IMOGES.

12. The ZERO hour will be notified later.

13. Battalion Headquarters will be with Divisional Headquarters at ST. IMOGES, opening at 6 a.m., 20th instant.

14. A C K N O W L E D G E.

[signature]

for Capt. & Adjt.,
51st (H) Battalion M.G.C.

ADMINISTRATIVE INSTRUCTIONS to ACCOMPANY OPERATION ORDER No.59.

1. **AMMUNITION:-** Ammunition supply will be as for open war-fare except that until the S.A.A.Section is able to deliver to Brigades, which is not likely to be before noon tomorrow, delivery will be made by lorry under arrangements which have already been notified to Brigadiers who will notify their attached M.G.Companies. Brigades have already been warned to send Orderlies from Brigade Transport giving their location and any change must be notified to "Q".
   No Divisional Small Arms Reserve Dump will be established at present.

2. Rations to make up to consumption 21st instant including Iron Rations or its equivalent have been drawn by the Divisional Train for delivery to Battalions today.

3. The Divisional Train will be parked at DIZY-MAGENTA. The Divisional Train will move there by 9 a.m. 20th. The S.A.A.Section on arrival will be at AY.

M. ~~The Divisional M.X.Company~~

4. **MEDICAL:-** The Advanced Main Dressing Station will be at ST.IMOGES. Main Dressing Station will be at CHAMPILLON. Walking Wounded Collecting Station will be at Briquoterie on Main Road, one mile North of CHAMPILLON.

Issued at 9 p.m.
" to:- 51st (H) Division "G".
    2 - "A" Coy.
    3 - "B" "
    4 - "C" Coy.
    5 - "D" "   ✱
    6 - 152nd Inf. Bde.
    7 - 153rd Inf. Bde.
    8 - 154th Inf. Bde.
    9 - Q.M.
    10 - T.O.
    11 - War Diary.
    12 - File.

✱ *only with maps.*

51st (H) Bn. M.G. Corps
OPERATION ORDER No. 41   22/7/18

Reference 1/20000 Sheet

1. The XXII Corps is to attack with a view to gaining ground in the valley of the River ARDRE.

2. The attack on the 51st Divisional front will be carried out by the 152nd Infantry Brigade.

3. The attached map shows the forming up line, objective, and flanks of attack.

4. By zero minus ten minutes the 154th Inf. Bde. will withdraw to the forming up line all troops in advance of that line.

5. The infantry of the 152nd Inf. Bde will be prepared to pass the forming up line immediately on the barrage lifting.

6. The troops of the 154th Inf. Bde. on the left flank of the attacking Battalion of the 152nd Inf. Bde. will advance in line with the latter & will establish a line running S.W. from ESPILLY cutting off the pocket which at present exists at this point. There will be no barrage on the west and this attack will be carried out without a barrage.

7. The Field Artillery barrage will open at ZERO hour and will be 200 yds to the west of the forming up line. At zero plus 10 mins. the barrage will begin to creep forward at the rate of 100 metres every 4 mins.

There will be one pause of 20 mins. during the attack during which the Field Artillery barrage will [ ] the Eastern face of the Bois de L'AULNAY.

The C.R.A. will arrange to bring fire to bear on LES HAIES, NAPPES and CHAUMUZY from Zero hour onwards.

8. "D" Coy will cover the advance by M.G. barrage in accordance with detailed instructions issued.

9. The attack will be assisted by 10 Tanks. These Tanks will assemble under cover of the woods about 500 metres S.S.W. of the Mont d'ARDRE and will be in position at this point by 3 a.m. tomorrow 23rd July. They will not leave the positions of assembly till Zero hour and their function is to follow up the infantry & to deal with any strong points which are holding up the

"2"

Tanks will move to the Northern edge of the BOIS DE COURTON in the neighbourhood of ESPILLY and fire to the neighbourhood of the BOIS D'AHLNAY.

The signal that assistance is required from the Tanks is the waving of a flag or handkerchief in the direction from which the opposition is being encountered. This signal will only be given by platoon commanders.

9. Zero hour will be 6 am 23rd inst. and time will be taken from the opening of the artillery barrage.

10. On completion of barrage Coy. will return to present location.

11. ACKNOWLEDGE.

for Adjt.
51 (H) Bn. M.G.C.

Issued at 5 pm
 D Coy
 Hd. Qrs.
 File.

SECRET.   Copy No...1...

51st (H) BATTALION, M. G. CORPS.

Operation Order No. 42.   26/7/18.

Reference map 1/20,000
and attached sketch.

---

1. An attack will be carried out to-morrow by the 51st and 62nd British Divisions, in conjunction with the 14th French Division.

2. **Dividing Lines & Objectives.**
The dividing lines between Brigades and the various objectives are shown on the attached sketch.

3. **Forming Up.**
The Infantry will be formed up on the jumping-off line by Zero hour.
As the barrage of the 62nd Division will fall on the Southern edge of the BOIS DE L'AULNAY, no troops of the 152nd Brigade will be within 250 yards of this line at Zero hour.
The barrage on the front of 153rd Brigade will fall on ESPILLY and on the track running S.W. from it. The troops of this Brigade will, therefore, form up on the Eastern face of the spit of wood S.E. of ESPILLY and on a line thence 200 yds. distant from the track mentioned.
Forming up lines will be taped out by the 152nd and 153rd Brigades in their respective areas.

4. **Artillery Barrage.**
The attack will be covered by an artillery barrage arranged in depth.
The barrage will open at Zero hour 200 yards in advance of the forming up line, and will commence to creep backwards at Zero plus 10 mins.
The points of junction of the barrage with that of the 14th French Division are :-
  Initial Barrage. - Junction of track from ESPILLY with the main drive through the wood.
  During pause on BROWN LINE. - On main track 200 metres S.E. of Cross Roads at point 243.2.

5. **General conduct of the attack:**
(a). The 153rd Infantry Brigade (less the troops in the spit of wood S.E. of ESPILLY) will advance at Zero plus 10 mins. in conjunction with the 14th French Division to the line shown in BROWN on the attached sketch, (approx. hour of arrival Z plus 86 mins.) leaving posts to watch the Northern face of the wood. The barrage during this advance will move at the rate of 100 metres every 6 mins.
The portion of the 153rd Brigade in the spit of wood S.E. of ESPILLY will advance with the 137th Brigade.
There will be a pause of 20 mins. on the BROWN LINE, after which, the advance of the 153rd Brigade will be resumed to the BLUE LINE (approx. hour of arrival Z plus 121 mins.)
(b). The 137th Brigade will pass through the troops of the 152nd Brigade on their front and advance from the jumping off line at Zero plus 86 mins. in time to move forward from the BROWN LINE with the 153rd Brigade.
(c). The 152nd Brigade will advance in line with the 137th Brigade (approx. hour of advance Zero plus 86 mins.)
(d). There will be a pause of 20 mins. while the Infantry are on the First Objective (BLUE LINE). At the end of this pause (i.e. at about Zero plus 141 mins.), the whole line will advance together under the barrage to the Second Objective (GREEN).
The pace of the barrage during this portion of the attack will be 100 metres every 7 mins.
(e). The portion of the 62nd Division to the North of the River ARDRE will swing forward in conjunction with the advance of the 152nd Bde., pivotting on the S.W. angle of the BOIS DU PETIT CHAMP.

- 2 -

6. There is a possibility of French Tanks co-operating on the front of the 62nd Division.

7. <u>Liaison with the 14th French Division.</u>
The 14th French Division are swinging forward the right flank of their attack to connect with the left flank of the 153rd Infantry Brigade.

8. <u>Consolidation.</u>
The First and Second Objectives will be consolidated and, in addition, the 153rd Inf. Brigade will consolidate the BROWN LINE.

9. <u>M. G. BARRAGE.</u>
"A," "B," & "C" Companies will be under the orders of the 152nd, 153rd and 154th Infantry Brigades respectively.
O.C. "D" Company in conjunction with a battery of 8 guns of "A" Company will arrange to cover the advance of the Infantry by a machine gun barrage in accordance with detailed instructions issued.

10. The C.R.E. will make a track through the wood from the jumping off line to the BROWN LINE.

11. The Headquarters of the 152nd and 153rd Inf. Brigades will remain at NANTEUIL.
The 137th Inf. Brigade will establish its Headquarters in the CHATEAU at NANTEUIL with an advanced report centre in the hollow road 200 yards S. of the third L of MOLIN MULLIN.

12. Zero hour will be at 8 a.m.
A synchronized watch will be taken from Divisional Headquarters to H.Q. 153rd Inf. Bde. at 7 p.m. to-day.

13. A C K N O W L E D G E.

Issued at 5 p.m.

2/Lieut. & Adjt.,
51st (H) Bn. M. G. C.

Copy No. 1 - "A" Coy.
" 2 - "B" "
" 3 - "D" "
" 4 - 152nd Inf. Bde.
" 5 - 153rd Inf. Bde.
" 6 - 51st (H) Div. "G."
" 7 - War Diary.
" 8 - File.

26/7/18.

51st (H) BATTALION, M.G. CORPS.

Detailed Instructions to Accompany Operation Order No. 42.

1. A barrage to cover the advance of the Infantry will be carried out by "D" Company in conjunction with a battery of 8 guns of "A" Company.

2. Map 1 is attached shewing areas to be dealt with.

3. Tracing 2 is attached shewing the Artillery barrage. The position of Infantry will be taken as 50 yds. behind the Artillery barrage and safety angles and time of lift will be calculated accordingly.

4. Barrage guns will be in position before dawn.

5. Rate of fire will be one belt per five minutes.

6. Completion of assembly will be reported to Bn. H.Q. by word "LEAVE."

7. On completion of barrage a battery of 8 guns of "D" Company will be moved forward into a position in front edge of the spit of wood S.E. of ESPILLY or other suitable position if this ground has been cleared of the enemy and will be laid on left S.O.S. barrage shewn in BROWN on attached map.

8. The remaining 8 guns of "D" Company will return to battle positions.

9. The battery of 8 guns of "A" Company will be laid on right S.O.S. barrage shewn in BROWN on attached map.

10. A C K N O W L E D G E.

2/Lieut. & Adjt.,
51st (H) Bn. M.G.C.

N O T E.

Reference 51st (H) Bn. M.G.C. Operation Order No. 42.

As the 187th Brigade may pass through the battery positions, arrangements must be made to cease fire until they are completely clear of the danger zone.

SECRET.   Copy No ...10...

51st (H) BATTALION, M.G. CORPS.

26.7.18

Operation Order No. 43.

Reference map
EPERNAY, 1/20,000.

1. *1*   Headquarters 51st (H) Bn. M.G.C. less Transport, will move to NANTEUIL, 27/7/18.

2. *2*   All reinforcements will move to area round track near stream 800 yards S.E. of NANTEUIL (222.7/265.4).

3. *3*   Transport, Quartermaster's Stores and Details will remain at HAUTVILLERS until further orders.

4. *4*   Valises and Packs of Reinforcements will be dumped at Quartermaster's Stores and a Guard detailed by the R.S.M. remain with them.

5. *5*   Lieut. HALL will be in charge of reinforcements during the move and will arrange time of parade.

6. *6*   Bn. H.Q. will be established at 6 p.m. in NANTEUIL at present Headquarters of "B" Company.

7. *7*   A C K N O W L E D G E.

Issued at 4 p.m.

                                          2/Lieut. & Adjt.,
                                      51st (H) Bn. M.G.C.

Copy No. 1 - "A" Coy.
        2 - "B" "
        3 - "C" "
        4 - "D" "
        5 - Lieut. Hall.
        6 - 51st (H) Div. "G."
        7 - 152nd Inf. Bde.
        8 - 153rd Inf. Bde.
        9 - 154th Inf. Bde.
       10 - War Diary.
       11 - File.
       12 - R.S.M.
       13 - Q.M.

SECRET   Copy 3

51st/7th Dn M.G.C.

OPERATION ORDER
No 44   7/7/18

By Major
JONEMENY [?]

1. I [...] the start of [...] as
   [...] in Wood 200 yds S.W.
   of Mon D'HENNE on night 7/8th
   July 1918

2. Coy will be prepared to
   move at short notice with
   [...] ready packed in
   limbers

3. Completion of concentration
   will be reported to Battn HQ

4. ACKNOWLEDGE

Issued 1/7 20/7   [signature]
                                                   adjt
         51st/7th M.G.C

SECRET.   Copy No. 9

51st (H) BATTALION, M. G. CORPS.

Operation Order No. 45.   29/7/18.

Reference Map
JONCHERY. 1/20,000.

1. **1**   "D" Company will come under the orders of the 154th Infantry Brigade and will be prepared to relieve the Companies in the line to-night.

2. **2**   "C" Company will come into Divisional Reserve and will take over the area occupied by "D" Company in wood 800 yards S.E. of Mdn. D'ARENE.

3. **3**   O. C. "D" Company will immediately get into touch with B.G.C. 154th Infantry Brigade.

4. **4**   A C K N O W L E D G E.

Issued at 7.15 p.m.

Copy No. 1 - "A" Coy.
         2 - "B" "
         3 - "C" "
         4 - "D" "
         5 - 51st (H) Div. "G."
         6 - 8 - Brigades.
         9 - War Diary.
        10 - File.

                                                 [signature]
                                              2/Lieut. & Adjt.,
                                              51st (H) Bn. M. G. C.

S E C R E T. Copy No. 13

51st (H) BATTALION, M. G. CORPS.

Operation Order No. 66.

Reference map
NEUFIS. 1/80,000.

31.7.18

1. 1   "C" Coy. will move to MARTEUIL area to-day, 31st July, 1918, leaving present location not before 6 p.m.

2. 2   A billeting party of One Officer and One Other Rank will be detailed to report to Battalion H.Q. at 2 p.m.

3. 3   On arrival in new area "C" Coy. will be attached to 154th Infantry Brigade Group and O. C. Coy. will report location of Headquarters to 154th Inf. Bde.

4. 4   "D" Company on arrival in new area will be attached to H. Q. Bn, M.G.

5. 5   A C K N O W L E D G E.

Issued at 11.15 p.m.

2/Lieut. & Adjt.,
51st (H) Bn. M. G. C.

Copy No. 1 - 4 - Companies.
       5 - 7 - Brigades.
       8 - 51st (H) Div. "G."
       9 -   "   "   "Q."
      10 - T.O.
      11 - Q.M.
      12 - R.S.M.
      13 - War Diary.
      14 - File.

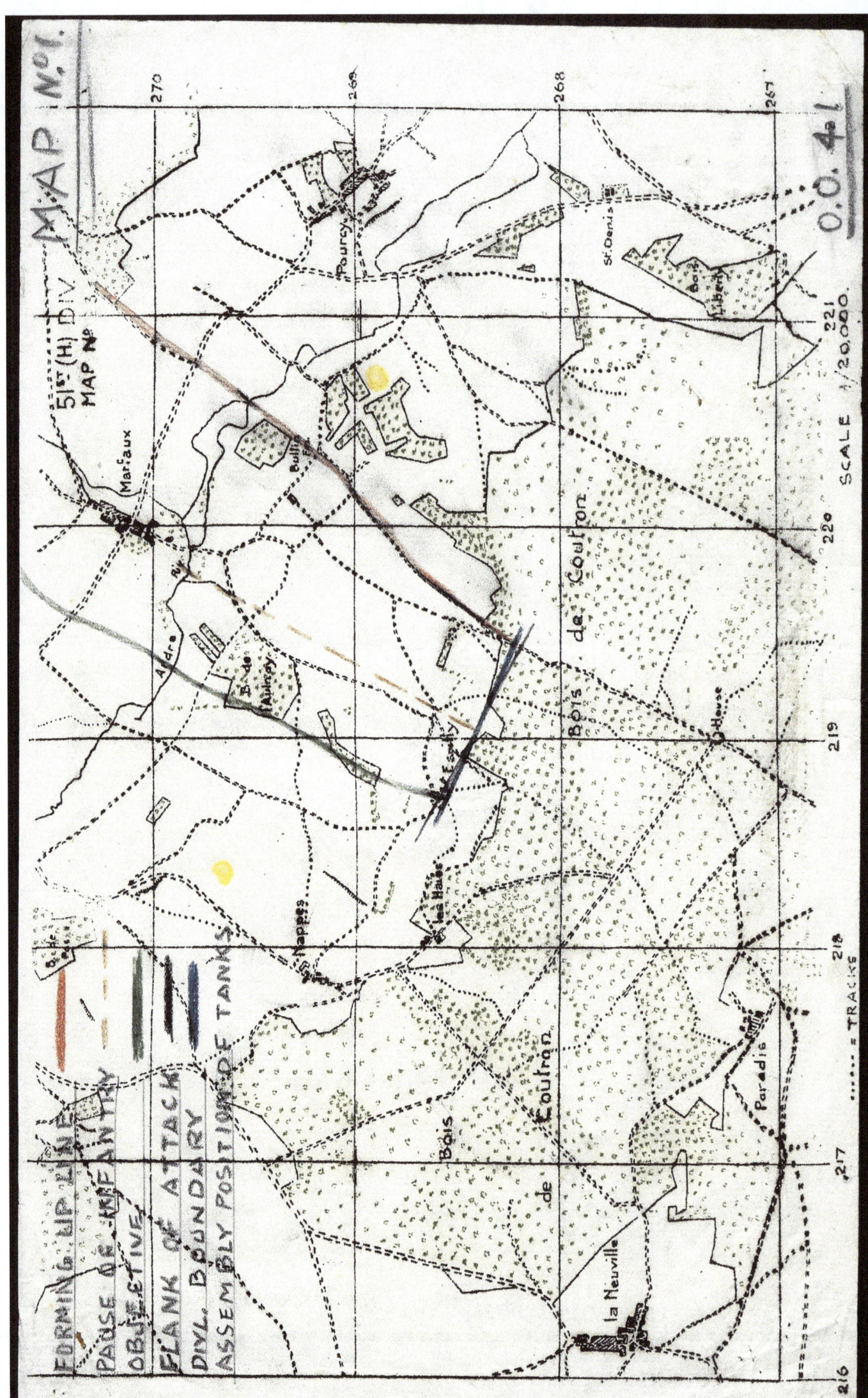

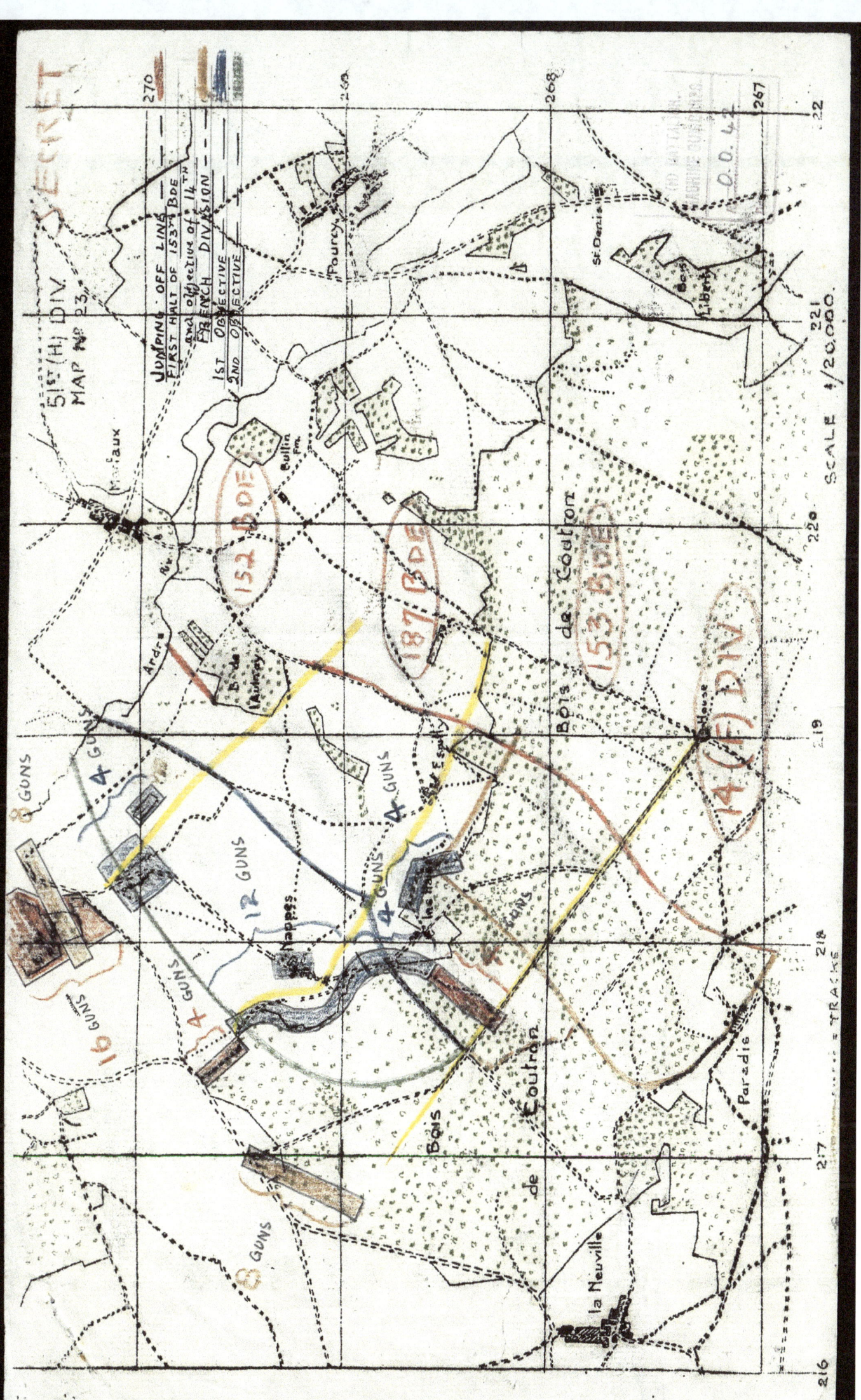

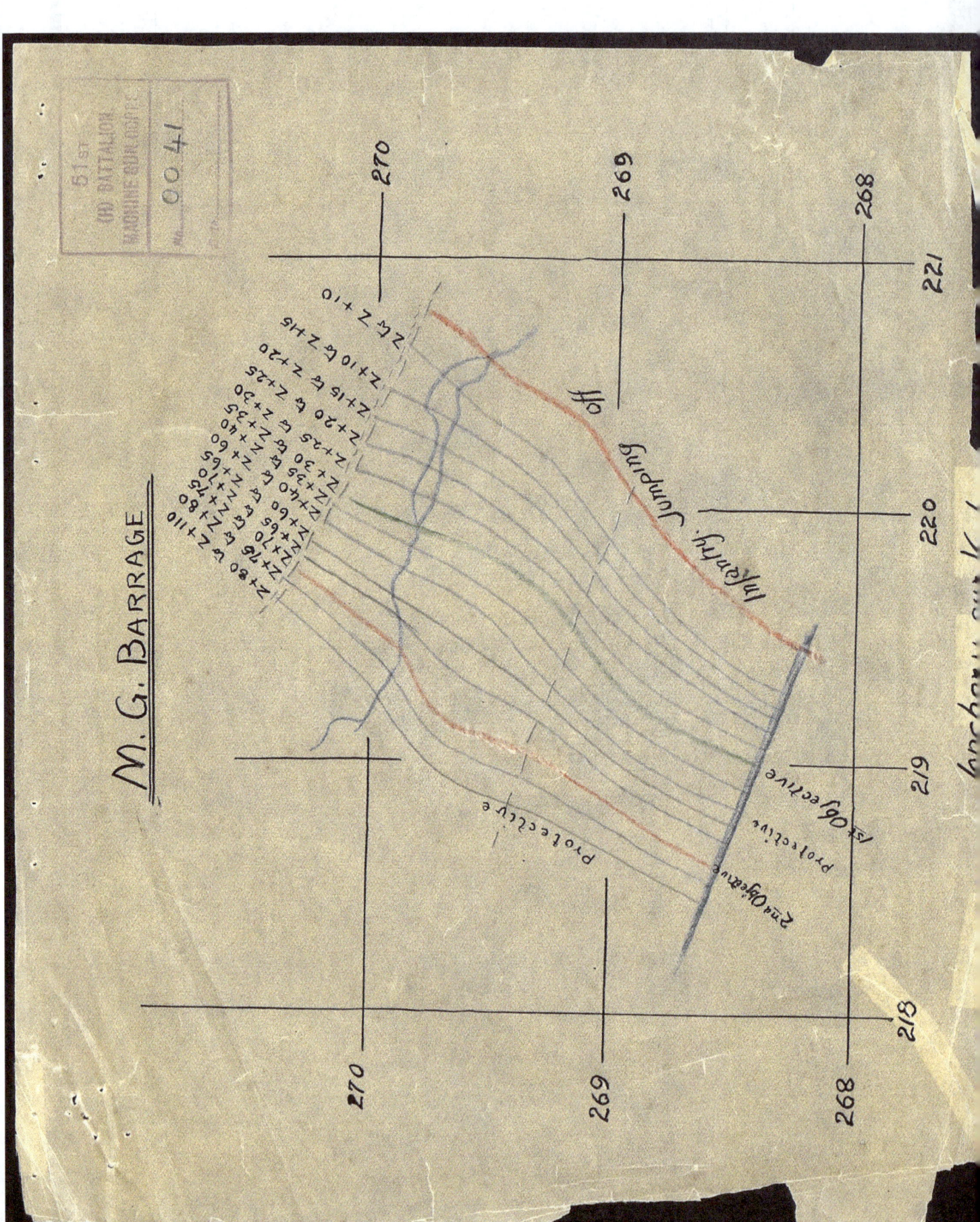

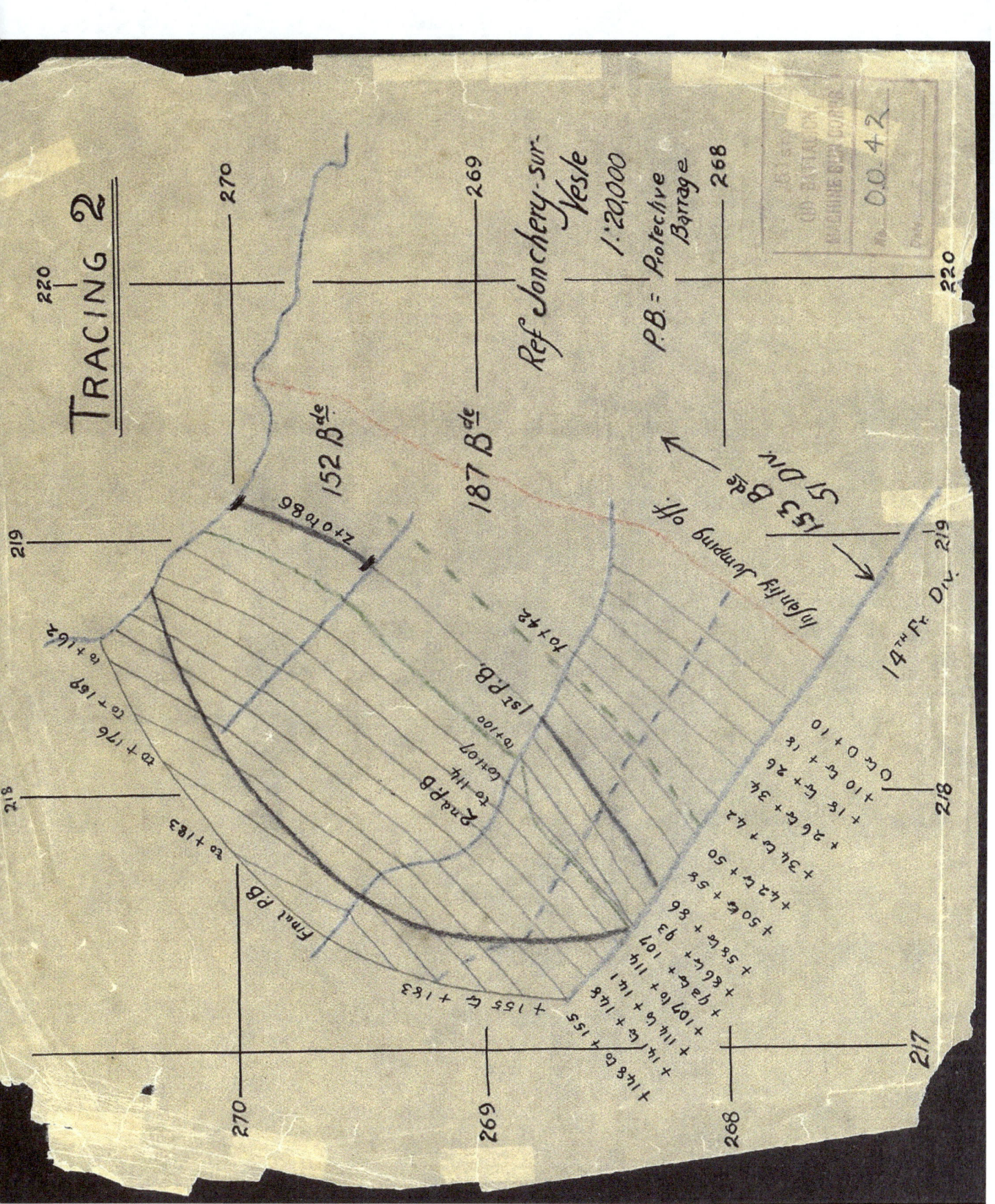

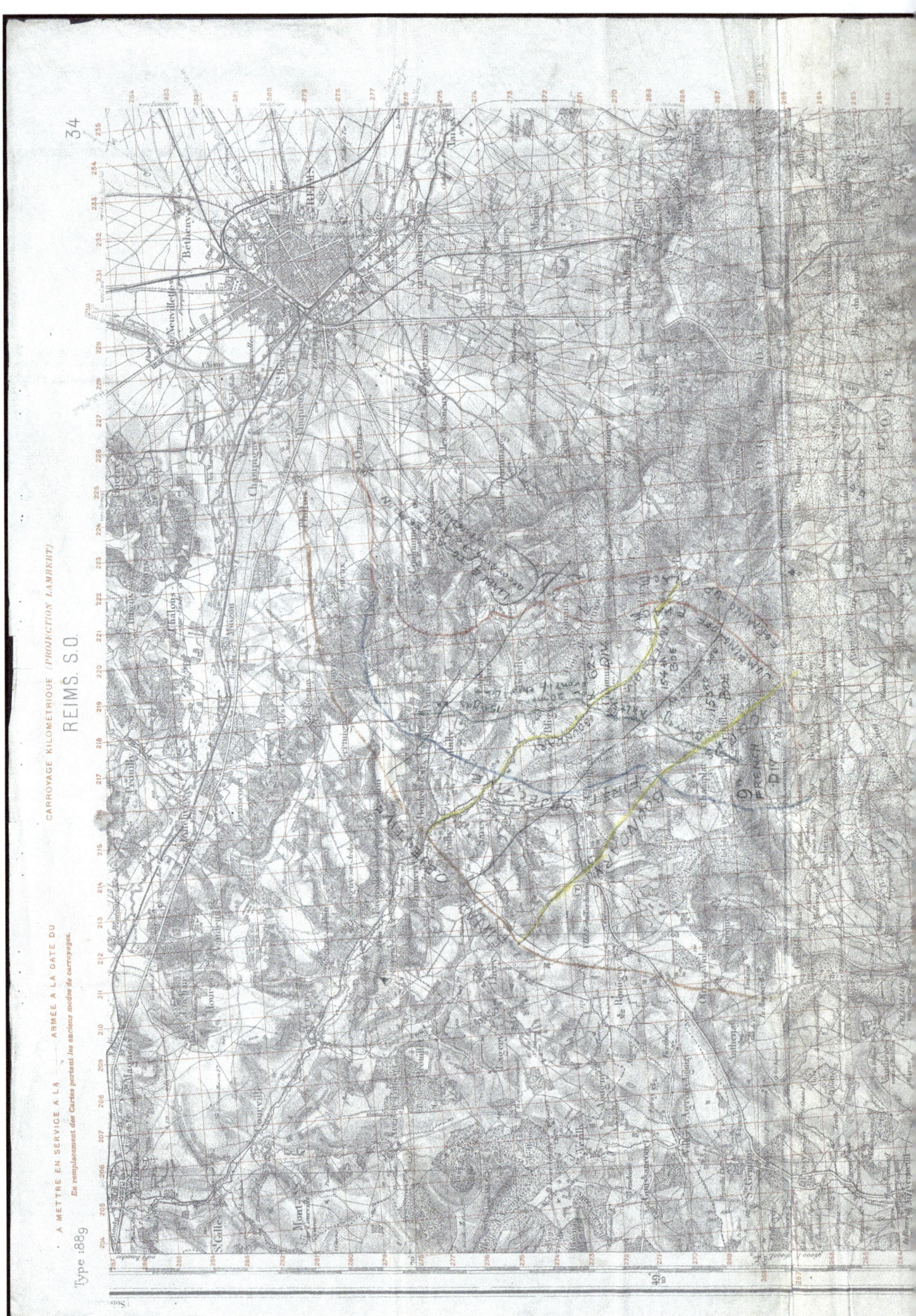

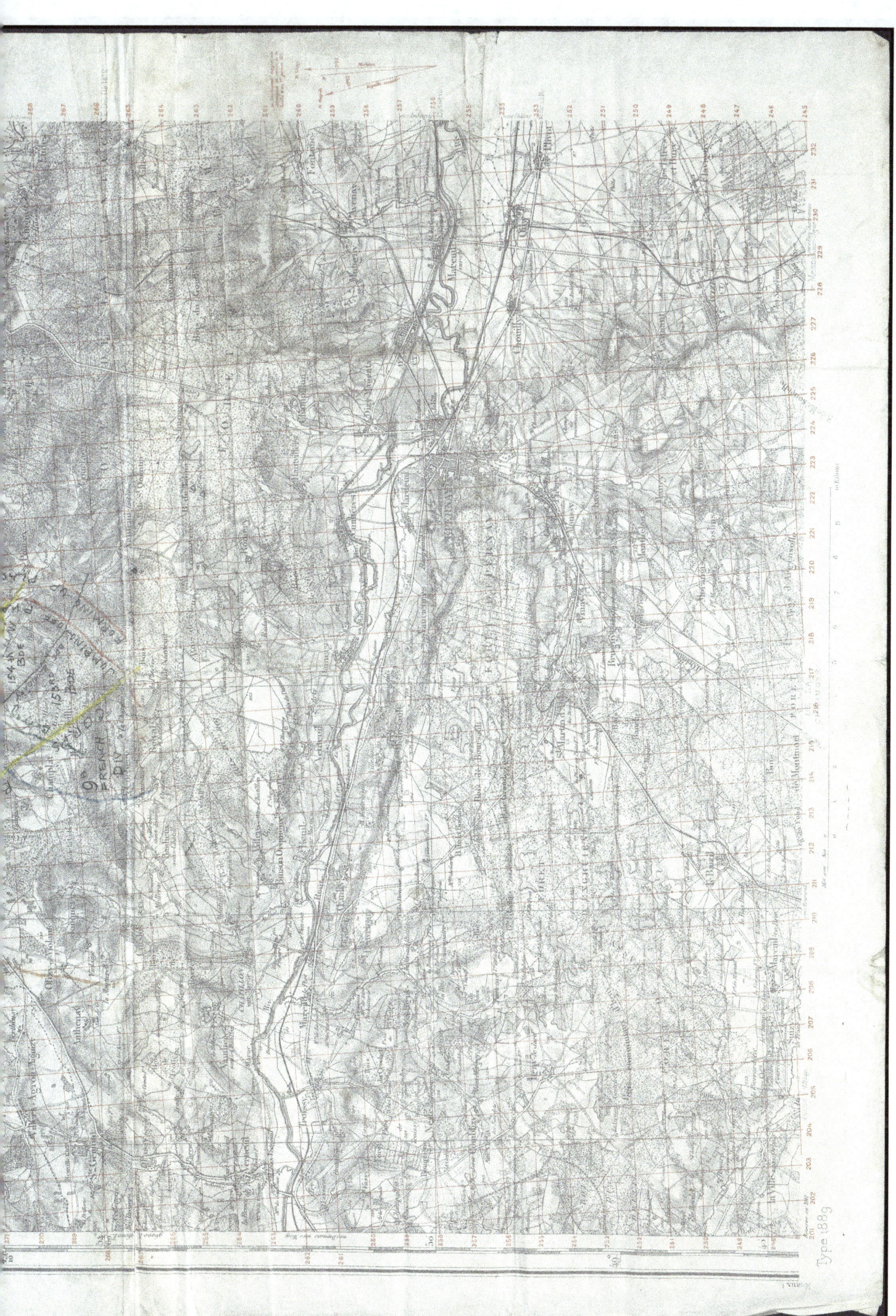

O.O. 39

COMBINED
REIMS & CHALONS
1/20,000

WITH OBJECTIVES AS
SHOWN ON DIVISIONAL MAP
DATED 19-7-18

DIVISIONAL MAP
21-7-18

O.O.40

JONCHERY
LARGE SCALE
SQUARED
1/20000

WITH OBJECTIVES SHOWN
FOR 21-7-18

51st (H) BATTALION, M.G. CORPS.,

REPORT on OPERATIONS, S.W. of RHEIMS, 19th/31st JULY, 1918.

Ref.Map:
JONCHERY-sur-VESLE, 1/20,000.

In the evening of the 19th July, orders were issued by the 51st Division for an attack at 8 a.m. on the 20th July.

The attack to be carried out by the 154th Brigade on the RIGHT and the 153rd Brigade on the LEFT, and the 152nd Brigade in Divisional Reserve.

The 62nd Division attacking on the RIGHT and the 9th French Division on the left of the Division.

"A" Coy., "B" Coy., and "C" Coy., were attached to the 152nd, 153rd, and 154th Infantry Brigades respectively and "D" Coy. was in Divisional Reserve.

"B" and "C" Companies assembled in Battle positions with the attacking Brigades on the night 19th/20th. "A" Coy. assembled with 152nd Infantry Brigade at BOIS de QUENTIN and "D" Company assembled in Divisional Reserve at BOIS de QUENTIN.

Battalion Headquarters were established beside Divisional Headquarters at ST. IMOGES.

The attack was carried out by the 154th Infantry Brigade on the RIGHT with the 4th Gordons on the left, 4th Seaforths on the right and the 7th A. & S.Hrs. to pass through to the final objective and by the 153rd Infantry Brigade on the left with the 7th Black Watch on the left and on the right 6th Bk Black Watch with the 7th Gordon Highrs. to pass through to the final objective.

The 154th Infantry Brigade attached a sub-section to each Battal holding ten guns in reserve. The 153rd Inf.Bde. attached a Section to each Battalion, holding a section in reserve.

The enemy put up a very strong resistance all along the line and in the afternoon, orders were issued to consolidate ground gained.

The guns of "C" Coy. were employed on the 20th as follows:-

Two guns on the Right advanced behind the 4th Seaforths and were able to bring direct overhead covering fire to bear on the enemy covering the advance and finally took up position in support of the Infantry in the N.E. end of Square 219/268 covering approach to MARFAUX.

Two guns on the left advancing behind the 4th Gordons but owing to the density of the woods, no opportunity arose to come into action and finally defensive positions were taken up in support of the Infantry consolidation about Square 219/267 central.

1.

Two guns advanced behind the 7th A.& S.Hrs. and took up position in front of Battalion H.Qrs. in Square 219/268. At 7 p.m. the enemy made a strong attempt to gain command of the high ground on the edge of BOIS DE COUTRON S.E. of ESPILLY, and had gained the fire control of the Ridge. Under the orders of the 7th A.& S.Hrs. these two guns reinforced the 7th A.& S.Hrs. at this point and regained the fire control of the Ridge thus enabling the 7th A.& S.Hrs. to re-occupy the commanding positions.

In the afternoon, three sub-sections were ordered forward by the Brigade to consolidate the ground from BULLIN FME. to the ARDRE.

The remaining four guns were held in Brigade Reserve.

The guns of "B" Coy. were employed on the 20th as follows:-

The three sections advanced in support of the Infantry but owing to the density of the woods no opportunity arose to come into action and finally they consolidated in support of Infantry in the Wood in Squares 215, 218/266.

In the afternoon, "A" Coy. moved with 152nd Infantry Brigade to BOIS de SARBRUGE.

In the evening of the 20th orders were issued by the Division for the 152nd Infantry Brigade to continue the attack to BOIS de COUTRON at 8 a.m. on the 21st, 153rd Brigade to form defensive flank on BOIS de COUTRON.

"A" Coy. were attached to 152nd Infantry Brigade and assembled in BOIS de COUTRON on the night 20/21st.

The attack was carried out by the 152nd Infantry Brigade, with the 6th Gordons on the right, 5th Seaforths on the left, and 6th Seaforths to pass through to the final objective. The 152nd Inf. Bde. attached one section to each Battalion retaining one section in Brigade reserve.

Strong M.G. opposition was encountered from the enemy. A line was consolidated running S.W. through S.E. corner of Square 219/268.

The guns of "A" Coy. were employed on the 21st as follows:-

Two sections with leading Battalions advanced behind the Infantry and took up position in Support.

The section attached to the 6th Seaforths was moved forward under orders of the Brigade to position on Road in Wood at 218/8 - 267/4 to deal with a heavy machine gun fire in that vicinity.

The section in Reserve remaining in Brigade reserve.

On the 22nd, orders were issued for the 152nd Inf.Bde to

attack at 6 a.m. on the 23rd and gain ground in the Valley of the ARDRE., the attack to be carried out covered by an artillery and M.G. barrage and to be assisted by tanks.

The 154th Inf.Bde. to advance on the left flank of the attacking Battalions of the 152nd Inf.Bde. and establish a line running S.W. from ESPILLY. This advance to be carried out without artillery barrage.

On the 22nd, the 154th Brigade extended its left flank into BOIS de COUTRON to join up with 153rd Inf.Bde. and the remaining M.G. Section in reserve took up positions on this flank.

The 152nd Inf.Bde. were withdrawn from the wood and were assembled for the attack during the night 22nd/23rd.

The attack was carried out by the 152nd Inf.Bde., with the 5th Seaforths on the Right and the 6th Seaforths in the centre and the 6th Gordons on the left.

The 152nd Inf.Bde. attached one section to each Battalion, retaining one Section in Reserve.

"D" Coy. were ordered to cover the advance of the 152nd Inf.Bde. and assembled on the night 22/23rd and carried out an intense barrage scheme, covering the advance, firing upwards of 70,000 rounds.

"A" Coy. were employed as follows:-

The three sections attached to Battalions took up positions and covered the advance of the Infantry by direct overhead fire, firing upwards of 20,000 rounds, very good effect being observed. Later, positions were consolidated on the forward slope of ridge running S.W. from BULLIN FME. During the morning, the Brigade reserve Section was also moved up into this line.

The attack in the valley had reached its objective but the village of ESPILLY and the wood at this point were still held by the enemy.

A section of "D" Coy. were allotted to the 152nd Brigade to assist the capture of ESPILLY by gaining the fire control of this position but this operation was not carried out.

A section of "D" Coy. was allotted to the 154th Brigade to strength their defence of the Wood S.E. of ESPILLY.

The remaining two sections of "D" Coy. were allotted to the 152nd Brigade.

During the night 23/24th, the M.G. defences on the Right sub-sector were re-organised. "A" Coy. being in position from the ARDRE to rectangular copse 600 yards E. of ESPILLY. "C" Coy. with 154th Inf.Brigade from that point to the left. "D" Coy. in reserve from MIN d'ARDRE from S.W. edge of Square 220/268.

During the 24th the 153rd Infantry Brigade with "B" Coy. was relieved by the 14th French Division and was concentrated in the neighbourhood of ST. IMOGES. The Divisional front was reorganised with the 152nd Infantry Brigade holding the right sector and the 154th Infantry Brigade holding the left sector.

Battalion H.Qrs. moved with Division to HAUT VILLERS.

On the night of the 24th/25th, the S.O.S. went up at 10-30 p.m. and the guns in the right sector opened fire on pre-arranged targets.

On the 26th, the 153rd Infantry Brigade and "B" Coy. M.G.C. relieved the 154th Inf.Bde. and "C" Coy. M.G.C. On the 26th, orders were issued for an attack on the 27th in conjunction with the 62nd Division.

The attack to be carried out by the 152nd Inf.Bde. on the Right with the 187th Inf.Bde. in the centre and 153rd Inf.Bde. on the left.

The 152nd Inf.Bde. attacked with the 5th Seaforths.

The 153rd Inf.Bde. attacked with the 7th Gordons on the Right and the 6th Black Watch on the left and 7th Black Watch to pass through these Battalions.

The advance was covered by an artillery and machine gun barrage.

"D" Coy. and a battery of eight guns of "A" Coy. carried out an intense barrage especially dealing with the edge of BOIS de COUTRON from West of ESPILLY to the N.E. of the Wood. Upwards of 120,000 rounds were fired in this barrage.

The advance was rapid and all objectives were gained.

A further advance was ordered by the Division to commence at 1 p.m. to occupy a line Ridge 200 yards N.W. of North corner of BOIS de COUTRON, to S.E. corner of BOIS des ECLISSES, to CHAUMUZY (inclusive) to point 173- 1500 metres N.E. of CHAUMUZY.

The 152nd Inf.Bde. continued the advance with the 6th Seaforths on the right and the 6th Gordons on the left.

The guns of "A" Coy. were employed on the 27th as follows:-

One section was attached to 5th Seaforths and advanced with them in the attack and consolidated positions 400 yards N.W. of BOIS D'AULNAY.

On the continuance of the advance, the two sections on completion of barrage were attached to the 6th Seaforths and 6th Gordons and advanced behind them and took up positions around CHAUMUZY.

The section with 5th Seaforths and with one gun of the remaining section (the other three having been put out of action) advanced and took up positions on a line about 1,000 yards S.E. of CHAUMUZY.

"B" Coy. were employed on the 27th as follows:-

One Section attached to the 7th Gordons advanced behind the Infantry and were able to cover the advance with direct fire.

One sub-section attached to the 6th Black Watch advanced behind the Infantry through BOIS DE COUTRON, but owing to the density of the wood, no opportunity arose.

One section attached to the 7th Black Watch advanced behind the Infantry through the BOIS de COUTRON but owing to the density of the wood no opportunity arose of coming into action.

These guns consolidated on a line running N.W. from the 'B' of the BOIS de COUTRON to point 210, on high ground South of BOIS DES ECLISSES.

The remaining Sub-section, as four guns of the Company were out of action, was held in Brigade Reserve and moved with Brigade during the night to CHAUMUZY.

On the 28th, the advance was continued through BOIS DES ECLISSES towards CHAMBRECY. The 152nd Inf.Bde. on the right, 153rd Inf.Bde. on the left, and the 62nd Division on the right of the Division.

The guns of "A" Company were employed on the 28th as follows:-

Two sections advanced behind the Infantry, and took up positions in the forward slopes of BOIS DES ECLISSES, covering CHAMBRECY.

During the day some excellent targets of the enemy retiring were engaged on the slopes N. of CHAMBRECY.

The remaining four guns took up positions in Reserve 800 yards N.W. of CHAUMUZY.

The Guns of "B" Company were employed on the 27th as follows:-

One section was attached to each Battalion and advanced behind the Infantry.

On reaching the forward slopes of BOIS DES ECLISSES, these guns were able to cover the advance of the Infantry, and got some good targets on the slopes N. of CHAMBRECY including one Field Gun which was firing at the advancing Infantry.

The guns consolidated in support to the Infantry on the forward slopes of BOIS des ECLISSES.

On the night 28th/29th, the 154th Infantry Brigade relieved the 152nd and 153rd Infantry Brigades, "D" Company taking over from "A" and "B" Companies, "C" Company coming into Divisional Reserve at MIN d'ARDRE.

On the 29th, the line was extended to include MONTAGNE DE BLIGNY and positions of a section of four guns adjusted accordingly.

"D" Company were relieved by the French on the 31st.

15/8/18.

Lt.Col.,
Cmdg., 51st (H) Battalion M.G.Corps.

Army Form W.3091.

Cover for Documents.

Nature of Enclosures,

Confidential

War Diary

of

51st (H) Bn. M.G. Corps

for Aug. 1918

Notes, or Letters written,

Army Form C. 2118.

WAR DIARY
or
INTELLIGENCE SUMMARY.
(Erase heading not required.)

Instructions regarding War Diaries and Intelligence Summaries are contained in F. S. Regs., Part II. and the Staff Manual respectively. Title pages will be prepared in manuscript.

Place	Date	Hour	Summary of Events and Information	Remarks and references to Appendices
	1918. Aug.		Reference maps :— CHALONS and REIMS, 1/50,000.	
			FRANCE 44B, 1/10,000.	
			LENS 11, 1/100,000.	
			MAROEUIL, 1/20,000.	
			FRANCE 51B. N.W., 1/20,000.	
			FRANCE 51C. N.E., 1/20,000.	
			OPPY and FAMPOUX, 1/10,000.	
			FAMPOUX, 1/10,000.	
	1.		B.H.Q. and "D" Coy. at NANTEUIL.	
			"A", "B" & "C" Coys. with respective Brigades in area around NANTEUIL.	
		12 noon.	B.H.Q. and "D" Coy. moved to PIERRY via HAUTVILLERS – DIZY MAGENTA – EPERNAY – arriving PIERRY 4 p.m. H.Q. at Billet 44.	
			"B" Coy. with 153rd Inf. Bde. marched past General Berthelot at DIZY MAGENTA.	
	2.	5.30 p.m.	Transport of B.H.Q. and "D" Coy. moved by march route to OIRY and entrained there.	
		7. 0 p.m.	B.H.Q. and "D" Coy. moved by march route to OIRY.	
		6. 0 p.m.	"C" Coy. entrained at EPERNAY.	
		4.36 p.m.	"A" " " AVIZE.	
		5.59 p.m.	"B" " " VERTUS.	
		11.12 p.m.	B.H.Q. and "D" Coy. entrained at OIRY.	
	3.		TRAVELLING ALL DAY.	
	4.	7. 0 a.m.	B.H.Q. AND "D" Coy. detrained at CALONNE.	
			"C" Coy. detrained at BRYAS.	
			"A" " " PERNES.	
			"B" " " CALONNE.	
		9. 0 a.m.	B.H.Q. and "D" Coy. moved by lorries to CAMBLIGNEUIL – arrived 11 a.m. Transport following (by Road).	
	5.		All Companies billeted in CAMBLIGNEUIL.	
	6-10.		Resting, re-equipping and cleaning up.	
	11.		Training.	
	12.		Church Parades. Kit Inspections.	
	13.		Training. Warning Order received intimating that 51st (H) Division were to relieve 52nd Division in the line, commencing night 14th/15th.	

Army Form C. 2118.

WAR DIARY
or
INTELLIGENCE SUMMARY.
(Erase heading not required.)

Instructions regarding War Diaries and Intelligence Summaries are contained in F. S. Regs., Part II. and the Staff Manual respectively. Title pages will be prepared in manuscript.

Place	Date	Hour	Summary of Events and Information	Remarks and references to Appendices
	14.		Companies completed preparations for line. "C" Coy. entrained at point W.20.b. (Sheet 44B. S.E.) on Light Railway, detrained at ECURIE and proceeded to line to relieve "B" Coy. 52nd Bn. M.G.C. in Right-Sub-Sector. Relief complete 1 a.m. 15th.	
	15.	1.30 p.m.	"C" Coy. Transport proceeded by march route to A.26.d.	
	16.	3. 0 p.m.	Relief of "A", "B" & "D" Companies held in abeyance.	
		5. 0 p.m.	Transport moved by march route to A.26.d.	
		7. 0 p.m.	Remainder of Battalion entrained at W.20.b. and moved by Light Railway to ECURIE.	
	17.	5.15 a.m.	B.H.Q., "A", "B" & "D" Companies at BRIGADE CAMP, A.26.b.2.6.	
		5.30 p.m.	"B" Coy. relieved "C" Coy. 57th Bn. M.G.C. in Left Sub-Sector of 57th Division. Relief complete.	
			"A" Coy. relieved "B" Coy. 57th Bn. M.G.C. in Centre Sub-Sector of 57th Division. Relief complete 1 a.m.	
			"D" Coy. in Divisional Reserve.	
	18.	10. 0 p.m.	"D" Coy. ordered to relieve "A" Coy. 57th Bn. M.G.C. in Sector held by 170th Bde., owing to extension of Divisional Right Boundary.	
		12.15 a.m.	Orders for extension of Divisional front cancelled. Move by "D" Coy. cancelled.	
		9. 0 p.m.	Enemy reported retiring N. and S. of the R. SCARPE. "A" Coy. received orders to co-operate with Canadians, who were to keep in touch with enemy retirement by means of strong fighting patrols.	
	19.	1. 0 a.m. to 1.40 a.m.	"A" Coy. assist in operation S. of R. SCARPE by carrying out an enfilade barrage on Indian and Italian Trenches.	
		1.40 a.m. to dawn.	"A" Coy. enfiladed CHINSTRAP LANE and S.W. of the area between LANCER TRENCH and R. SCARPE.	
	20.		Enemy found to have evacuated his front line. Advance continued with fluctuating success. Warning Order received that 1st (L.G.) Bn. M.G. Regt. will relieve "C" Coy. night 22nd/23rd.	
	21.	1.30 a.m.	152nd Inf. Bde. carried out successful minor operation, driving enemy out of FAMPOUX. 12 guns of "A" Coy. co-operating fired on Railway Bank from H.23.b.3.3. to junction of Railway with COLT Trench, thence along COLT Trench to the QUARRY, I.13.a.0.3.	

WAR DIARY
or
INTELLIGENCE SUMMARY.
(Erase heading not required.)

Army Form C. 2118.

Place	Date	Hour	Summary of Events and Information	Remarks and references to Appendices
	21 (Contd.)		For this purpose 4 guns of "A" Coy. moved to positions in PUDDING Trench, H.16.b. 6 guns of "B" Coy. fired on area JUTLAND Trench and COLT Trench to the QUARRY, I.13.a.0.5. 4 guns of "D" Coy. assisted "A" Coy. in operation.	
	22.		Relief of "C" Coy. by 1st (L.G.) Bn. M.G. Regt. cancelled.	
	23.		One Section of "D" Coy. (4 guns) moved into line to assist in operation to be carried out by 153rd Inf. Bde.	
	24.		153rd Inf. Bde. carried out an operation to establish the line ZION ALLEY - HYDERABAD along Support Line to H.5.d.8.1. Operation assisted by 8 guns of "A" Coy., 10 guns of "B" Coy., 8 guns of "C" Coy. and 4 guns of "D" Coy.	
		Night.	Operation successful except on left flank, where considerable bombing was encountered. "C" Coy. relieved in line by "D" Coy. and withdrawn to billets at BRIGADE CAMP, A.26.b.2.6. Relief complete 12.30 a.m. 25th.	
			"C" Coy. in Divisional Reserve. 4 guns of "C" Coy. formed the Anti-Aircraft defence of the Bn. at BRIGADE CAMP, A.26.b.2.6.	
	25.	6.0 a.m.	Operation carried out by 153rd Inf. Bde. 4 guns of "A" Coy., 6 guns of "B" Coy. and 6 guns of "D" Coy. co-operated in attack.	
	26.		Operations carried out by 152nd and 153rd Inf. Bdes. Action of M.G's. as follows :- Two batteries of 8 guns each of "A" Coy. and a battery of 8 guns of "D" Coy. 1st (L.G.) Bn. M.G. Regt..fired barrage on LANCER Trench and concentrated on area, E. of R. SCARPE and S. of the Railway. "B" Coy. less 2 Sections, "D" Coy. and "C" Coy. 1st (L.G.) Bn. M.G. Regt., as per organisation orders. Two Sections of "B" Coy. to consolidate ground captured by 153rd Inf. Bde. Two Sections of "D" Coy. 1st (L.G.) Bn. M.G. Regt. in 152nd Inf. Bde. Reserve. "C" Coy. at tactical disposal of 154th Inf. Bde.	
	27.	3.0 p.m.	H.Q. closed at BRIGADE CAMP and opened at H.14.a.0.7.	
		2.0 p.m.	"C" and "D" Coys. 1st (L.G.) Bn. M.G. Regt. withdrawn from line to rejoin Battn. at HAUTE AVESNES.	
			"A" Coy. 101st Bn. M.G.C. under orders of 51st (H) Bn. M.G.C. and take up positions in vicinity of COSSACK Trench and DEE Trench in H.15.d. and H.16.a.	
		Night.	"C" and "D" Coys. relieved in Left Sector by a M.G. Company of the 8th Division.	

Army Form C. 2118.

WAR DIARY
or
INTELLIGENCE SUMMARY.
(Erase heading not required.)

Instructions regarding War Diaries and Intelligence Summaries are contained in F. S. Regs., Part II. and the Staff Manual respectively. Title pages will be prepared in manuscript.

Place	Date	Hour	Summary of Events and Information	Remarks and references to Appendices
	27.	(Contd.)	"C" Coy. come under orders of 153rd Inf. Bde., 8 guns being placed into CADIZ - CALF - CHICKEN Reserve Line and 8 guns in MISSOURI Trench.	
	28.	Night.	"D" Coy. in Divisional Reserve at H.14.a.0.7. 153rd Inf. Bde. relieved by 154th Inf. Bde. in the line. Front of 152nd Inf. Bde. N. of CLOD Trench also taken over by 154th Inf. Bde. "B" and "C" Coys. come under orders of 154th Inf. Bde.	
	29.	6.30 p.m.	Attack carried out by 154th Inf. Bde. to gain the crest of GREENLAND HILL from CLOD Trench, I.15.a.2.5. to WILLOW Trench I.8.b.3.3. Attack supported by 8 guns of "A" Coy. in vicinity of CORRONA SUPPORT and firing on high ground S. of the Railway from CLOD Trench to DELBAR WOOD. Two Sections of "C" Coy. in reserve in MISSOURI Trench assembled in vicinity of CROCK ALLEY, I.13.b. with the object of advancing by bounds behind the Infantry and consolidating the ground astride the Railway. One Section of "B" Coy. in position in CHALK RESERVE to move forward in vicinity of NOSE, I.1.d. on capture of final objective. Warning Order issued. 152nd Inf. Bde. to attack at dawn on 30th HAUSA and DELBAR WOODS to gain command of the high ground between the R. SCARPE and CYRIL Trench, I.21.a. and I.15.c. Warning Order cancelled. HAUSA and DELBAR WOODS being in our possession. "D" Coy. relieved guns of "A" and "C" Coys. and "A" Coy. 101st Bn. M.G.C. as follows :-	
			2 guns of "D" Coy. relieved 2 guns of "A" Coy. 51st (H) Bn. M.G.C. at approx: I.13.b.3.8.	
			2 " " "D" " " 2 " " "A" " " " " " " I.13.b.9.0.	
			2 " " "D" " " 2 " " "A" " " " " " " I.13.d.8.4.	
			2 " " "D" " " 2 " " "A" " " " " " " I.21.a.9.3.	
			2 " " "D" " " 2 " " "C" " " " " " " I.14.b.4.6.	
			2 " " "D" " " 2 " " "B" " " " " " " I.8.d.4.4.	
			4 " " "D" " " 2 " " from each of the two forward Sections of "A" Coy. 101st Bn. M.G.C.	
	31.		Relieved teams of "A" and "C" Coys. moved to billets vacated by "D" Coy. at H.14.a.0.7.	

Army Form C. 2118.

WAR DIARY
or
INTELLIGENCE SUMMARY.
(Erase heading not required.)

Instructions regarding War Diaries and Intelligence Summaries are contained in F. S. Regs., Part II. and the Staff Manual respectively. Title pages will be prepared in manuscript.

Place	Date	Hour	Summary of Events and Information	Remarks and references to Appendices
			HONOURS AND AWARDS.	
			THE MILITARY CROSS.	
			2/Lieut. F.C. FENTON.	
			2/Lieut. J.C. McDERMOTT.	
			THE DISTINGUISHED CONDUCT MEDAL.	
			20258, Sgt. SMITH, H.	
			[signature]	
			Major,	
			Comdg. 51st (H) Bn. M.G.C.	

SECRET.   Copy No... 11

51st (H) BATTALION, M. G. CORPS.

Operation Order No. 48.   1/8/18.

Reference map
CHALONS, 1/50,000.

1. Battalion Headquarters and "D" Company will move to OIRY to-morrow, 2/8/18, for the purpose of entraining. The programme of entrainment previously issued is cancelled and the Battalion will entrain in accordance with attached programme.

2. Transport will move independently under the orders of the B.T.O. to arrive at OIRY not later than 8 p.m. All limbers must be packed ready for moving off by 7.30 p.m.

3. Battalion H.Q. and "D" Coy. will parade ready to move off at 7 p.m.

4. Marching out States will be rendered before moving off.

5. All billets will be left in a clean condition and "D" Coy. will render a certificate to this effect before leaving.

6. Billeting parties of One Officer and One Other Rank per Company and Bn. H.Q. will be detailed and will travel by the train leaving OIRY at 7.12 p.m.

7. Picquets (detailed by the R.S.M. from Battalion H.Q.) will be provided at all stops for each end of the train to prevent troops leaving.

8. All doors of covered trucks and carriages on the right hand side of the train when on the main line will be kept closed.

9. ACKNOWLEDGE.

Issued at 7 P.M.

Copies No. 1 - 4 - Companies.   2/Lieut. & Adjt.,
         5 - 7 - Brigades.   51st (H) Bn. M. G. C.
             8 - 51st (H) Div. "G."
             9 - T.O.
            10 - Q.M.
            11 - War Diary.
            12 - File.
            13 - R.S.M.

SECRET.   51st (H) BATTALION, M.G.CORPS.   Copy No. 13.
           OPERATION ORDER No. 49.
                                             13/8/18.

Ref. Map:
FRANCE, 44.B., 1/10,000.
"   LENS 11, 1/100,000.

1. The 51st (H) Division will be transferred to the XVII Corps and will relieve the 52nd (Lowland) Division in the line, as follows:-

Date.	Sub-Sector.	Brigade.
August 15th	Centre	152nd Inf. Bde.
" 16th	Left	153rd Inf. Bde.
" 17th	Right	154th Inf. Bde.

The 51st (H) Battalion M.G.C. will relieve the 52nd Battalion M.G.C. in the line as follows:-

14th August:-
"A" Coy. 51st (H) Bn. M.G.C. will relieve "D" Coy. 52nd Bn. M.G.C. in the CENTRE Sub-sector.

15th August:-
"B" Coy.   do.   do.   do.   "C" " 52nd Bn. M.G.C. in LEFT Sub-sector.
"C" "   do.   do.   do.   "B" " 52nd Bn. M.G.C. in RIGHT Sub-Sector.
"D" "   do.   do.   do.   "A" " 52nd Bn. M.G.C. in RESERVE.
H.Qrs.   do.   do.   do.   H.Qrs. 52nd Bn. M.G.C.

2. All details of the relief will be arranged between Os.C. Coys. concerned.

3. RATIONS: Reserve Rations will be taken over by farming Coys. who will give receipts only after checking the numbers. A list of Reserve Rations, Trench Stores, and ammunition taken over in the line will be forwarded to Battalion H.Qrs. by noon, 17th instant.

4. Dismounted personnel will move by light railway from W.30.b. Mounted personnel by march route, the usual intervals being maintained on the line of march.

5. Light railway arrangements will be notified later.

6. There will be no movement by day EAST of the top of the Ridge (POINT DU JOUR - THELUS RIDGE Line) before 8 p.m.

7. Completion of relief will be reported to H.Qrs. of both 51st and 52nd M.G.Battalions.

8. On completion of relief, the 57th Division will be on the RIGHT and the 8th Division (VIII Corps) on the left of the 51st Division.

9. A C K N O W L E D G E.

Issued at 11 p.m. to:-
Copy No. 1-4 - Coys.
         5-7 - Brigades.   51st (H) Battalion, M.G.Corps.
         8 - 51st (H) Div."G".
         9 - 52nd M.G.Bn.
         10 - T.O.
         11 - Q.M.
         12 - S.O.
         13 - War Diary.
         14 - File.

SECRET.   51st (H) BATTALION, M.G.CORPS.
        AMENDMENT of OPERATION ORDER No. 49.   14/8/18.
                   ****

Order of Reliefs in

1. Operation Order No.49 is cancelled.

2. The only relief to be carried out on the 14th August, 1918, will be:-

"C" Coy. 51st (H) Bn.M.G.C. will relieve "B" Coy. 52nd Bn.M.G.C. in the
                                                    RIGHT Sub-Sector.

Details to be arranged between Os.C.Coys. concerned.

    Further orders later.

                                                        Adjt.,
                                        51st (H) Battalion, M.G.Corps.

Addressed All recipients of O.O.49.

51st (H) Battalion M.G.CORPS.   Copy No. 14
OPERATION ORDER No. 50
                                                                 15/8/18
Ref. Maps:
XXXXXX, XXXX, XXXX X/XX,XXX. FRANCE, 44.B., 1/40,000
     XXXX. XX X/XXX,XXX. HAZEBROUCK,   1/20,000

1. The 51st (H) Division will relieve the Right Brigade (152th Inf.
Bde.) of the 52nd (Lowland) Division and the Left (172nd Inf.Bde.) and
Centre (171st Inf.Bde.) Brigades of the 57th Division as follows:-
16/8/18. 154th Inf.Bde. will take over RIGHT Sub-sector of 52nd Division.
17/8/18. 153rd Inf.Bde.   "   "   "   LEFT   "   "   " 57th   "
18/8/18. 152nd Inf.Bde.   "   "   "   CENTRE "   "   " 57th   "

2.   The 51st (H) Bn. M.G.Corps, less "C" Company, will move tomorrow
to BRIGADE CAMP, A20.d.5.2. Dismounted personnel will move by light
railway; transport and mounted personnel by march route, the usual
intervals being maintained on the line of march.

3.   The 51st (H) Bn. M.G.C. will carry out the following reliefs:-
16th August:-
"B" Coy. 51st (H) Bn.M.G.C. will relieve "C" Coy. of the 57th Bn.M.G.C.
                                              in LEFT Sub-Sector of
                                              57th Division.
17th August:-
"A" Coy. 51st (H) Bn.M.G.C. will relieve "B" Coy. of the 57th Bn.M.G.C.
                                              in CENTRE Sub-sector of
                                              57th Division.

4.   All details of the relief will be arranged between Os.C.Coys.
concerned.

5.   "D" Company will be in Divisional Reserve at Brigade Camp,A20.d.5.2.

6.   RATIONS; Reserve Rations will be taken over by Companies who will
give receipts only after checking the numbers. A list of Reserve
Rations, Trench Stores, and ammunition taken over in the line will be
forwarded to Battalion H.QRS. by noon, 18th inst.

7.   Light railway arrangements will be notified later.

8.   Completion of reliefs will be reported to H.Qrs. of the Machine
Gun Battalions concerned by the word "ROPE".

9.   Battalion H.Qrs. will open at BRIGADE CAMP (A20.d.5.2.) at 8 p.m. 16th inst.

10.   ACKNOWLEDGE.

                                                    [signature]
                                                               Adjt.
Issued at 8-50 p.m.   51st (H) Bn. M.G.Corps.
Issued to:- Coys.
   No.5 - Div. "G"
   Nos.6-9- Bdes.
      No.10- 52nd M.G.Bn.
      No.11- 57th " " "
      No.12- T.O.
      No.13- Q.M.
      No.14- S.O.
      No.15- War Diary.
      No.16- File.

51st (H) Battalion M.G.CORPS.   Copy No....
OPERATION ORDER No. 50
13/8/18

Ref. Maps:
WYTSCHAETE, FRANCE, 44.B., 1/10,000
Y.   IN 1/100,000, WAROMUIL, 1/20,000

1. The 51st (H) Division will relieve the Right Brigade (156th Inf. Bde.) of the 52nd (Lowland) Division and the Left (172nd Inf.Bde.) and Centre (171st Inf.Bde.) Brigades of the 57th Division as follows:-
16/8/18. 154th Inf.Bde. will take over RIGHT Sub-sector of 52nd Division.
17/8/18. 153rd Inf.Bde.   "   "   "   LEFT   "   "   " 57th   "
18/8/18. #152nd Inf.Bde. "   "   "   CENTRE "   "   " 57th   "

2.   The 51st (H) Bn. M.G.Corps, less "C" Company, will move tomorrow to BRIGADE CAMP, A20.d.7.8. Dismounted personnel will move by light railway; transport and mounted personnel by march route, the usual intervals being maintained on the line of march.

3.   The 51st (H) Bn. M.G.C. will carry out the following reliefs:-
16th August:-
"B" Coy. 51st (H) Bn. M.G.C. will relieve "C" Coy. of the 57th Bn.M.G.C.
                                                 in LEFT Sub-Sector of
                                                 57th Division.

17th August:-
"A" Coy. 51st (H) Bn. M.G.C. will relieve "B" Coy. of the 57th Bn.M.G.C.
                                                 in CENTRE Sub-sector of
                                                 57th Division.

4.   All details of the relief will be arranged between Os.C.Coys. concerned.

5.   "D" Company will be in Divisional Reserve at Brigade Camp, A20.d.7.8.

6.   RATIONS; Reserve Rations will be taken over by Companies who will give receipts only after checking the numbers. A list of Reserve Rations, Trench Stores, and ammunition taken over in the line will be forwarded to Battalion H.Qrs. by noon, 18th inst.

7.   Light railway arrangements will be notified later.

8.   Completion of reliefs will be reported to H.Qrs. of the Machine Gun Battalions concerned by the word "ROPE".

9.   Battalion H.Qrs. will open at BRIGADE CAMP (A20.d.7.8.) at 8 p.m..

10. ACK'O LEDGE.

Issued at 9-50 p.m.   Adjt.
Issued to:- Coys.   51st (H) Bn. M.G.Corps.
    No.5 - Div. "G"
   Nos.6-8- Bdes.
    No.10- 52nd M.G.Bn.
    No.11- 57th " " "
    No.12- T.O.
    No.13- Q.M.
    No.14- S.O.
    No.15- War Diary.
    No.16- File.

"A" Form
MESSAGES AND SIGNALS.

Army Form C. 2121
(in pads of 100).

TO: O.C. "A", "B" & "D" Coys.
Copy — "C" Coy, T.O., M.G.R.S.M.

Sender's Number: OO 80/a
Day of Month: 16th
AAA

Companies will parade under Company arrangements, and march to entraining point in succession, to reach entraining point at 2-45 p.m. Dress - Full Marching Order with Balmorals.

2/Lt. — SCOTT will act as entraining Officer.

Transport will move by march route under orders of the T.O. The usual distances will be maintained.

All billets will be left scrupulously clean, and certificate to this effect will be rendered to Battalion Orderly Room before moving.

Marching Out state will be rendered by 1-30 p.m.

From: 51st (H) Bn. M.G.C.
Place:
Time:

SECRET. 51st (H) BATTALION, M.G.CORPS. Copy No. 13
OPERATION ORDER No. 51.
17/8/18.

Ref.Map:
FRANCE, Sheet 51B.N.W.,1/20,000.

1. On the night 18/19th inst. the Division will take over the front at present held by the 170th Brigade, extending as far S. as X H.23.c.9.2.

2. Inter-Brigade boundaries will be adjusted in accordance with map issued to all concerned.

3. "D" Coy., 51st (H) Battalion M.G.C. will relieve "A" Coy. 57th Battalion M.G.C. in sector at present held by the 170th Inf.Bde.

4. Details of relief will be arranged between Os.C.Coys. concerned.

5. Relief will be carried out as far as possible by day.

7. A complete return of ammunition, reserve rations, and trench stores, etc., taken over will be rendered to Battalion H.Q. by noon, 20th instant.

8. Completion of relief will be reported to Battalion H.Q. of Battalions concerned by code word "BANK".

9. A C K N O W L E D G E.

Issued at 10 p.m.

[signature]
Adjt.,
51st (H) Battalion M.G.Corps.

Issued to:-

Copy No. 1-4 - Coys.
     5 - Division "G"
    6-8 - Brigades.
     9 - 57th Bn.M.G.C.
    10 - M.
    11 - S.O.
    12 - T.O.
    13 - War Diary.
    14 - File.

Cancelled.
12-15 a.m.
18/8/18

SECRET

Copy No. 6

61st (U) Battalion M.G. Corps.
OPERATION ORDER NO. 32
==============================

Ref. Map:
TRENCH Sheet 51B N.I. 3/12,000   19/1/10

1)   In cooperation with operations taking place against 11/20th Hun
     on 20/21st. "B" and "D" Coys, 61 (U) M.G. Bn will arrange to carry
     out indirect barrage fire on days and nights of 20/21st, on objective

     N 14 7 - 0 12 d 5

     T 13 4 - 14 Centr1.

                CALIBRE RELATIVE TO CAL
                between hours 1800 and 2100 hours.

2)   From hour - 3 R.A.M.

3) ACKNOWLEDGE.

Issued out - 0 3.05.   [signature]
Isue Nos.   No: 1   No: 6 ("B") (O) Lt. Col 61 MG
             No: 2   No: 7
             No: 3   Inter LG. Off.
             No: 4   Itours
             No: 5   War Diary.
                             File.

                                        [signature]
                                        Adjt (a) Bn, 61 M.G. Corps.

SECRET.   51st (H) BATTALION, M.G.CORPS.   Copy No. 9

OPERATION ORDER No. 54.

20/8/18.

Reference Map:
FRANCE, 51.B., N.W., 1/20,000.

1. One Company of the 1st (Life Guards) Battalion M.G.Regt. will relieve "C" Company, 51st (H) Battalion M.G.C. in the LEFT Sub-sector of the Divisional front on night 22nd/23rd August, 1918.

2. Details of the relief will be arranged between Officers Commanding Companies concerned.

3. All Harassing Fire Schemes and concentrations will be handed over and care must be taken that full particulars are given of all night firing and battle positions.

4. Reserve rations will be handed over and a complete list of Trench Stores etc. handed over will be returned to Battalion H.Q. by 12 noon, 23rd instant.

5. Completion of relief will be notified to Battalion H.Q. by code word "WEBB".

6. On completion of relief, "C" Company, 51st (H) Battalion M.G.C. will be withdrawn into Divisional Reserve.

7. ACKNOWLEDGE.

Adjt.,
51st (H) Battalion, M.G.C.

Issued at 9 p.m.
To:- Nos. 1-4 - Coys.
        5 - 1st (Life Guards) Bn.M.G.Regt.
        6 - 154th Inf.Bde.
        7-8 - 51st (H) Division, "G" & "Q".
        9 - War Diary.
        10 - File.

51st (H) BATTALION, M.G. CORPS.
OPERATION ORDER No.55.

Copy No. 10
20/8/18.

Ref. Map:
FRANCE, 51C. N.E., 1/20,000.

1. On the night 20th/21st August, 1918, the 152nd Inf.Bde. will carry out operations to seize the line marked in BLUE on the attached map (issued to Coys. only).

2. The operations will be covered by an Artillery Barrage.

3. The 51st (H)Battalion M.G.C. will co-operate as follows:-

(a) i) "A" Coy. will arrange for 12 guns to deal with the Railway Bank from H.23.b.3.3. to Junction of Railway with COLT TRENCH - thence along COLT TRENCH to the QUARRY, I.13.a.0.3.

ii) For this purpose 4 guns will be moved to positions in PUDDING TRENCH or PORT TRENCH, H.16.b.

iii) A section of 4 guns of "D" Coy. will be placed at the disposal of O.C., "A" Coy.

iv) The following points will be specially dealt with:-
    The QUARRY, I.13.a.
    JUNCTION of RAILWAY with CRASH TRENCH.

v) After daylight the 4 guns moved to H.16.b. will be ready to deal with any enemy activity or enemy M.Gs. which may open fire.

(b) "B" Coy. will arrange for 8 guns to deal with JUTLAND TRENCH and COLT TRENCH to the QUARRY, I.13.a.

4. Rates of fire will be:-   Z. to Z.plus 10 - 1 belt per 2 mins.
                             Z.plus 10 to Z.plus 40 - 1 belt per 4 mins.

5. Zero hour, will be at 1-30 a.m.

6. ACKNOWLEDGE.

Issued at 5 p.m.

(Adjt.,
51st (H) Battalion, M.G.C.

Issued to:- 1-4 - Coys.
            5 - 51st (H) Division "G".
            6-8 - Brigades.
            9 - 170th Inf.Bde.
            10 - War Diary. ✓
            11 - File.

SECRET.   51st (H) BATTALION, M.G. CORPS.   COPY No. 10

WARNING ORDER.

21/3/18.

Reference Map:
Sheet 51B.N.W., 1/20,000.

1. At a date and time to be notified later, the 153rd Infantry Brigade will carry out operations to seize the line shown in BROWN on the map issued to Companies concerned.

2. The 51st (H) Battalion M.G.Corps will co-operate as follows:-

   (a) "A" Coy. will arrange for 8 guns to bring fire to bear from junction of COLT TRENCH and CAMEL AVENUE to Junction of HAVANA TRENCH and CADIZ RESERVE to enfilade CLYDE AVENUE to Junction of CADIZ RESERVE and CLYDE AVENUE.

   (b) "B" Coy. will arrange for 10 guns to enfilade CALEDONIAN AVENUE and CIVIL AVENUE to Junctions with CHICKEN RESERVE.

   (c) "C" Coy. will arrange for 6 guns to enfilade CHILI AVENUE to Junction with CHALK RESERVE and for 2 guns to fire on Junction of CALEDONIAN AVENUE and HAGGARD TRENCH.

3. A section of 4 guns of "D" Company will be placed at the disposal of O.C. "B" Company and will move into position on Z minus 1 day.

4. Positions for barrage guns should be reconnoitred and constructed forthwith. O.C. "D" Company will arrange with O.C. "B" Company for necessary working parties to construct positions for guns of the section of "D" Coy.

5. Company Commanders will make arrangements for the necessary ammunition to be drawn and got into position on an estimate of 5,000 rounds per gun.

6. A C K N O W L E D G E.

2/Lieut. & Adjt.,
51st (H) Battalion M.G.Corps.

Issued at 5 p.m.
Issued to:-
    Copy No. 1-4 - Coys.
             5-7 - Brigades.
               8 - 51st (H) Division, "G".
               9 - T.O.
              10 - War Diary.
              11 - File.

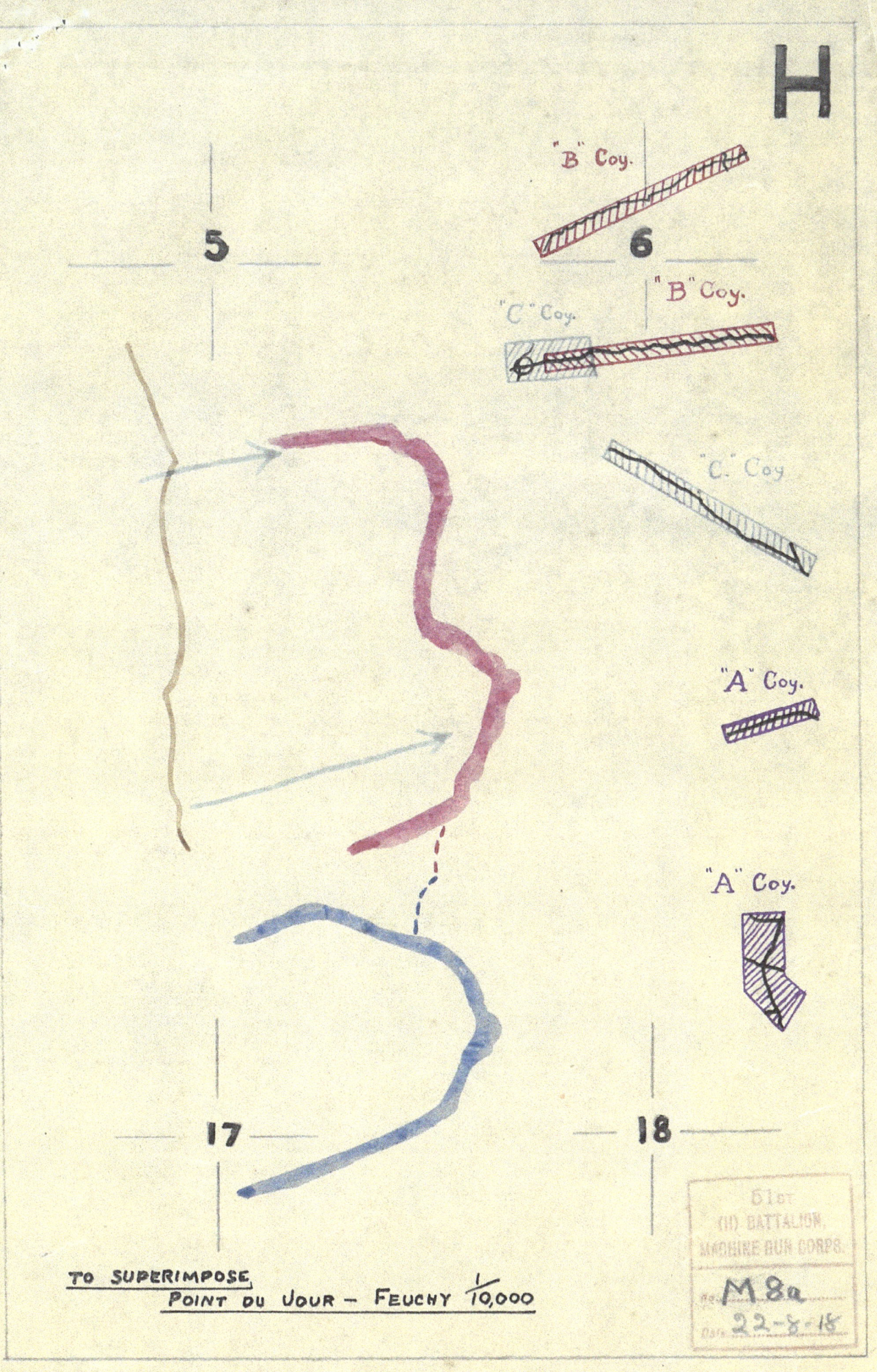

SECRET.   51st (H) BATTALION, M.G. CORPS.   Copy No. 13

OPERATION ORDER No. 53.   23/8/18.
****

Ref. Map:
FRANCE,
Sheet 51B.N.W., 1/20,000.

1. On the night 24th/25th August, 1918, the following Inter-Company relief will take place:-

   "D" Coy. will relieve "C" Coy.

2. The necessary detail of arrangement will be made between Company Commanders concerned.

3. Tripods, 10 Belt Boxes per gun, Trench Stores and Work in Hand will be handed over and receipts obtained for Trench Stores and Note of Work will be handed into Battalion H.Q. by 5 p.m., 25th August, 1918.

4. All Harassing Fire Schemes and Intelligence Reports will be handed over by "C" Coy. to "D" Coy. as a going concern. There will be no intermission due to relief.

5. On completion of relief, "C" Coy. will withdraw to billets in BRIGADE CAMP, A.26.b.2.6.

6. Completion of relief will be notified to Battalion H.Q. by code word "COURT".

7. "C" Coy. will become Divisional Reserve and Officers and as many N.C.Os. as possible will reconnoitre Reserve positions.

8. "C" Coy. will take over the Anti-Aircraft Defence of BRIGADE CAMP.

9. A C K N O W L E D G E.

Issued at 10 a.m.
                                                    Adjt.,
                                         51st (H) Battalion M.G. Corps.

Issued to:-
   1-4 - Coys.
     5 - 51st (H) Division "G".
   6-8 - Brigades.
     9 - T.O.
    10 - Q.M.
    11 - War Diary.
    12 - File.

SECRET.   51st (H) BATTALION, M.G.CORPS.   Copy No. 9.

OPERATION ORDER No. 56.   25/3/18.

Reference Map:-
SHEET 51.B.N.E., 1/20,000.

1. An operation will be carried out by the 153rd Infantry Brigade on a date to be notified later, with a view to establishing a line shown in RED on tracing issued to all concerned, and joining up with 152nd Infantry Brigade along ZION ALLEY.

2. The operation will be carried out by the 7th BLACK WATCH on a two-Company front, under Artillery and M.G.Barrage.

3. The 51st (H) Battalion M.G.Corps will co-operate as follows, the limits of ground to be barraged being shown on tracing issued:-

(a) "A" Coy. will arrange for 8 guns to bring fire to bear from junction of GOLF TRENCH and CAMEL AVENUE to Junction of HAVANA TRENCH and CADIZ RESERVE and to enfilade CLYDE AVENUE to Junction of CADIZ RESERVE and CLYDE AVENUE.

(b) "B" Coy. will arrange for 10 guns to enfilade CALEDONIAN AVENUE and CIVIL AVENUE to Junctions with CHICKEN RESERVE.

(c) "C" Coy. will arrange for 6 guns to enfilade CHILI AVENUE to Junction with CHALK RESERVE and for 2 guns to fire on Junction of CALEDONIAN AVENUE and HAGGARD TRENCH.

4. Rates of fire will be:-
  Zero to Zero plus 30 .... 1 belt per 4 mins.
  Zero plus 30 to Zero plus 40. 1 belt per 5 mins.

5. A section of 4 guns of the Reserve Company will be placed at the disposal of O.C. "B" Coy. and will move into position on Zero minus 1 day.

6. Positions for barrage guns will be fully prepared, and the necessary ammunition will be placed in position.

7. M.G.Company Commanders will arrange to send representatives to 153rd Bde. Headquarters, G.12.b.85.35. at 2 p.m. and 8 p.m. on the day before operation, for synchronisation.

8. Date and time will be notified later to Companies concerned.

9. A C K N O W L E D G E.

2/Lieut. & Adjt.,
51st (H) Battalion M.G.Corps.

Issued at 5-30 p.m.
TO:- 1-4 - Coys.
     5-7 - Bdes.
       8 - Div."G".
       9 - War Diary 10 - File.

SECRET.　　　　　　　51st (H) BATTALION, M.G.CORPS.　　　　　Copy No..5..

OPERATION ORDER No. 57.　　　　　　　24/3/18.

Reference Map:
PAMPOUX, 1/10,000.

1. The 3rd CANADIAN DIVISION are attacking the enemy's positions SOUTH of the River SCARPE at a date and hour to be notified later.

2. The 51st (H) Division are co-operating on the NORTH of the River but will not be attacking.

3. The attack will be a surprise attack under a rolling barrage. There will be no preliminary barrage.

4. "A" Coy. of 51st (H) Battalion M.G.C. along with a half-Company of the 1st (Life Guards) Battalion M.G.Regt. attached, will co-operate by covering the LEFT flank with concentrated M.G.fire from the high ground N.W. of PAMPOUX.

5. Action of Machine Guns:-

(a) Barrage positions:- CAM AVENUE - PEPPER TRENCH - PUDDING TRENCH and PORT TRENCH in E.16.b. and E.16.d.

(b) Area to be dealt with is shown on Map issued to Company Commander concerned.

(c) Barrage map giving times of lifts has been forwarded to Company Commander concerned.

(d) Watches will be synchronised on Y/Z night and time will be taken from opening of Artillery barrage.

6. On completion of barrage on LANCER TRENCH in accordance with times of lifts, fire will be concentrated on the area shown on the EAST of the River SCARPE and SOUTH of the Railway until completion of barrage.

7. On completion of barrage, guns will remain at barrage positions until further orders.

8. O.C.Company concerned will report by wire to Battalion H.Q. when all preparations are complete by code words "N.O.S received".

9. Date and hour will be notified later to Company Commander concerned.

10. A C K N O W L E D G E.

Issued at .. 7-30 p.m.
Issued to No.1 - "A" Coy.
　　　　　　　2 - 152nd Inf.Bde.
　　　　　　　3 - 51st (H) Div."Q".
　　　　　　　4 - 3rd Bn. M.G.C. (Canadian).
　　　　5-6 - War Diary & File.
　　　　　　　7 - Coy.(L.G.) M.G.Bn.

2/Lieut. & Adjt.,
51st (H) Battalion, M.G.Corps.

SECRET.

51st (H) BATTALION M.G. CORPS.
ADDENDUM TO OPERATION ORDER No.57.

25/8/18.

1. Amended Barrage Map is attached.

2. Rates of fire will be :-

   ZERO to ZERO plus 60 .... 1 Belt per 4 mins.

   ZERO plus 60 to ZERO plus 100 .... No firing unless enemy activity on targets.

   ZERO plus 100. .... Cease fire.

3. Zero hour will be notified as soon as known.

[signature]

2/Lieut. & Adjt.,
51st (H) Battalion M.G.C.

Issued at 6-30 p.m.
Issued to :-
   O.C. "A" Coy.
   O.C. "C" Coy. 1st (L.G.) Bn. M.G. Regt.
   War Diary.
   File.

SECRET.   51st (H) BATTALION, M.G.CORPS.   Copy No. 7.
                                                              Ref.D.385.

                    =   WARNING ORDER.   =   24/3/18.

Reference Maps:
OPPY & FAMPOUX, 1/10,000.

1.   The 153rd Infantry Brigade are carrying out an operation at an
early date, probably tonight, with a view to seizing the line shown
in RED on tracing "A" issued to all concerned.

2.   The 51st (H) Battalion M.G.C. will co-operate as follows:-

   (a) "A" Coy. will arrange for 4 guns to bring fire to bear on the
       junction of CHALK RESERVE and CHILI AVENUE.

   (b) "B" Coy. will arrange for 6 guns to bring fire to bear on the
       junction of CHICKEN RESERVE and CALEDONIA AVENUE and on
       junctions of NAVAL TRENCH and SUPPORT with the GAVRELLE-
       ST. LAURENT Road.

   (c) "C" Coy. will arrange for 3 guns to enfilade Communication
       Trench running from B.30.a.5.0. to ECCLES TRENCH, -
       B.30.d.5.5., and to bring fire to bear on the junctions of
       ECCLES TRENCH and BURNIE TRENCH with TOM ALLEN.

       The ground to be barraged is shown on Tracing "A".

3.   The necessary ammunition will be drawn on an estimate of
2,500 rounds per gun.

4.   O.C., "B" Coy. will keep in close touch with 153rd Inf.Bde.
and will arrange to warn Os.C., "A" and "C" Coys. of ZERO hour as
soon as this is known.

5.   Date and time of operation will be notified later.

6.   A C K N O W L E D G E.

                                            [signature]
                                            2/Lieut. & Adjt.,
Issued at 2 p.m.   51st (H) Battalion M.G.C.
Issued to:-
    Copy No. 1-4 - Coys.
            5 - 153rd Inf.Bde.
            6 - 51st (H) Division "G".
            7 - War Diary.
            8 - File.

SECRET.   51st (H) Bn, M.G.Corps.
                           Operation Order No...

                                                    24.8.18

Reference Maps:-
      TRESCAULT, 1/10,000.

1.   The 152rd Infantry Brigade will carry out an operation tomorrow
for the purpose of occupying the line of NOAH, NAOMAND, and NAVAL
Trenches, as far North as R.C.A.7.7. and thence the line of NEWTON
Trench to its junction with IVRY Alley.

2.   At the same time, the 154th Infantry Brigade will push out along
IVRY Alley to its junction with NEWTON Trench, and will hold IVRY ALLEY
as a defensive flank.

3.   The attack will be made under a creeping barrage which will open
at ZERO hour.

4.   The 51st (H) Bn. M.G.C. will co-operate as follows:-

(a)   "A" Coy. will arrange for 4 guns to bring fire to bear on the
      junction of CHILI TRENCH and CHILLI AVENUE.

(b)   "B" Coy. will arrange for 4 guns to bring fire to bear on the
      junction of CHICKEN TRENCH and CALEDONIAN AVENUE and on
      junctions of NAVAL TRENCH and SUPPORT with the BAPAUME
      - CAMBRAI Road.

(c)   "D" Coy. will arrange for 4 guns to enfilade Communication
      Trench running from R.30.a.8.8. to HOULIN TRENCH - R.30.d.8.8.
      and to bring fire to bear on the junctions of NAOMAN TRENCH
      and NEWTON TRENCH with IVRY ALLEY.

      The ground to be barraged is shown on tracing "A" already issued.

5.   Rates of fire will be:-

          ZERO to ZERO plus 30 .... 1 Belt per 4 mins.
          ZERO plus 30 to ZERO at completion
             of Artillery barrage 1   "   " 8 mins.

          ZERO hour will be 5 a.m.

6.   O.C. "D" Coy. will ensure that the period of the Artillery barrage
is made known to O's.C. "A" and "B" Coys.

7.   ACKNOWLEDGE.

                                              (Sgd) Walpole

Issued at 11-45 p.m.   2/Lieut.& Adjt.,
Issued to:-   51st (H) Bn. M.G.Corps.
      No.1-4 - Coys.
         5 - 152rd Inf. Bde.
         6 - 51st (H) Div. "G".
         7 - War Diary.
         8 - File.

"A" Form
MESSAGES AND SIGNALS.

Army Form C. 2121 (in pads of 100.)

TO: OC "C" Coy.

Sender's Number: OK.653
Day of Month: 25
AAA

Your Company is placed at the tactical disposal of 154 Inf Bd. Major H.G. HARCOURT will report to B.G.C. 154 Inf. Bde. tonight 6pm

From: 51 (H) Bn M.G.C
Time: 4.30pm

SECRET.   51st (H) BATTALION M.G.CORPS.   Copy No...17
          OPERATION ORDER No.59.
                                             25/8/18.
Reference Map
SHEET, 51B.F.W.1/20,000.

1.   The success of our Third Army in the neighbourhood of BAPAUME and HENIN is developing to such an extent that the Canadians are extending their objectives of tomorrow's operation, and hope to capture MONCHY and to press on several miles to the East of it.
        It is the intention that another Division should be used to carry on the advance North of the SCARPE, but meanwhile, in case the Canadians have a great success tomorrow, the 51st Division must be prepared to do more that has hitherto been contemplated.

2.   In view of an extended success South of the SCARPE, the main objective North of that River is GREENLAND HILL. The lower ground at MOUNT PLEASANT and near MUSA WOOD is of minor importance.

3.   The first stage of tomorrow's operation will be as already outlined, and will aim at seizing the line from CORDITE TRENCH, through CALF RESERVE and CHICKEN RESERVE to TOTT ALLEY.
        In case the 152nd Brigade cannot occupy MOUNT PLEASANT by means of strong patrols, the G.O.C. does not propose to launch a real attack against it. In this case the 152nd Brigade will occupy the Railway Embankment from the River SCARPE to COLT TRENCH as a flank, facing Southwards.

4.   The next step in the event of a big success South of the River will be for the 153rd Brigade to capture the line CALICO and COPPER Trenches and CORK SUPPORT, forming a left flank on CIVIL AVENUE; the 152nd Brigade occupied CAMEL to its Junction with CALICO.
        This operation would probably take place tomorrow evening, and would be exploited with a view to occupying our old front line, with the defensive flank along the railway found by the 152nd Brigade.

5.   The next stage of the operation would be to capture the old German front line and the line of WEB, WAVE, LEG, and WOOL Trenches, connecting with our old front line at I.1.b.7.0. and with the Right flank along the Railway.

6.   The action of the 152nd Inf.Bde. in these operations depends on whether they have succeeded in occupying MOUNT PLEASANT or not. In case they have done so they will move forward in conjunction with the advance in the centre to CORONA SUPPORT, and possibly further forward.
        In case they have not been able to occupy MOUNT PLEASANT, their function will be confined to forming a defensive flank along the railway and exploiting Southwards from this line as much as possible.
        The function of the 154th Brigade will be to form a defensive flank facing Northwards, and they will be prepared to hold this flank lightly.

7.   Map showing Objectives of Operations is attached for all Companies concerned.

8.   The action of M.Gs. will be as follows:-
(a) Two batteries of EIGHT guns each of "A" Coy. 51st (H) Bn.M.G.C. in conjunction with one battery of EIGHT guns of "D" Coy. of the 1st (L.G.) Bn. M.G.Regt. will act in accordance with instructions already issued under O.O.57.
        On completion of the barrage, these batteries will remain in position ready to assist any operations of the 152nd Inf.Bde. which may take place.

-1-

-2-

(b) "B" Coy. 51st (H) Battalion M.G.C. less TWO Sections, "D" Coy. 51st (H) Bn. M.G.C. and "C" Coy. 1st (L.G.) Bn.M.G.Regt. will carry out a barrage to cover the advance of the 153rd Brigade as per Fire Organisation Orders issued to Companies; on completion of task these the batteries will be prepared on receipt of orders to advance to area of STOKE TRENCH to assist in further operations.

(c) TWO Sections of "B" Coy. 51st (H) Bn. M.G.C. will consolidate ground captured by the 153rd Inf.Bde. and TWO Sections of "D" Coy. 1st (L.G.) Bn. M.G.Regt. will be in 152nd Inf.Bde. Reserve.

(d) "C" Coy. 51st (H) Bn. M.G.C. will be at the tactical disposal of 154th Inf.Bde.

9. Os.C. Companies will be responsible that all guns are in position tonight and that all preparations for S.A.A., Water Supply, and Communications are made.
Barrage Group Commanders will ensure that everything is in readiness tonight and will wire completion by codewords "M.G.26 Received."

10. Barrage map and rates of fire will be issued later to Companies concerned.

11. ACKNOWLEDGE.

/Lieut.& Adjt.,
51st (H) Battalion M.G.Corps.

Issued at 6-30 p.m.
Issued to:-
Copy No.1-4 - Coys.
      5-6 - "C" and "D" Coys. 1st (L.G.) Bn.M.G.Regt.
      7-9 - Brigades.
      10 - 51st (H) Division, "G".
      11 - 3rd Canadian M.G.Bn.
      12 - War Diary.
      13 - File.

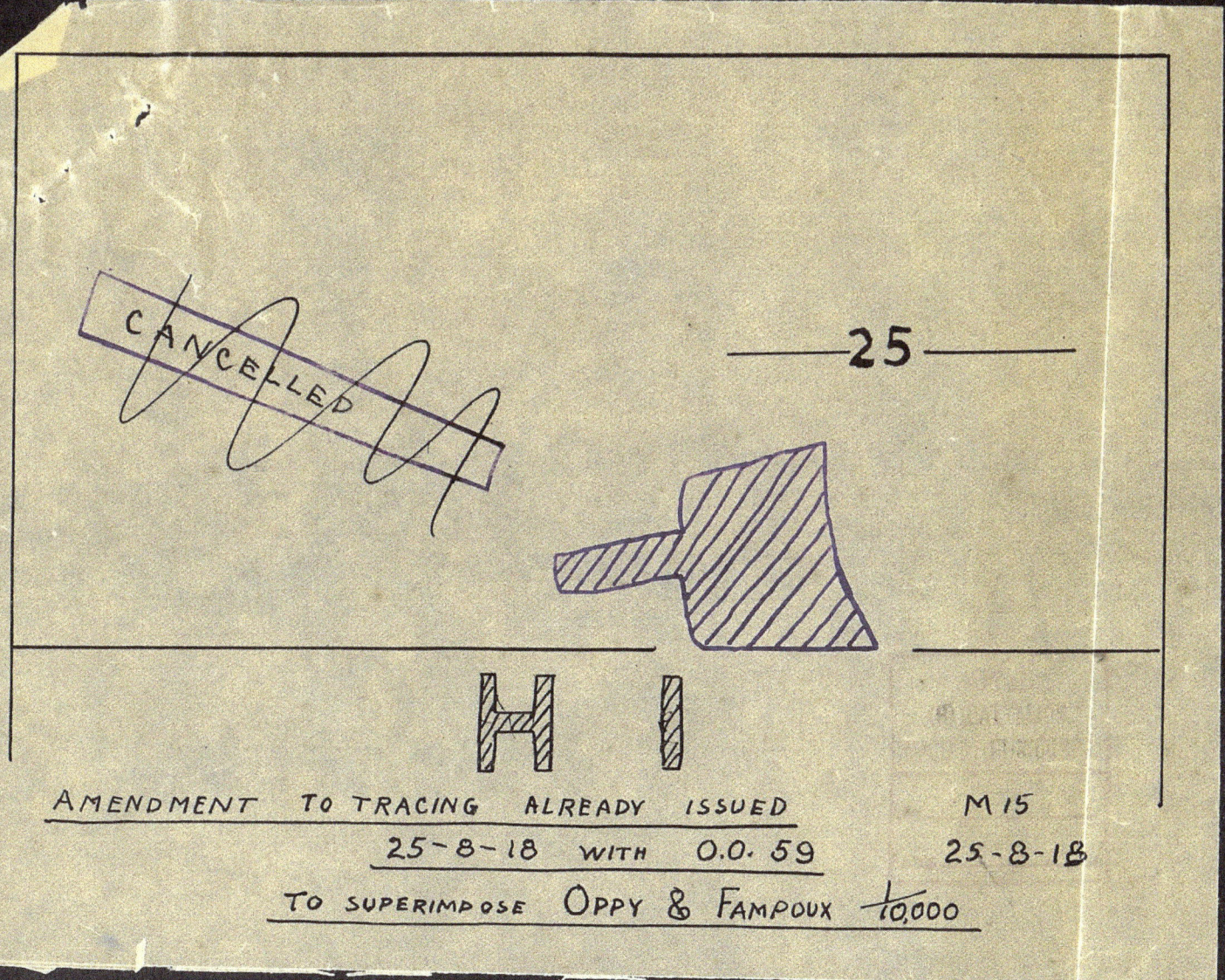

AMENDMENT TO TRACING ALREADY ISSUED   M 15
     25-8-18 WITH O.O. 59   25-8-18
TO SUPERIMPOSE OPPY & FAMPOUX 1/10,000

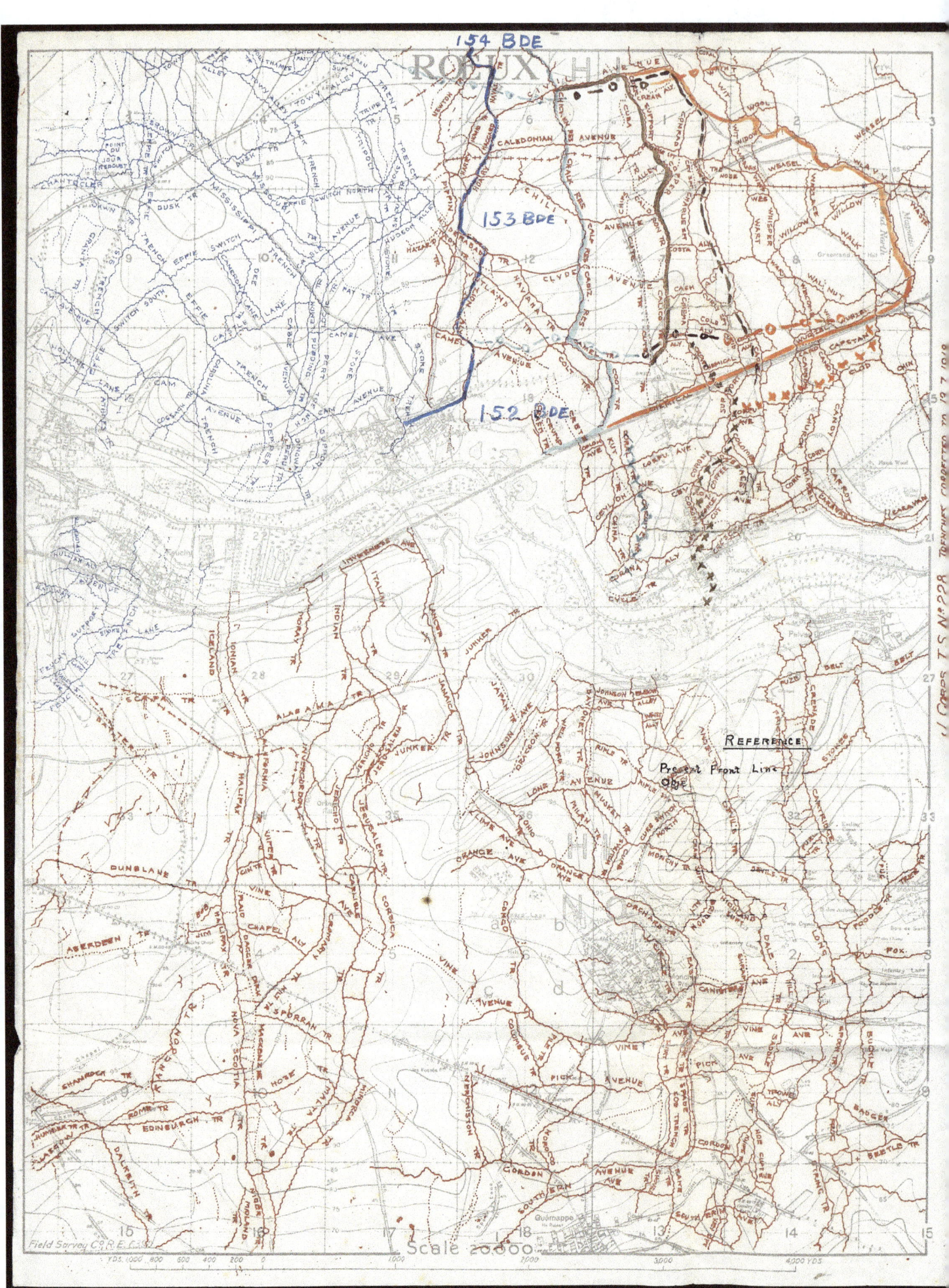

51st (H) Bn M.G.C
FIRE ORGANISATION ORDERS

To Accompany O.O. No.59., 35/8/18.
****

GROUP	GROUP CMDR	LOCATION APPROX	COMPOSITION	REMARKS
1	Major C.H Ross	H.11.c.6.6. H.11.c.0.9 H.10.b.8.2	3 guns of C Coy 1st (L.g)Bn 3 " C " 1st (L.g)Bn 3 " B " 51st Bn.	
2	Major H.H. Pearson M.C.	B.29.a.f.3. B.28.a.4.3.	3 guns of D Coy 51st Bn.	

SECRET.

51st (H) BATTALION, M.G. CORPS.

FIRE ORGANISATION ORDERS to Accompany O.O. 59.
25th Aug. 1918.

Group.	Group Commander.	Location (approx).	Composition.	Remarks
1.	Major C.H. ROSE.	H.11.c.0.6. H.11.c.0.9. H.10.b.8.2.	8 guns of "C" Coy. 1st (L.G) Bn. 8 " " "C" " 1st (L.G) Bn. 8 " " "B" " 51st (H) Bn.	
2.	Major A.H. PEARSON. (MC)	B.28.a.6.3.) or) B.28.a.4.3.)	16 guns of "D" Coy. 51st (H) Bn.	

SECRET.   Copy No. 11

51st (H) BATTALION, M. G. CORPS.

Operation Order No. 60.   26/8/18.

Ref: maps:-
FRANCE, SB.N.W.1/20,000.
LENS, 11, 1/100,000.

---

1. "C" and "D" Coys. 1st (Life Guards) Bn. M.G.Regt. will be withdrawn from the line at 2 p.m. tomorrow, 27th August, 1918, and will rejoin their unit at HAUT AVESNES by daylight.

2. Limber Transport for guns and equipment will be provided by the 51st (H) Bn. M.G.C. as far as 51st (H) Bn. M.G.C. Transport Lines, G.15.b.8.8.

3. Officers Commanding "C" and "D" Coy. 1st (Life Guards) Bn. M.G. Regt. will detail one guide per section to report to 51st (H) Bn. M.G.C. Headquarters at M.14.a.0.7. at 2 p.m. tomorrow.
   These guides will conduct limbers to places selected by O's.C. "C" and "D" Coys. 1st (L.G.) Bn. M.G.Regt. for the collection of their guns and equipment. Points to which limbers will be guided must be reported to 51st (H) Battalion M.G.C. Headquarters as soon as possible.

4. Completion of withdrawal will be reported to 51st (H) Bn. M.G.C. by Company Commanders on arrival at 51st (H) Bn. M.G.C. Transport Lines by code word "LORRY".

5. 1st (L.G.)Bn. M.G.Regt. will arrange for necessary motor transport to be at 51st (H) Bn. M.G.C. Transport Lines, G.15.b.8.8. at 4 p.m.

6.   A C K N O W L E D G E.

                                                    [signature]
                                                    Lieut. & Adjt.,
Issued at 9 p.m.   51st (H) Battalion, M.G.Corps.
TO:-
    Nos. 1 - "A" Coy.
         2 - "B" "
         3 - "C" Coy. 1st (L.G.) Bn. M.G.Regt.
         4 - "D" "   "   "   "   "   "
         5 - 51st (H) Division "G".
         6 - 152nd Inf.Bde.
         7 - 153rd Inf.Bde.
         8 - T.O.
         9 - Q.M.

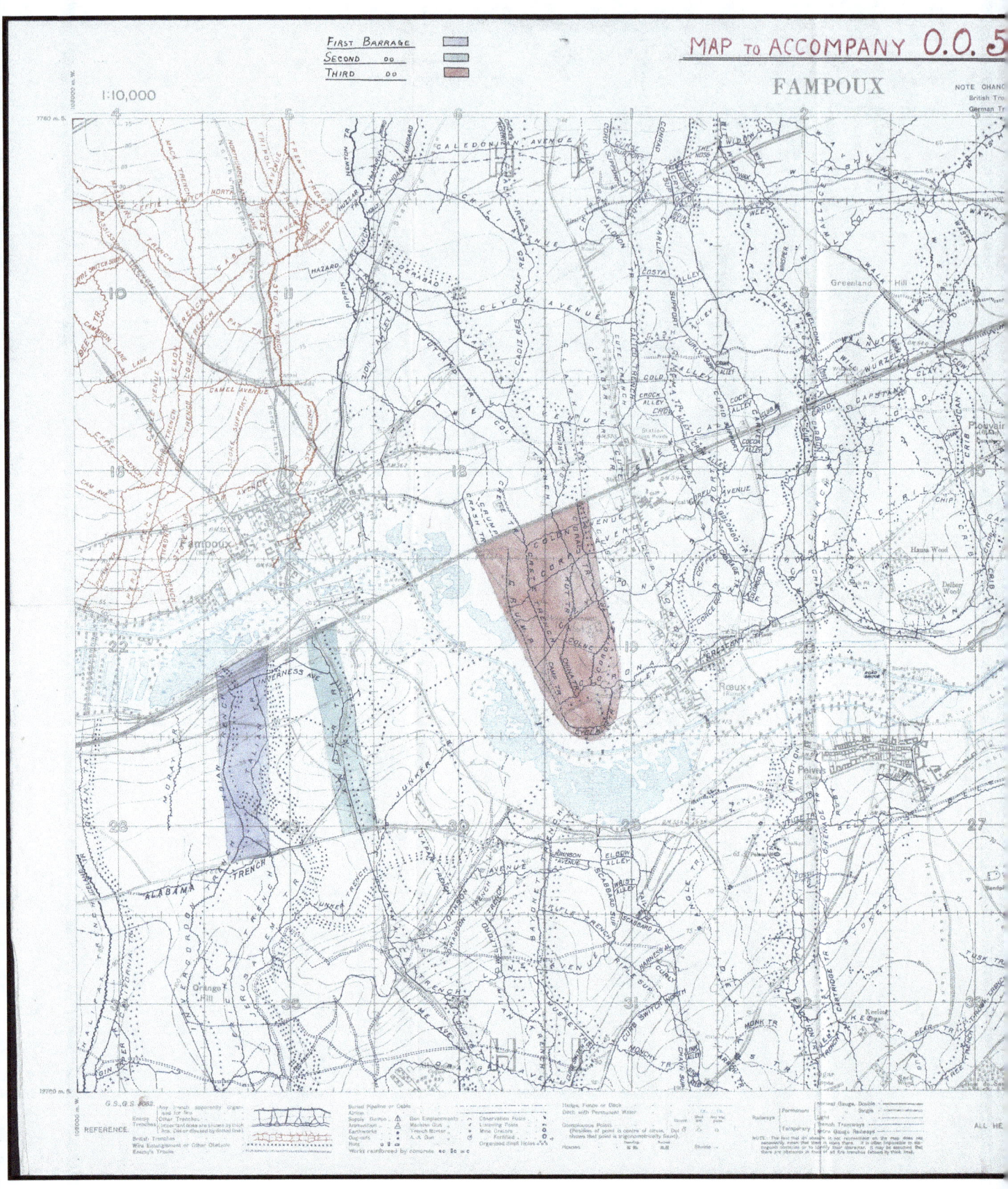

Secret

O.O. 57

SECRET. 27th August, 1918.

TO:-
 O.C. "A" Coy.
 101st Bn. M.G.Corps.

Reference Map: FRANCE, SHEET, 51B.N.W., 1/20,000.

1. Your Coy. will be in 51st (H) Divisional Reserve, and will take up positions in the vicinity of COSSACK TRENCH and DEE TRENCH in H.15.d. and H.16.a.

2. After dawn tomorrow, you will have the area forward to the old British Front Line reconnoitred by Officers.

3. You will send an Orderly to be attached to 51st (H) Battalion M.G.C Headquarters at H.14.a.0.7.

4. Completion of move and location of your Company and Company Headquarters will be reported by this Orderly.

5. A C K N O W L E D G E.

[signature]
Lieut. & Adjt.
51st (H) Battalion, M.G.Corps.

SECRET.   Copy No...7...

51st (H) BATTALION, M.G. CORPS.

Operation Order No. 61.   27/8/18.

Ref: map :—
FRANCE, 51.b., N.W.,
1/20,000

1. 154th Infantry Brigade will be relieved in the line by a Brigade of the 8th Division on the night 27/28th August, 1918.

2. One Machine Gun Company of the 8th Division will relieve "C" and "D" Companies of the 51st (H) Bn. M.G.C. in the line on the same night.

3. "C" Company will come under the orders of the 153rd Infantry Brigade and will side-slip 8 guns into the CADIZ-CALF-CHICKEN RESERVE Line and 8 guns into MISSOURI TRENCH.

4. Headquarters of "C" Company will move to the vicinity of the 153rd Infantry Brigade Headquarters.

5. "D" Company, on relief, will come into Divisional Reserve and will move to the vicinity of the present M.G. Battalion Headquarters (H.14.a.0.7.)

6. All details of relief have been arranged between Company Commanders concerned.

7. Completion of relief will be reported to Bn. H.Q. by Officers Commanding "C" and "D" Companies by Code Words "HARCOURT" and "PEARSON," respectively.

8. A C K N O W L E D G E.

Issued at 7 p.m.

Copy No. 1 - "C" Coy.
      2 - "D" "
      3 - 153 Infantry Bde.
      4 - 154 Infantry Bde.
      5 - 51st (H) Div. "G."
      6 - 8th M.G. Bn.
      7 - War Diary.
      8 - File.

Lieut. & Adjt.,
51st (H) Bn. M.G.C.

SECRET.

51st (H) BATTALION, M.G. CORPS.

FRANCE, Sheet 51B.N.W.   Operation Order No. 62.   29/8/18.
1/20,000.

Copy No... 10

1. The 154th Infantry Brigade are relieving the 152nd Infantry Brigade in the line and are taking over the front of the 152nd Infantry Brigade North of SLOB Trench, tonight.
    The 154th Infantry Brigade will attack tomorrow morning at 5-30 a.m. with a view to gaining the high ground at GREENLAND HILL astride the ARRAS – DOUAI Railway.

2. Map showing definite objectives of attack will be forwarded later to Coys. concerned.

3. On completion of inter-Brigade relief, "B" and "C" Coys. will come under the orders of the 154th Infantry Brigade and the Headquarters of these Coys. will be established near the 154th Infantry Brigade Headquarters.

4. The action of Machine Guns will be as follows:-

(a) 1. EIGHT guns of "A" Coy. from positions in the vicinity of CORONA SUPPORT will bring intense M.G.fire to bear on the high ground South of the Railway from SLOB Trench to BILBAO WOOD as shown in attached tracing "A".

    2. The approximate location of our front line is shown in tracing "A" but will be verified from the 152nd Infantry Bde. by O.C. "A" Coy.

(b) 1. TWO sections of "B" Coy. at present in reserve in KITCHEN TRENCH will assemble in the vicinity of CROCK ALLEY, I.13.b. tonight.
    Completion of assembly will be notified to Battalion H.Q. by code word "SNOWY".

    2. These guns will advance by bounds behind the Infantry and will consolidate the ground gained astride the Railway.

    3. Approximate consolidation positions will be:-

TWO guns in WALNUT Trench (I.8.d.5.4.) These positions will be on the
TWO guns in CAPSTAN   "   (I.14.b.5.8) forward slopes of GREENLAND HILL.

TWO guns in GARDEN Trench (I.14.D.)
TWO guns in WAG   Trench (I.8.d.)

These sections are for the defence of the forward slopes of GREENLAND HILL and for the protection of the flank from HAWKS and BILBAO WOOD through PLOUVAIN to the Railway.

(c) On the capture of the final objective the section of "B" Coy. at present in position in BRAKE REDOUBT will move forward to the vicinity of the BOSKE (I.1.d.) with a field of fire North and East.

5. ACKNOWLEDGE.

Issued at 7-30 p.m.
To:- 1 – Coys.
     5-7 – Brigades.
     8 – 51st (H) Division "G".
     9 – "A" Coy. 101st Bn. M.G.C.
     10 – War Diary.
     11 – File.

Lieut. & Adjt.,
51st (H) Battalion, M.G.Corps.

TO SUPERIMPOSE **FAMPOUX** 1/10,000.

14 | 15

20 | 21

TRACING A.   0.0.62.

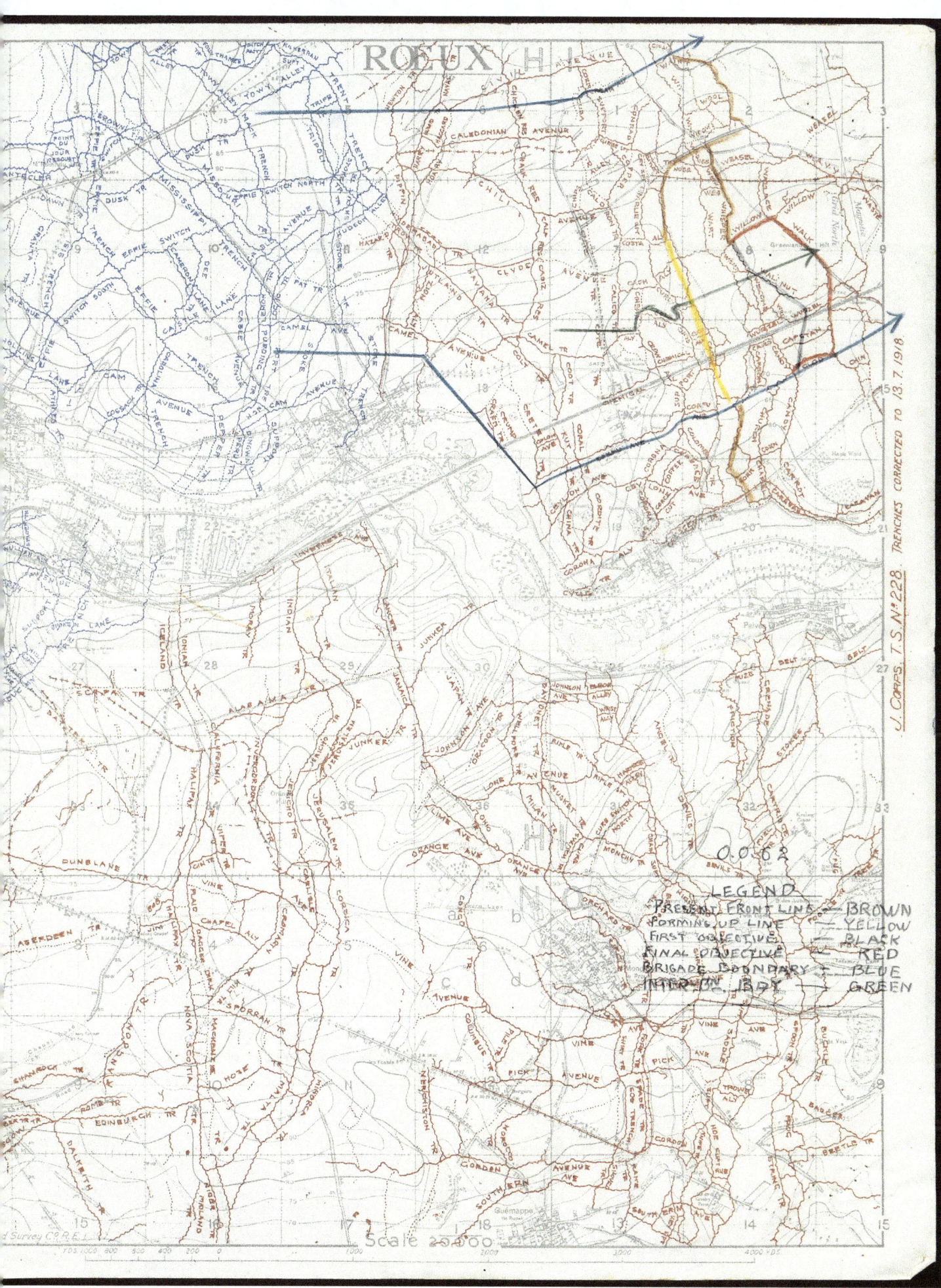

O. C., "A" Coy.,
101st Bn. M.G.C.

Reference WARNING ORDER G.404 of to-day, HAUSA and BELGIAN WOODS are now in our possession.

Your Company is placed at the disposal of the 152nd Infantry Brigade; please get in touch at once with H.Q., 152nd Infantry Brigade in CAM VALLEY.

W Walgrady
Lieut. & Adjt.,
101st (H) Bn. M.G.C.

29/9/18.

Copy to all recipients of Warning Order.

S E C R E T.   Copy No. 8..

                   81st (M) BATTALION, M. G. CORPS.
                   ─────────────────────────────────

Ref: map :-   Warning Order.   S.404.
FRENCH 51.S., V.B..   29/8/18.
1/10,000.
─────────

1.   The 182nd Infantry Brigade will be attacking probably at
        dawn to-morrow, 30/8/18, HANGA and BELGAN WOODS to gain command
        of the high ground between the River DUANES and CYRIL Trench,
        I.21.a. and I.15.c.

2.   The attack will be carried out under a creeping barrage.

3.   The attacking troops will be assembling in a line COW Trench
        and CYRIL Trench, I.14.d.
              CYRIL

4.   "A" Coy., 101st Bn. M.G.C. will be attached to the 182nd
        Infantry Brigade and will be employed as follows :-

(a). 1.   A battery of eight guns will assemble in the vicinity
           of the Southern end of CHUCK Trench.

      2.   These guns will cover the advance of the Infantry by
           bringing direct concentrated fire to bear on HANGA and
           BELGAN WOODS in accordance with the attached map issued to
           Company concerned.

      3.   The time will be calculated in accordance with artillery
           barrage map, a copy of which will be issued later to Company
           concerned and by direct observation of the advancing Infantry.

      4.   Rate of fire will be ONE belt per FOUR minutes.

      5.   On completion of task a Section of these guns will
           consolidate in vicinity of battery position and a Section
           will consolidate in CHUCK Trench, I.14.d.

(b). 1.   EIGHT guns will assemble in CHUCK Trench in I.14.c.
           and advance by bounds behind the attacking Infantry.

      2.   These guns will consolidate the forward slopes of the
           high ground in I.21.a. and I.15.c.

      3.   Approximate consolidation positions will be :-

TWO guns at I.21.a.6.0.)   Field of fire E. & S.E.
TWO guns at I.20.c.4.0.)

TWO guns at I.15.c.8.9.)   Field of fire N. & N.E.
TWO guns at I.15.c.8.4.)

5.   ZERO hour will probably be at dawn.

6.   A C K N O W L E D G E.

        Issued at 8 p.m.

        Copy Nos. 1 - 4 - Coys.
                     5 - "A" Coy.,
                         101 Bn. M.G.C.
                     6 - 81st Div. "G."
                     7 - 182nd Inf. Bde.
                     8 - War Diary.
                     9 - File.

                                         [signature]
                                         Lieut. & Adjt.,
                                         81st (M) Bn. M. G. C.

SECRET.   51st (H) BATTALION, M.G.CORPS.   Copy No. 15

OPERATION ORDER No. 65.   30/8/18.

Reference Map:
FRANCE, 51.J.,N.,
1/20,000.

1.   On night 31st Aug./1st Sept., "D" Coy. 51st (H) Battalion M.G.C. will relieve guns of "A" and "C" Coys. 51st (H) Battalion M.G.C. and "A" Coy. 101st Bn. M.G.C. in the line in accordance with the attached Chart.

2.   On the night 1st/2nd Sept. the following reliefs and supplements will be carried out in accordance with attached Chart:-

    (a)   "A" Coy. 103rd Bn. M.G.C. will relieve guns of "A" Coy. 51st (H) Bn. M.G.C. and "A" Coy. 101st Bn. M.G.C. and supplement guns of "D" Coy. 51st (H) Battalion, M.G.C.

    (b)   "B" Coy. 103rd Bn. M.G.C. will relieve guns of "C" Coy. 51st (H) Bn. M.G.C. and "A" Coy. 101st Bn. M.G.C. and will supplement guns of "D" Coy. 51st (H) Bn. M.G.C.

    (c)   "C" Coy. 103rd Bn. M.G.C. will relieve guns of "C" Coy. 51st (H) Bn. M.G.C. and supplement the Left Sub-Sector.

3.   Reliefs will be carried out as far as possible by daylight.

4.   All details of reliefs will be arranged between Os.C. Coys. concerned.

5.   Positions will be reconnoitred by Officers of the 103rd Bn. M.G.C. tomorrow afternoon.

6.   On night 31st Aug./1st Sept., the relieved sections will take over billets vacated by "D" Coy. 51st (H) Bn. M.G.C. at H.14.a.0.7.
        Billets for sections relieved subsequently will be notified later.

7.   Completion of relief will be reported to H.Q. 51st (H) Battalion M.G.C. by code word "CHINA" prefixed by the Company and number of Battalion, e.g., "B.103.CHINA."

8.   A C K N O W L E D G E.

                                                W M Grasby
                                                Lieut. & Adjt.,
Issued at 11-30 P.M.   51st (H) Battalion M.G.Corps.
Issued to:-
    Copy No.1-4 - Coys.
           5   - "A" Coy. 101st Bn. M.G.C.
           6-8 - "A", "B" & "C" Coys. 103rd Bn. M.G.C.
           9   - 103rd Bn. M.G.C.
           10   - 51st (H) Division, "G".
           11   - 51st (H) Division "Q".
           12-14 - Brigades.
           15-16 - War Diary & File.
           17-18 - T.O. & Spare

SECRET.

O.C., "A" Coy.
 "   "B" "
 "   "C" "
 "   "D" "
"C" Coy. 1st (L.G.) Bn. M.G.Regt.
"D" "   "   "   "   "   "   "
War Diary.
File.

O.O.59/1.

Maps 1/10,000 OPPY and FAMPOUX shewing barrage.

Rates of fire will be as follows:-

ZERO to ZERO plus 30 .... 1 Belt per 4 mins.
ZERO plus 30 to ZERO plus 40 .... 1 Belt per 5 mins.

O.C. Companies of Barrage Batteries referred to will arrange close liaison with 153rd Inf.Bde. Headquarters, so that they will get the ZERO hour as soon as possible.

O.C. "B" Coy. will ensure that O.C. "D" Coy. 51st (H) Bn. M.G.C. gets the time and any alterations in time that may be made.

[signature]

2/Lieut. & Adjt.,

25th August, 1918.   51st (H) Battalion, M.G.Corps.

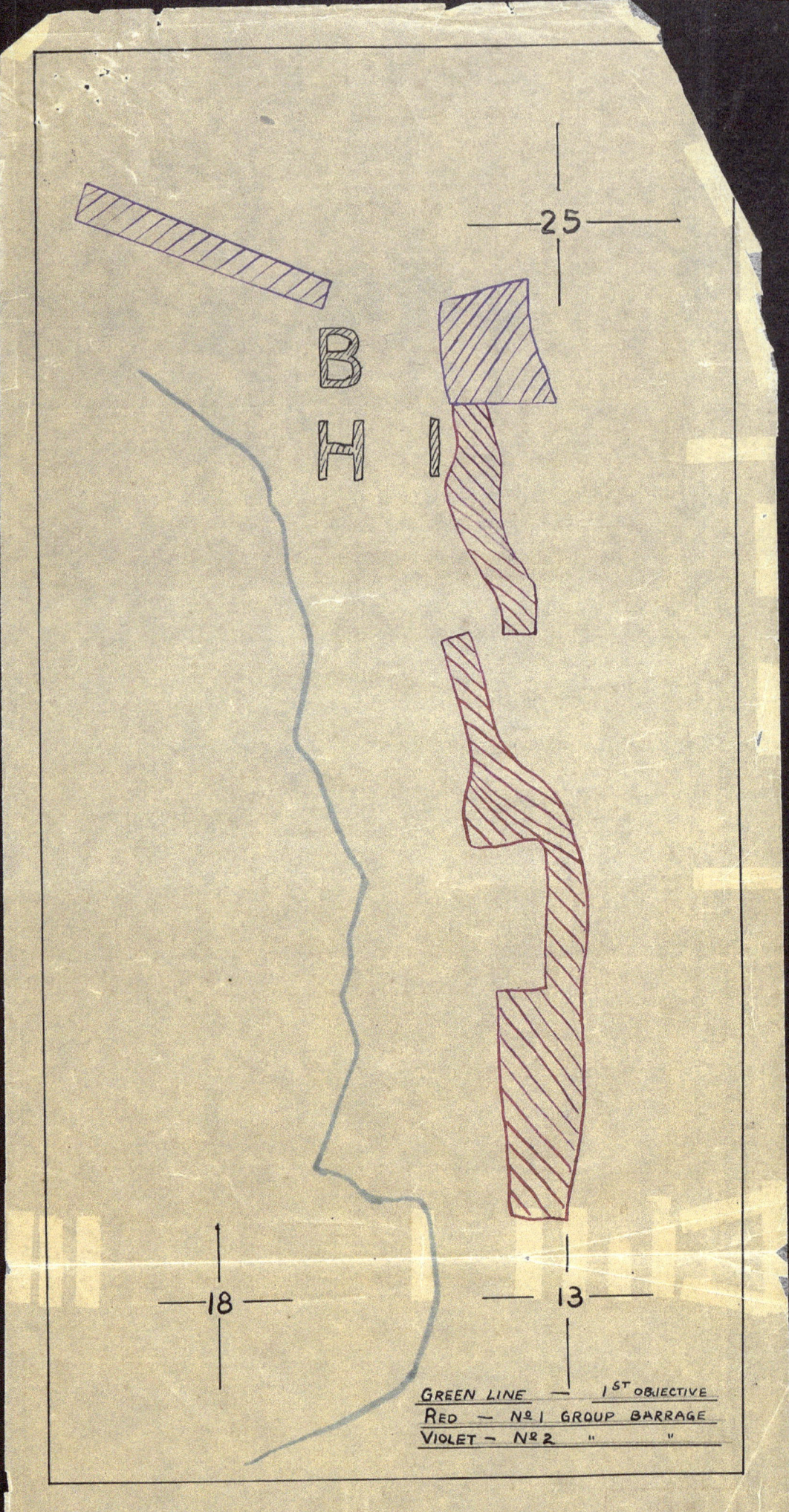

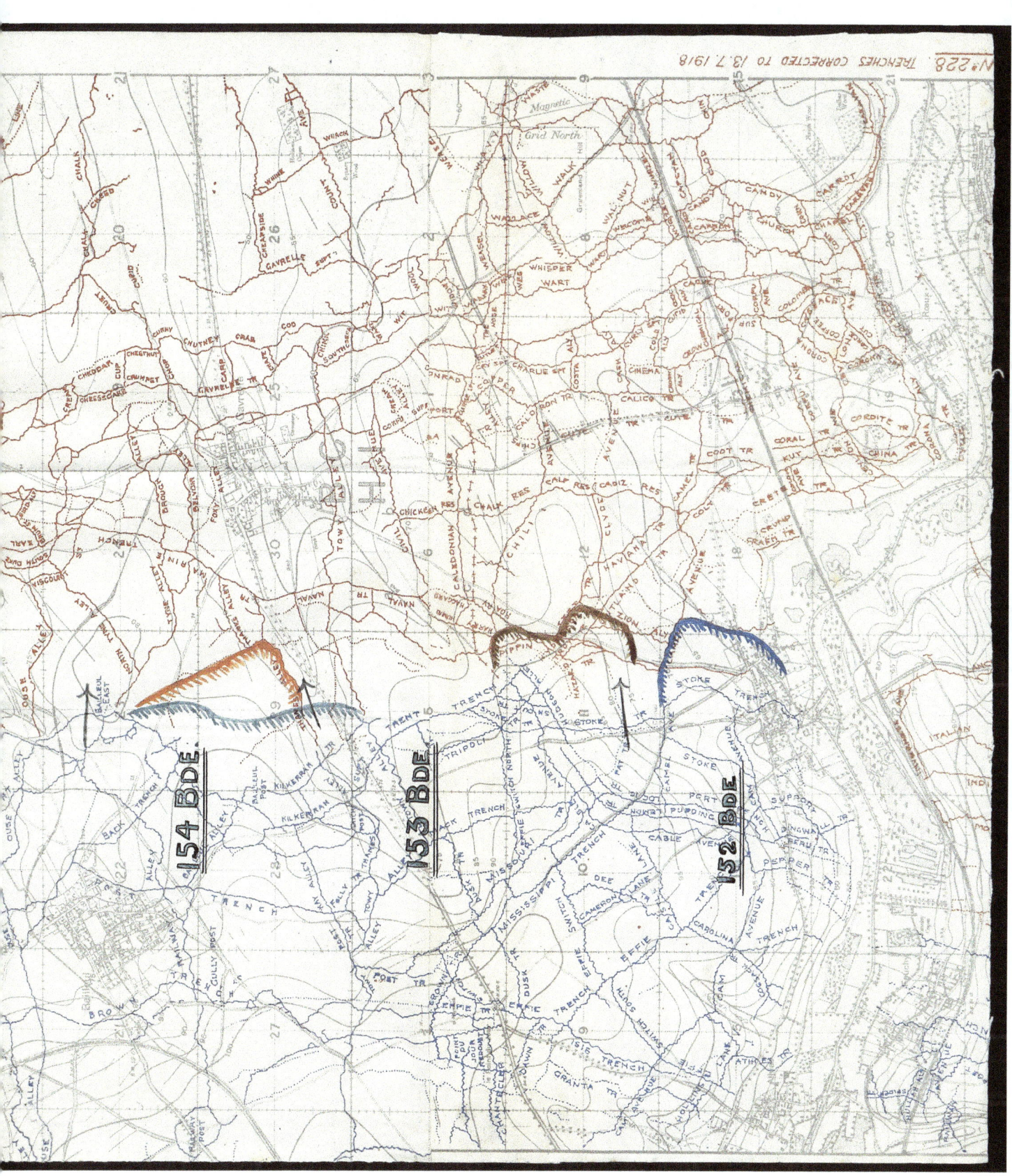

EUX
1/20,000

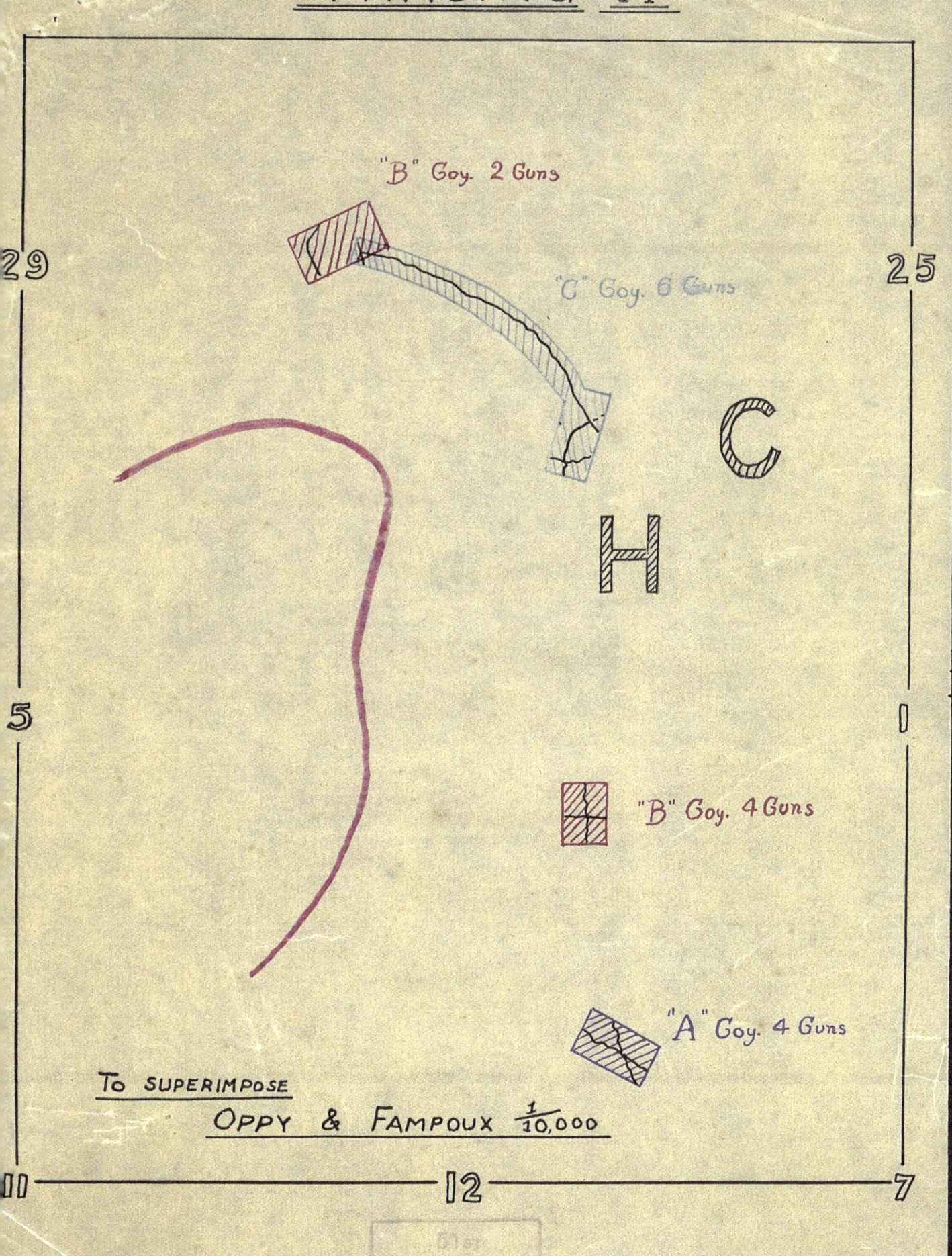

SECRET.

51st (H) BATTALION, M. G. CORPS.

AMENDMENT TO OPERATION ORDER No. 63, DATED 30/8/18.

1. In all cases where "A" Coy., 103rd Bn. M.G.C. is referred to, please read "D" Coy., 103rd Bn. M.G.C.

Lieut. & Adjt.,
51st (H) Bn. M.G.C.

Distribution :-
   To all recipients of O.O. 63.

S E C R E T.

51st (H) Battalion, M. G. Corps.

R E L I E F C H A R T.

To accompany O.O. 63.

30/8/18.

31 Aug/ 1 Sept.	2 guns of "D" Coy. 51 Battn. will relieve 2 guns of "A" Coy. 51 Battn. at approx:	T.13.b.3.0.
	2 " " " " " " " " 2 " " "A" " " " "	T.13.b.9.0.
	2 " " " " " " " " 2 " " "A" " " " "	T.13.d.8.4.
	2 " " " " " " " " 2 " " "A" " " " "	T.21.a.9.3.
	2 " " " " " " " " 2 " " "B" " " " "	T.14.b.4.5.
	4 " " " " " " " " 2 " " "B" " " " "	T.3.d.4.4.
	"A" Coy. 101st Bn. M.G.C. from each of the 2 forward sections of	
1/2nd Sept.	4 guns of "A" Coy. 105th Battn. will relieve 4 guns of "A" Coy. 51st Bn. in CORDITE Trench.	
	4 " " " " " " " " 4 " " "A" " " " in CORONA SUPPORT.	
	4 " " " " " " " " remaining 2 guns from each of the two forward Sections of "A" Coy. 101st Bn. M.G.C.	
	2 guns of "A" Coy. 105th Battn. will supplement 2 guns of "D" Coy. 51 Battn. at	T.15.d.0.4.
	2 " " " " " " " " 2 " " "D" " " " "	T.21.a.9.3.
	2 guns of "D" Coy. 105th Battn. will relieve 2 guns of "D" Coy. 51 Battn. at app:	T.14.b.2.8.
	4 " " " " " " " " 4 " " "A" " " " "	T.8.d.0.6.
	8 " " " " " " " " 8 " " " 101st Bn. in Reserve.	
	2 " " " " " " " " supplement 2 guns of "D" Coy. 51st Battn. at	T.13.b.5.3.
	2 " " " " " " " " " " " "	T.13.b.9.0.
	2 guns of "B" Coy. 105th Battn. will relieve 2 guns of "B" Coy. 51 Bn. in CADIZ-GILCHRIST Res. Line.	
	4 " " " " " " " " supplement CADIZ-GILCHRIST RESERVE Line at	H.13.b.9.5.
	4 " " " " " " " " Line at CORP SUPPORT. -	T.1.a.4.6.
	"B" Coy. 51st (H) Bn. M.G.C. will provide the necessary guide for these Supplementary positions.	

SECRET.   INSTRUCTIONS for ENTRAINMENT of   Copy No. ......
           51st (H) DIVISION, ...
                    on
              2nd August, 1915.   S1/9/15.
           ==================

1. "A", "B" and "C" Coys. will move under orders of the 152nd,
    153rd and 154th Infantry Brigades respectively in accordance with
    the attached time table.

2. The Commander of each train is responsible for the entrainment
    and detraining of his train.

3. Transport will arrive at the entraining Stations 3½ hours
    and personnel 2 hours before the times of departure shown in the
    table.
        The entrainment must be completed half-an-hour before the
    departure time of the train when it will be shunted from the siding.

4. Trains are composed as follows:-

            1 Officers' carriage.
            17 flat trucks.
            30 covered trucks, to take 40 men, 8 H.D. or 2 O.D.
            1 Brake Van (in which no personnel or stores may
                        travel).

5. A complete nominal roll showing the number of men,
    horses, G.S. Limbers, G.S. Wagons, two-wheeled vehicles, and bicycles,
    will be rendered with the forecast of every convoy so that
    accommodation in the train can be checked by the entraining officer
    or N.C.O.

6. Breast ropes for horse trucks must be provided by Coys. themselves.

7. Supply and Baggage wagons will accompany their own Coys. Empty
    wagons will travel full.

8. The train journey is expected to take 24 hours.

9. In addition to the current day's ration and those carried in the
    Supply wagons, one extra one day's iron ration will be drawn at the
    entraining stations for the journey.

10. Sufficient food for cooking on the day of arrival will be taken
    on the train by companies.

11. Companies will arrange for picquets guns to be kept in readiness
    for instant action during the train journey.

12. Units of the Division will be grouped as under for the move by
    rail:-

152nd Inf. Bde. Group:-   153rd Inf. Bde. Group:-

152nd Inf. Bde.   153rd Inf. Bde.
"A" Coy. 51st Dn. E.M.G.   "B" Coy. 51st Dn. ..... .
400th Fd. Coy. R.E.   401st Fd. Coy. R.E.
1/2nd H. Field Amb.   1/3rd H. Field Amb.
Div. Reception Camp.   9th H.Mobile & Delousing Sec.
No. 4 Coy. Div. Train.   No. 5 Coy. Div. Train.
1/1st Mob. Vet. Section.   Hdqrs. 2."C" Coy. 51st (H) Bn.M.G.C.

                 153rd Infantry Brigade:-

                153th Inf.Bde.
                "C" Coy. 51st (H) Bn. M.G.C.
                403th Fd.Coy. R.E.
                1/1st H. Field Amb.
                No.6 Coy. Divisional Train.

1

13. Brigades will issue all orders for entrainment and orders on detrainment to Units in their Brigade Group.

14. Billeting parties should proceed in the first train in each Group.

15. AERODROMES.

                                                                            [signature]
                                                                            Adjt.,
Issued at 9-30 p.m.   51st (H) Battalion H.L.I.

Copy No. 1 — Coys.
        2-4 — Brigades.
        5 — Division "A".
        9 — Col.
        10 — 2.0.
        11 — War Diary.
        12 — File.

ORDER OF MARCHING.

Starting Point - RUDGE.		Interval Report - AVING.		Billet Report - VERNE.	
Hour & Date.	Unit.	Hour & Date.	Unit.	Hour & Date.	Unit.
10.00 hrs. 2/8/18. (Column 7 hrs.)	Bn. 61 Div.Arty. Tps. - No. 2 Sn	15.30 hrs. 2/8/18.	Bn. 64-in Hy.Bde.RGA. 1st Bde. RHA.Inn. 2nd Bde. RHA.Inn. Sqt Cav. L.H. Bn. 1st Fld. Ambt.	21.30 hrs. 2/8/18.	H.Q. 1st Bde. 3rd Bde. RHA.Inn. 4th Sqn. CAV. L.H. Bn. CAV. L.H. Bn. 1st Fld. Ambt.
10.00 hrs. 3/8/18.	H.Q.,1st Inf.Bde. 1st Bde.-Arty.Gp. 4pr Co. S.A. Bn. 1st Fld. Ambt.			12.00 hrs. 3/8/18.	H.Q.,Div. Train. 1st & Eng. Co. Fld. Hy.

* Billeting parties will meet at these points.

NOTE: Boundary stations. RUDGE - AVING - VERNE - GLOUKS.

S E C R E T.

Copy No. ...9...

51st (H) BATTALION, M. G. CORPS.

Reference maps
CHALONS & REIMS,
1/50,000.

Operation Order No. 47.

31/7/18.

1. Battalion H.Q. and "D" Company, 51st (H) Bn. M. G. C. will move at 12 noon 1st August, 1918, to PIERRY to reach HAUTVILLERS at 1 p.m.

2. Order of March will be - "D" Company - Battalion H.Q. - Transport. 100 yards intervals will be maintained between personnel and transport.

3. An early dinner will be arranged.

4. Dress :- Fighting Order with Balmorals.

5. Battn. Transport Officer will arrange for stores of B.H.Q. and "D" Coy., now at DIZY MAGENTA, to be collected and removed to PIERRY.

6. All billets and areas occupied will be left scrupulously clean. "D" Coy. will render a certificate to this effect before marching out.

7. A billeting party of One Officer and One Other Rank will be detailed by O. C. "D" Coy. to report with horses or cycles to Bn. H.Q. by 9 a.m.

8. A C K N O W L E D G E.

Issued at 4.30 p.m.

2/Lieut. & Adjt.,
51st (H) Bn. M. G. C.

Copy No. 1 - "D" Coy.
2 - 51st (H) Div. "G."
3 - T.O.
4 - S.O.
5 - Q.M.
6 - A.S.H. 51st (H) Div. "Q."
7 - War Diary.
8 - File.

WAR DIARY
or
INTELLIGENCE SUMMARY.
(Erase heading not required.)

Army Form C. 2118.

51 Bn. M.G. Corps

Place	Date	Hour	Summary of Events and Information	Remarks and references to Appendices
Field.	1918. Sept. 1.		**Dispositions of Machine Guns :-** The 51st (H) Bn. M.G.C. have 52 guns in the line and 12 guns in Reserve and 1 Company of the 101st Bn. M.G.C., which are at the tactical disposal of the 51st (H) Division has 12 guns in the line and 4 in Reserve. Bn. H.Q. at H.14.a.0.7.	
	1st/2nd.		2 Companies of 103rd Bn. M.G.C. relieved 12 guns of 101st Bn. M.G.C. and 20 guns of 51st (H) Bn. M.G.C. and 1 Company reinforced the Divisional frontage. 2 Companies 51st (H) Bn. M.G.C. in line and 2 Companies in Reserve at BRIGADE CAMP, A.26.b.2.6.	
	2.		3 Companies 103rd Bn. M.G.C. in line and 1 in Reserve at ANZIN. 1 Company 101st Bn. M.G.C. rejoined its Battalion.	
	5.		"A" Coy. 51st (H) Bn. M.G.C. relieved "B" Coy. 51st (H) Bn. M.G.C. in line. "B" Coy. moved to BRIGADE CAMP, A.26.b.2.6. in Divisional Reserve.	
	6.		"C" Coy. 51st (H) Bn. M.G.C. relieved "D" Coy. 51st (H) Bn. M.G.C. in line. "D" Coy. moved to BRIGADE CAMP, A.26.b.2.6. in Divisional Reserve.	
	8-10. 11.	10.30 a.m.	Divisional Order received that 51st Division will be relieved by the 49th Division on the 12th/14th Sept. and on relief move to CHATEAU DE LA HAIE - MONT ST. ELOY - CAMBLAIN L'ABBE area with Divisional H.Q. at VILLERS AU BOIS. One Company of M. G. Battalion to move with each Brigade, and H.Q. and one Company M.G. Bn. to move to AUBIGNY.	
	12.	9. a.m.	"A" Coy. 49th Bn. M.G.C. relieved "C" Coy. 51st (H) Bn. M.G.C. in the line, the latter Company moving to LE PENDU arriving at 3.0 a.m. 13th. Amended Order that Bn. H.Q. will move to VILLERS AU BOIS received. "D" Coy. 49th Bn. M.G.C. relieves "D" Coy. 51st (H) Bn. M.G.C. in Reserve at BRIGADE CAMP, A.26.b.2.6. Latter Company proceeding by march route to AUBIGNY. "B" Coy. 49th Bn. M.G.C. relieves "B" Coy. 51st (H) Bn. M.G.C. in Reserve at BRIGADE CAMP, A.26.b.2.6. Latter Company proceeding by march route to CAMBLAIN L'ABBE. "C" Coy. 49th Bn. M.G.C. relieves "A" Coy. 51st (H) Bn. M.G.C. in line. Latter Company proceeding from CAMP VAILLY by lorry to GOUY SERVINS.	
	14.	5 a.m.		

Army Form C. 2118.

WAR DIARY
or
INTELLIGENCE SUMMARY.
(Erase heading not required.)

Instructions regarding War Diaries and Intelligence Summaries are contained in F.S. Regs. Part II. and the Staff Manual respectively. Title pages will be prepared in manuscript.

Place	Date	Hour	Summary of Events and Information	Remarks and references to Appendices
	14.	10.0 a.m.	51st (H) Bn. M.G.C. H.Q. relieved by 49th Bn. M.G.C. and moved to VILLERS AU BOIS.	
	16.		Battalion cleaning up and Baths.	
	16-21.		Training.	
	21.		Order received for 51st (H) Division to relieve 49th Division in the line. Relief to be complete by 24/9/18.	
	22.	11.30 a.m.	Orders for move postponed for 24 hours.	
		8.0 p.m.	Further orders received. Relief of 49th Division now to be complete by 25/9/18.	
	23.	10.30 a.m.	"A" Coy. proceeded by march route from PETIT SERVINS to BRIGADE CAMP, relieving "B" Coy. 49th Bn. M.G.C. Relief complete 8.30 p.m.	
		5.0 p.m.	"B" Coy. proceeds by lorry from CAMBLAIN L'ABBE to the line, relieving "A" Coy. 49th Bn. M.G.C. in the Right Sub-Sector. Relief complete. 11.0 p.m.	
	24.	2.0 p.m.	Transport by march route to BRIGADE CAMP, A.26.b.2.6.	
			"C" Coy. and Transport moved by march route from LE PENDU to BRIGADE CAMP, A.26.b.2.6. relieving "D" Coy. 49th Bn. M.G.C.	
		4.0 p.m.	"D" Coy. proceeded by Light Railway from AUBIGNY relieving "C" Coy. 49th Bn. M.G.C. in the Left Sub-Sector. Relief complete midnight.	
	25.	8.30 a.m.	Bn. H.Q. relieved 49th Bn. H.Q. at H.14.a.0.7.	
			Dispositions :- Right Sector. "B" Coy. 51st (H) Bn. M.G.C.	
			"A" Coy. 103rd Bn. M.G.C.	
			Left Sector. "D" Coy. 51st (H) Bn. M.G.C.	
			"D" Coy. 103rd Bn. M.G.C.	
			Two Coys. 51st (H) Bn. M.G.C. in Reserve at BRIGADE CAMP, A.26.b.2.6.	
			" " 103rd Bn. M.G.C. " " at ANZIN.	
	27.	5.35 a.m.	"Chinese" Attack carried out by 51st Division in conjunction with Divisions on the flanks. Machine Guns of "B" Coy. 51st (H) Bn. M.G.C. carry out enfilade fire on COB and WHALE Trenches, I.10.d.6.5. to I.4.c.4.7.	
	28-30.		Dispositions of Companies unchanged.	

P.M.A... Lieut. Colonel,
Commanding,
51st (H) Bn. M.G.C.

SECRET.   Copy No. 14.

51st (A) Battalion, M. G. Corps.

Ref: msg :—   OPERATION ORDER No. 64.   1/5/18.
FRANCE 1:5., N.W.,
1/20,000.

1. Rear Battalion Headquarters and Sections of "A" and "C" Companies at present in Railway Cutting, R.14.d.6.7., will move under Company arrangements to billets in BRIGADE CAMP, A.20.d.6.8., to-day.

2.   "A" and "C" Coys. Transports will move from present location to BRIGADE CAMP under arrangements of the S.T.O.

3.   Time of arrival at BRIGADE CAMP will not be before 2-30 p.m.

4.   2/Adjut. ROWE will act as Billeting Officer.

5.   All present billets will be left in a clean condition and a certificate rendered to Battn. Orderly Room that this has been done.

6.   Completion of move will be reported to Battn. H.Q.

7.   ACKNOWLEDGE.

                                            [signature]
                                            Lieut. & Adjt.,
                                            51st (A) Bn. M. G. Corps.

Copy 1 - 4 - Companies.
      5 - 8 - Rear H.Q. Coys.
          9 - Division, "G."
         10 - B.T.O.
         11 - Q.M.
         12 - S.O. SOFFE
         13 - R/Lr.
         14 - War Diary.
         15 - File.

SECRET.

51st (H) BATTALION, M.G.CORPS.
AMENDMENT No.2. at OPERATION ORDER No.63.

1. Reference para.6., on completion of reliefs night 1st/2nd September, relieved sections will proceed to billets in BRIGADE CAMP, A.26.b.2.6.
   Relieved sections of the 101st Bn. M.G.C. will occupy billets at Battalion H.Q., H.14.a.0.7.
2. A C K N O W L E D G E.

1st Sept. 1918.

Lieut. & Adjt.,
51st (H) Battalion M.G.Corps.

Addressed all recipients of O.O.63.

SECRET. Copy No 14.

51st (H) BATTALION, M. G. CORPS.

DEFENCE SCHEME. B.429.

EMPLOYMENT OF MACHINE GUN COMPANIES IN DIVISIONAL RESERVE.

1. On receipt of the order "MAN BATTLE STATIONS" the Companies in Divisional Reserve will be prepared to move as follows :-

    (a). One Company 51st (H) Bn. M.G.C. will be prepared to reinforce the main line of resistance in positions which will be earmarked by O. C. 51st (H) Bn. M.G.C.

    (b). One Company 51st (H) Bn. M.G.C. will be prepared to assemble in MISSOURI TRENCH.

    (c). One Company 103rd Bn. M.G.C. will be prepared to assemble in LEMON TRENCH.

2. Reinforcing positions will be constructed in, or immediately in rear of, the main line of resistance and will be marked with boards with large letters "V.G." 10,000 rounds S.A.A. will be placed at each double gun position.

3. Companies in Divisional Reserve will arrange for all Officers and as many N.C.Os. as possible to reconnoitre routes to the necessary reinforcing and assembly positions.

4. Before a Company is relieved in the line and becomes a Company in Divisional Reserve, the Company Commanders will obtain full particulars from the relieving Company Commander and will arrange for as many Officers and N.C.Os. as possible to make the necessary reconnaissances.

3rd September, 1918.

Lieut. & Adjt.,
51st (H) Bn. M.G.C.

Copies 1-4 - All Coys. 51st Bn. M.G.C.
    5-8 - All Coys.103rd Bn. M.G.C.
    9-11- Brigades.
    12 - 51st (H) Division "G."
    13 - 103rd Bn. M.G.C.
    14 - War Diary.
    17 - File.

SECRET.

51st (H) BATTALION, M. G. CORPS.

OPERATION ORDER No. 65.

Copy No. 14.

5/9/18.

Ref: Map :-
FRANCE, 51B.N.W., 1/20,000.

1. On the night 5th/6th September, 1918, the following Inter-Company relief will take place :-

   "A" Coy. 51st Bn. M.G.C. will relieve "B" Coy. 51st Bn. M.G.C.

2. Tripods, 10 belt boxes per gun, trench stores and work in hand will be handed over and receipts obtained will be forwarded to reach Battn. H.Q. by 5 p.m. 6th September, 1918.

3. Fire Schemes and Intelligence Reports will be handed over. There will be no intermission due to relief.

4. All further details will be arranged between Company Commanders concerned.

5. On completion of relief "B" Company will withdraw to billets in BRIGADE CAMP, A.26.b.2.6. and will become Divisional Reserve.

6. Completion of relief will be notified to Battn. H.Q. by code phrase "O.R.21 noted".

7. A C K N O W L E D G E.

W. Walmesley
Lieut. & Adjt.,
51st H. Bn. M. G. C.

Issued at 2 p.m.

Copies 1-4 - "A" "B" & "C" Coys., 51st Bn. M.G.C.
       5-7 - "B" "C" & "D" Coys., 103rd Bn. M.G.C.
         8 - 103rd Bn. M.G.C.
         9 - 152nd Inf. Bde.
        10 - 153rd Inf. Bde.
        11 - 51st (H) Division, "G."
        12 - T.O.
        13 - Q.M.
        14 - War Diary.
        15 - File.

SECRET.   Copy No. ......

51st (H) BATTALION, M. G. CORPS.

Operation Order No. 66.

Ref: map:-
FRANCE 51B. N.W.
1/20,000.   4/9/18.

1. On the night 6th/7th September, 1918, the following Inter-Company relief will take place :-

   "C" Coy. 51st Bn. M.G.C. will relieve "D" Coy. 51st Bn. M.G.C.

2. Tripods, 10 bolt boxes per gun, trench stores and work in hand will be handed over and receipts obtained will be forwarded to reach Battn. H.Q. by 5 p.m. 7th September, 1918.

3. Fire Schemes and Intelligence Reports will be handed over. There will be no intermission due to relief.

4. All further details will be arranged between Company Commanders concerned.

5. On completion of relief "D" Company will withdraw to billets in BRIGADE CAMP, A.26.b.2.6. and will become Divisional Reserve.

6. Completion of relief will be notified to Battn. H.Q. by code phrase "R.O.66. RECEIVED."

7. A C K N O W L E D G E.

                                                       [signature]
                                                    Lieut. & Adjt.,
                                                    51st (H) Bn. M.G.C.

Issued at 2 p.m.

Copies 1-4 - "A" "B" "C" & "D" Coys. 51st Bn. M.G.C.
       5-7 - "B" "C" & "D" Coys. 103rd Bn. M.G.C.
         8 - 103rd Bn. M.G.C.
         9 - 152nd Inf. Bde.
        10 - 153rd Inf. Bde.
        11 - 51st (H) Division "G."
        12 - T.O.
        13 - A.M.
        14 - War Diary.
        15 - File.

S E C R E T.   Copy No. 17

                          51st (H) Battalion, M. G. Corps.

                          OPERATION ORDER No. 67.   Cancelled   9/9/18.
                          *****************************   Noon
                                                               11/9/18
Ref: Map :-
FRANCE 51 . N.W. 1/20,000.

1. On the night 11/12th September, 1918, the following Inter-Company
    relief will take place :-

    "D" Coy. 51st (H) Bn. M.G.C. will relieve "A" Coy. 51st (H) Bn. M.G.C.

2. Tripods, belt boxes, trench stores and work in hand will be handed
    over and receipts obtained will be forwarded to reach Battn.
    H.Q. by 5 p.m. 12th September, 1918.

3. Fire Schemes, Intelligence Reports and particulars of Working
    Parties will be handed over.   There will be no intermission
    due to relief.

4. All further details will be arranged between Company Commanders
    concerned.

5. On completion of relief "A" Coy. will withdraw to billets in
    BRIGADE CAMP, A.20.D.2.6. and will become Divisional Reserve.

6. Completion of relief will be notified to Battn. H.Q. by code word
    "LEAGUE."

7. A C K N O W L E D G E.

                                                    [signature]
                                                    Lieut. & Adjt.,
    Issued at 9 p.m.   51st (H) Bn. M. G. C.

    Copies 1-4 - All Coys. 51st (H) Bn. M.G.C.
           5-8 - All Coys. 103rd Bn. M.G.C.
             9 - 103rd Bn. M.G.C.
            10 - 152nd Inf. Bde.
            11 - 153rd Inf. Bde.
            12 - 154th Inf. Bde.
            13 - T.C.
            14 - 51st (H) Division "G."
            15 - Q.M.
            16 - C.O.
            17 - War Diary.
            18 - File.

cancelled
now
11/9/18

Copy No. 12.

SECRET.

51st (H) BATTALION, M. G. CORPS.

OPERATION ORDER No. 80.   10/9/18.

Ref: MAP :-
FRANCE 51B. S.W. 1/20,000.

1. On the night 15/16th September, 1918, the following Inter-Company relief will take place :-

   "D" Coy, 51st (H) Bn, M.G.C. will relieve "C" Coy, 51st (H) Bn, M.G.C.

2. Tripods, belt boxes, trench stores and work in hand will be handed over and receipts obtained will be forwarded to reach Battn. H.Q. by 6 p.m. 16th September, 1918.

3. Fire Schemes, Intelligence Reports and particulars of working parties and Reconnaissances will be handed over. There will be no intermission due to relief.

4. All further details will be arranged between Company Commanders concerned.

5. On completion of relief "C" Company will withdraw to billets in BRIGADE CAMP, A.23.b.8.8, and will become Divisional Reserve.

6. Completion of relief will be notified to Battn. H.Q. by code word "PINTO."

7. ACKNOWLEDGE.

W R Grasby
Lieut. & Adjt.,
51st (H) Bn. M. G. Corps.

Issued at 1 p.m.

Copy 1-4 - All Coys, 51st (H) Bn, M.G.C.
     5-8 - All Coys, 103rd Bn, M. G. C.
       9 - 103rd Bn. M.G.C.
      10 - 152nd Inf. Bde.
      11 - 153rd Inf. Bde.
      12 - 154th Inf. Bde.
      13 - 51st (H) Division, "G."
      14 - T.O.
      15 - Q. .
      16 - S.O.
      17 - War Diary.
      18 - File.

S E C R E T.   Cancelled Copy No. 17.
                                                                                          noon
                        51st (H) BATTALION, M. G. CORPS.   11/9/18

                        AMENDMENT TO OPERATION ORDER No. 67.
                        ************************************   11/9/18.

1.   Para. 1 - line 1 :-   For   11/12th September, 1918,
                                read   14/15th September, 1918.

2.   Para. 2 - line 3 :-   For 12th September, 1918,
                                read 15th September, 1918.

3.   ACKNOWLEDGE.

                                                            [signature]
Issued at 10 a.m.   Lieut. & Adjt.,
Addressed all recipients of O.O.67.   51st (H) Battalion, M. G. Corps.

SECRET.   Copy No. 18

51st (H) BATTALION, M. G. CORPS.

OPERATION ORDER No. 69.

11/9/18.

Ref: maps :-
FRANCE 51B, N.W. 1/20,000,
LENS 11, 1/100,000.

1. The 51st (H) Division will be relieved in the line by the 49th Division and will move on relief to the CHATEAU de la HAIE – MONT ST. ELOI and CAMBLAIN L'ABBE area, with Divisional Headquarters at VILLERS AU BOIS.

2. The 1st Divl. M.G. Battn. will be relieved by the 49th Divl. M.G. Battn. in accordance with the attached table.

3. Fourteen belt boxes per gun, trench stores, work in hand, Defence Schemes, Intelligence Reports, and Fire Schemes will be handed over and receipts obtained will be forwarded to Battn. H.Q. Tripods will not be handed over.

4. All further details will be arranged between Company Commanders concerned.

5. Completion of relief will be notified to Battn. H.Q. by code word "SUMMER."

6. On completion of relief Companies will move to billeting areas in accordance with the attached table. One Company will be in each Infantry Brigade area; one Company and Battn. H.Q. will be at AUBIGNY.

7. Company Transports will move under Company arrangements, 100 yds. intervals being maintained between units and transports.

8. Packs will be withdrawn from Battalion Dump at BRIGADE CAMP.

9. Billeting parties will be detailed by Companies, and sent on in advance to take over billets.

10. Arrival in billets will be notified to Battn. H.Q.

11. Battn. H.Q. will close at H.14.a.0.7. at 10 a.m. 14th inst. and will open at AUBIGNY CHATEAU.

12. A C K N O W L E D G E.

W.A.Grasby
Lieut. & Adjt.,
51st (H) Bn. M.G.C.

Issued at 10.15 p.m.

Copies 1- 4 – All Coys. 51st (H) Bn. M.G.C.
        5- 7 – "A" "B" & "C" Coys. 103rd Bn. M.G.C.
           8 – 103rd Bn. M.G.C.
           9 – 49th Bn. M.G.C.
          10 – 51st (H) Div. "G."
          11 – 51st (H) Div. "Q."
       12-14 – Brigades.
          15 – Q.M.
          16 – T.O.
          17 – S.O.
          18 – War Diary.
          19 – File.

SECRET.

51st (H) BATTALION, M. G. CORPS.
****

TABLE TO ACCOMPANY OPERATION ORDER No. 69, DATED 11/9/18.
_____

Date.	Unit.	From.	To.	Relieving.	Moves to.	Remarks.
12/13th.	"A" Company, 49th Bn. M.G.C.	H.14.a.0.7.	Line.	"C" Company, 51st (H) Bn. M.G.C.	LE PENDU.	By lorry/from CAL VALLEY at 12.5 a.m. 13th.
13th.	"D" Company, 49th Bn. M.G.C.	AUBIGNY.	A.26.b.5.6.	"D" Company, 51st (H) Bn. M.G.C.	AUBIGNY.	By march route. Companies to be clear of present billets by 9 a.m. 13th.
	"B" Company, 49th Bn. M.G.C.	ONTRATH LIAISE	A.26.d.8.3.	"B" Company, 51st (H) Bn. M.G.C.	CALBLAIR LIAISE.	
13/14th.	"C" Company, 49th Bn. M.G.C.	H.14.a.0.7.	Line.	"A" Company, 51st (H) Bn. M.G.C.	SOUX SHRVIES.	By lorry from CAL VALLEY at 12.5 a.m. 14th.
14th.	Battn. H.Q., 49th Bn. M.G.C.	AUBIGNY.	H.14.a.0.7.	Battn. H.Q., 51st (H) Bn. M.G.C.	AUBIGNY.	By march route.

NOTE: (i). Rear Battalion Headquarters will move with "D" Coy., 51st (H) Bn. M.G.C.

(ii). "A" & "C" Coys., 51st (H) Bn. M.G.C. will detail an Officer to meet the lorries at CAL VALLEY.

Five lorries will be provided by 51st (H) Division for each of these Companies.

****

War Diary.

Reference O.O. 89, dated yesterday.

Rear Battalion H.Q. will not now move with "D" Company, but will move independently on the morning of the 14th instant, to be clear of BRIGADE CAMP by 9 a.m.

Lieut. & Adjt.,
51st (H) Bn. M. G. C.

12/9/18.

Copies to "B" Coy
"D" "
a/q & m/m G C
T O
Q M
S O
War Diary
File

[Stamp: 51st (H) BATTALION, MACHINE GUN CORPS.]

S.O.R.N.

First (1) BATTALION. A. & CORPS.

ADDITION TO OPERATION ORDER No. 69.
****

12/6/18.

1. Delete Paragraph 11 and substitute the following:-

Battalion H.Q. will close at 1st.a.0.5. at 10 a.m. 14th inst.
and will open at VILLERS AU BOIS.

[signed]
Lieut. & Adjt.,
1st (I) Bn. A.& C.

Issued at 9 p.m.
Addresses all receiving copy of O.O. 69.

SECRET.

51st (H) BATTALION, M. G. CORPS.

Copy No.......

OPERATION ORDER No. 70.   21/9/18.

Refce: map :-
FRANCE 51B, N.W. 1/20,000.
LENS II, 1/100,000.

1. The 51st (H) Division will relieve the 49th Division in the line, relief to be completed by 10 a.m. 24th instant, at which hour the command of the Divisional front will pass to G.O.C. 51st (H) Division.

2. The 51st (H) Bn. M.G.C. will relieve the 49th Bn. M.G.C. in the line in accordance with the attached table.

3. Companies will come under orders of G.O.C. 49th Division from time of arrival in 49th Divisional area until 10 a.m. 24th September, 1918, when H.Q. 51st (H) Bn. M.G.C. will open at H.14.a.0.7.

4. Trench Stores, Maps, Aeroplane Photographs, Defence Schemes, Intelligence Reports, Fire Schemes and Work in Hand will be taken over. Details of Trench Stores, etc, taken over will be forwarded to reach Battalion H.Q. not later than 10 a.m. 26th instant.

5. All further details will be arranged by Company Commanders concerned.

6. Completion of relief will be notified to H.Q. of 49th Bn. M.G.C. and 51st (H) Bn. M.G.C. by code phrase "M.G.23 received."

7. Company Transports will move under Company arrangements in accordance with table and will take over Horse Lines from the 49th Bn. M.G.C. in the vicinty of BRIGADE CAMP.

8. During the move the distances laid down in Para. 19 of S.S.724 will be maintained and special care will be taken to prevent the enemy observing undue movement during or subsequent to the relief.

9. All billets must be left in a clean condition and a certificate that this has been done will be rendered to Battalion Orderly Room.

10. The Reserve Companies will send forward billeting parties to take over billets from the 49th Bn. M.G.C. at BRIGADE CAMP.

11. ACKNOWLEDGE.

W.M.Grasby
Lieut. & Adjt.,
51st (H) Bn. M.G.C.

Issued at 11 a.m.

Copies 1-4 - All Companies.
       5-7 - Brigades.
         8 - Division "G."
         9 - Division "Q."
        10 - 49th Bn. M.G.C.
        11 - 103rd Bn. M.G.C.
        12 - Q.
        13 - T.O.
        14 - S.O.
        15 - War Diary.
        16 - File.

S E C R E T.

Copy No........

51st (H) BATTALION, M. G. CORPS.

RELIEF CHART TO ACCOMPANY OPERATION ORDER No. 70, DATED 21/9/18.

Date.	Serial No.	Unit.	From.	To.	Relieving.	Remarks.
22nd.	3.	"D" Coy. 51st (H) Bn. M.G.C.	AUBIGNY.	Right Sub-Sector.	"N" Coy. 49th Bn. M.G.C.	Personnel by Light Railway, arriving ATHIES about 6 p.m. Transport to be East of MONT ST. ELOI by 2 p.m.
23rd.	1.	"B" Coy. 51st (H) Bn. M.G.C.	GAUCHAIN L'ABBE.	Left Sub-Sector.	"P" Coy. 49th Bn. M.G.C.	Personnel by Light Railway, arriving ATHIES about 6 p.m. Transport to pass MONT ST. ELOI at 10.15 a.m.
	2.	"A" Coy. 51st (H) Bn. M.G.C.	PETIT SERVINS.	BRIGADE CAMP. A.26.b.2.6.	"B" Coy. 49th Bn. M.G.C.	By march route under orders to be issued by G.O.C. 152nd Inf. Bde.
24th.	4.	"C" Coy. 51st (H) Bn. M.G.C.	LE PENDU.	do.	"D" Coy. 49th Bn. M.G.C.	By march route at 10 a.m.

DETAILED TRAIN ARRANGEMENTS WILL BE NOTIFIED LATER.

51st (H) Battalion, M. G. Corps.

AMENDMENT TO OPERATION ORDER No. 70, DATED 21/9/18.

Reference Relief Chart :-

Serial 1 - For Right Sub-Sector read LEFT Sub-Sector.
" " "A" Coy., 40th Bn. M.G.C. read "C" Coy., 40th Bn. M.G.C.

" 2 - For Left Sub-Sector read RIGHT Sub-Sector.
" " "C" Coy., 49th Bn. M.G.C. read "A" Coy., 49th Bn. M.G.C.

Addressed all recipients of O.O.70.   Lieut. & Adjt.,
21/9/18.   51st (H) Bn. M.G.C.

SECRET.   Copy No..... 15

51st (H) BATTALION, M. G. CORPS.

OPERATION ORDER No. 71.
                                                                       22/9/18.
Ref. Maps:
FRANCE 51b.N.W., 1/20,000.
LENS 11, 1/100,000.

Operation Order No. 70 cancelled and the following substituted :-

1. The 51st (H) Division will relieve the 49th Division in the line, relief to be completed by 10 a.m., 23th instant, at which hour the command of the Divisional front will pass to G.O.C., 51st (H) Division.

2. The 51st (H) Battalion M.G.C. will relieve the 49th Bn. M.G.C. in the line in accordance with the attached table.

3. Companies will come under orders of G.O.C.,49th Division from time of arrival in 49th Divisional area until 10 a.m., 23th Septr.,1918., when H.Qrs. 51st (H) Bn. M.G.C. will open at H.14.a.O.7.

4. Trench Stores, Maps, Aeroplane Photographs, Defence Schemes, Intelligence Reports, Fire Schemes, and Work in Hand will be taken over. Details of Trench Stores etc. taken over will be forwarded to reach Battalion H.Q. not later than 10 a.m., 23th instant.

5. All further details will be arranged between Coy.Commanders concerned.

6. Completion of Relief will be notified to H.Q. of 49th Bn. M.G.C., and 51st (H) Bn. M.G.C. by code phrase "M.G.23 RECEIVED".

7. Company Transports will move under Coy. arrangements in accordance with Table and will take over Horse Lines from the 49th Bn. M.G.C. in the vicinity of BRIGADE CAMP.

8. During the move the distances laid down in para. 19 of S.S.724 will be maintained and special care will be taken to prevent the enemy observing undue movement during or subsequent to the relief.

9. All billets must be left in a clean condition and a certificate that this has been done will be rendered to Battalion Orderly Room.

10. The Reserve Companies will send forward Billeting Parties to take over billets from the 49th Bn. M.G.C. at BRIGADE CAMP.

11. A C K N O W L E D G E.

                                                   [signature]
                                                   Lieut.& Adjt.,
                                           51st (H) Battalion, M.G.Corps.

Issued at 9 p.m.

Copies 1-4 - Corps.
       5-7 - Brigades.
       8-9 - 51st (H) Div. "G" & "Q".
       10 - 49th Bn. M.G.C.
       11 - 103rd Bn. M.G.C.
       12 - Q..
       13 - T.O.
       14 - C.O.
       15 - War Diary.
       16 - File.

SECRET.

51st (H) BATTALION, M.G. CORPS.

RELIEF CHART TO ACCOMPANY OPERATION ORDER No. 71, DATED 22/9/18.

Date.	Serial No.	Unit.	From.	To.	Relieving.	Remarks.
23rd.	1.	"B" Coy. 51st (H) Bn. M.G.C.	GAUBLAIN L'ABBE.	Right Sub-Sector.	"A" Coy. 49th Bn. M.G.C.	Personnel by Light Railway, arriving ATHIES about 6 p.m. Transport to pass MONT ST. ELOI at 10.15 a.m.
	2.	"A" Coy. 51st (H) Bn. M.G.C.	PETIT SERVINS.	BRIGADE CAMP, A.26.b.8.8.	"B" Coy. 49th Bn. M.G.C.	By march route under orders to be issued by O.C. 152nd Inf. Bde.
24th.	3.	"D" Coy. 51st (H) Bn. M.G.C.	AUBIGNY.	Left Sub-Sector.	"C" Coy. 49th Bn. M.G.C.	Personnel by Light Railway, arriving ATHIES about 8 p.m. Transport to be East of MONT ST. ELOI by 2 p.m.
24th.	4.	"C" Coy. 51st (H) Bn. M.G.C.	LE FERDU.	BRIGADE CAMP, A.23.1.2.3.	"D" Coy. 49th Bn. M.G.C.	By march route at 10 a.m.

DETAILED TRAIN ARRANGEMENTS WILL BE NOTIFIED LATER.

SECRET.   Copy No. 10

51st (H) BATTALION, M. G. CORPS.

OPERATION ORDER No. 72.

26/9/18.

Reference map :-
FRANCE, 51B. N.W. & N.E. (combined sheet).

1. On a date and at a time to be notified later the Division will carry out a "Chinese Attack" against the FRESNES - ROUVROY Line, in co-operation with the 4th Division on the South and the 8th Division on the North.

2. The "Chinese Attack" will consist of :-

      (a) a barrage.
      (b) the exposure of dummy figures.

3. For the barrage the Divisional Artillery will make the GAVRELLE-FRESNES Road their left boundary.
    The barrage will open at ZERO hour on normal S.O.S. lines and will move with the following lifts :-

Falls on the FRESNES-ROUVROY Line.	Z plus 12'
Lifts off the FRESNES-ROUVROY Line.	Z plus 20'
Jumps back on to the FRESNES-ROUVROY Line.	Z plus 50'
Lifts off the FRESNES-ROUVROY Line.	Z plus 55'
Barrage ceases.	Z plus 60'

4. The dummies will be exposed under arrangements to be made by the 153rd and 154th Brigades between ZERO and ZERO plus 50 minutes. During this time the dummies will be alternately raised and lowered for periods of about a minute.

5. O. C. "B" Company, 51st (H) Battalion, M.G. Corps will arrange for six guns in I.16.d. to bring enfilade fire to bear on COB and WHALE Trenches, I.10.d.6.5. to I.4.c.4.7., between ZERO plus 25 to ZERO plus 30, and between ZERO plus 45 to ZERO plus 50.

6. Rate of fire - One belt per two minutes.

7. Company Commanders will arrange that until all hostile retaliation has ceased, all men not on duty at the guns are kept under shell-proof cover.

8. ACKNOWLEDGE.

                                                      Lieut. & Adjt.,
Issued at 9.0 a.m.   51st (H) Bn. M.G.C.

Copy 1-5 - Coys. in line.
     6 - 51st Division "G."
  7-8 - 153rd and 154th Brigades.
     9 - 103rd Bn. M.G.C.
10-11 - War Diary and File.

SECRET.   Copy No......10

ADDENDUM to 51st (H) BATTALION M.G.CORPS
OPERATION ORDER No.72.

                                                               26/9/18.

1.   With reference to 51st (H) Battalion M.G.Corps Operation Order No.72 dated 26th September, 1918, ZERO hour will be 5-35 a.m. tomorrow, 27th instant.

2.   ACKNOWLEDGE.

                                                  [signature]

                                                         Lt. & Adjt.,
Issued at 6-30 p.m.   51st (H) Battalion M.G.C.

Addressed all recipients of O.O.72.

S E C R E T.

51st (H) BATTALION, M. G. CORPS.   B.597.

Instructions in case of Enemy Withdrawal.

27/9/18.

1. The enemy may carry out either a partial or general withdrawal on the front with which the Division is concerned.

(a). A partial withdrawal would probably entail his abandoning the FRESNES - ROUVROY Line between FRESNES and the RIVER SCARPE and occupying a switch line North of GOSTER WOOD and VITRY MARSH.

(b). A general withdrawal from the FRESNES - ROUVROY Line to the DROCOURT - QUEANT Line followed possibly by a further withdrawal to the line of the HAUTE-DEULE CANAL in the neighbourhood of DOUAI.

2. In the event of any withdrawal on the Corps front contact must be regained with the enemy on the initiatives of Brigades in the line, the present Main Line of Resistance remaining unaltered until receipt of orders from Divisional Headquarters.

3. The Divisional Boundaries in case of advance will be as follows :-

Right Boundary.   RIVER SCARPE.

Left Boundary.   COUNT AVENUE (inclusive) RAILWAY WOOD

(inclusive) - FRESNES (exclusive) - GLOUCESTER WOOD

(inclusive), thence to D.10.central - DOUAI (inclusive).

The Inter-Brigade Boundary will be the track running through I.10.a. and b., I.4.d., I.5.c., d. and b., I.6.a., thence to the point where the FRESNES - BREBIERES Road crosses the front trench of the DROCOURT - QUEANT Line at D.25.b.3.7. thence along this road to the cross roads at D.26.a. - 7.5.

4. The VIII Corps orders legislate for an advance by bounds as under :-

FIRST BOUND. The extension of the present line of observation northwards through C.20.Central to OPPY SUPPORT Trench.

SECOND BOUND. From C.29.c.8.0. - C.23.a.0.0. - C.15.a.5.5.

5. STAGES OF ADVANCE.

On the 51st Divisional front, the advance will be carried out by bounds as under :-

(a). FIRST BOUND. The FRESNES - ROUVROY Line from the RIVER SCARPE to the junction with COUNT AVENUE.
This line will be occupied on the initiatives of Brigades in the line as soon as the enemy is found to have evacuated it.
As soon as this line has been securely occupied patrols will be pushed forward to examine BIACHE, BIACHE STATION and RAILWAY COPSE; if found unoccupied by the enemy, these positions will be occupied as outpost positions by Brigades in the line.

(b) SECOND BOUND. The South-Western edge of VIMY MARSH and GLOUCESTER WOOD.
The move forward to this objective will not be commenced without reference to Divisional Headquarters.

6. FORWARD MACHINE GUNS. The following Machine Guns will be at the Tactical disposal of Brigades for use in the forward area:-

Right Brigade. Two Sections of Right Company 103rd M. G. Battalion at present in position in CORAL and CORDITE Trenches and at ROEUX CHATEAU, I.13.d.1.1.

Left Brigade. Two Sections of Left Company 103rd M. G. Battalion at present in position at CADIZ, CALF and CHICKEN RESERVE.

The remaining Machine Guns in the line will not move without orders from Divisional Headquarters.

7. HEADQUARTERS.

The first forward bound of Headquarters will be to the following positions :- These moves will take place on orders from Div. H.Q. probably as soon as the first bound is completed.
Divisional Headquarters. - Railway Embankment, H.14.a.

Right Brigade H.Q. — Junction of CALICO and CROOK, I.13.b.1.8.

Left Brigade H.Q. — Present Right Battalion H.Q. at junction of CALICO and CASH, I.7.d.1.4.

(a). M.G. Battalion H.Q. — Will remain in present location, H.14.a.0.7.

(b). M. G. Company H.Q. — (At present in the line). Will move with Brigades to the vicinity of :-

    1. Right Company - I.13.b.1.3.
    2. Left   "   - I.7.d.1.4.

(c). Reserve Brigade H.Q. — Will move to present Left Brigade H.Q. at H.12.c.1.8.

8. MOVES. Two Companies of 51st (H) Bn. M.G.C. in Reserve at BRIGADE CAMP will move TRAMWAY VALLEY, H.14.a. on receipt from Bn. H.Q. of order "CARRY OUT ADVANCE MOVE."

Fighting Transport will accompany Reserve M. G. Companies and Fighting Transport of Companies in the line will move to MUSKETRY VALLEY on receipt of order "CARRY OUT ADVANCE MOVES."

Instructions for the movement of remaining Transport will be issued under Administrative Instructions.

9. ROADS. The Roads selected to be repaired and maintained will be detailed later and maps will be forwarded showing tracks and roads suitable for gun limbers

11. ENEMY TRAPS. Three parties each of one Officer and ten Other Ranks are being detailed by the 172nd Tunnelling Co. R.E. to search for enemy booby traps. Each member of these parties will wear a distinguishing badge on both sleeves consisting of a red strip of cloth one inch wide extending from the point of the shoulder to the cuff.

The following measures will be adopted by Search Parties when examining captured ground :-

Dugouts which have been passed at the first examination will be marked at the entrance with green chalk, the word "examined" and the date and signature of the unit concerned.

                              e.g.   (Green)
                              Examined.
                              (date)
                        Blank Company R.E. (Unit).

-3-

After the final examination for delayed action mines has been completed, a White tin sign will be nailed up, lettered in black as follows:-

> Considered safe.

Dugouts in which booby traps are found, or which are considered dangerous, will be marked either in RED CHALK as follows:-

○ (Red)
Mined - Dangerous.
(date)
Blank Company R.E. (Unit).

or will have a Red tin sign nailed up, lettered in Black as follows:-

> Mined Dangerous.

Roads will be marked as follows:-

DANGER.

White letters on RED board. This board to be erected if road has not been inspected or has been found mined.

 Movable arrow.

This board will be erected when road has been inspected and found safe for traffic.

11. A C K N O W L E D G E.

Lieut. & Adjt.,
51st (H) Battalion M.G.Corps.

Copy No. 1-4 - All Coys. 51st (H) Bn. M.G.C.
5-6 - "B" & "D" Coys. 103rd Bn. M.G.C.
7 - 51st (H) Division "G".
8 - 51st (H) Division "Q".
9 - 4th Division.
10 - 8th Division.
11-13 - Brigades.
14 - 103rd Bn. M.G.C.
15 - C.R.G.O.
16 - D.P.O.
17 - S.O.
18 - Q.M.
19 - War Diary.
20 - File.

Army Form W.3091.

Cover for Documents.

Nature of Enclosures.

Confidential

War Diary
of
51st (H) Bn. M.G. Corps
for
October, 1918.

Notes, or Letters written.

Army Form C. 2118.

WAR DIARY
or
INTELLIGENCE SUMMARY.
(Erase heading not required.)

Instructions regarding War Diaries and Intelligence Summaries are contained in F.S. Regs., Part II. and the Staff Manual respectively. Title pages will be prepared in manuscript.

Place	Date	Hour	Summary of Events and Information	Remarks and references to Appendices
	1918. Oct.		Reference maps :- FRANCE 51.B. 1/40,000. FRANCE 57.C. 1/40,000. FRANCE 51.A. 1/40,000.	
	1.		Orders received that 8th Division is to take over the front held by the 51st Division. 20 guns of 51st (H) Bn. M.G.C. relieved by 20 guns of 103rd Bn. M.G.C. 12 guns of 51st (H) Bn. M.G.C. withdrew from the line without relief. Complete relief accomplished by 21.30 hours.	See O.O.75.
	3.	10.00	Relieved Companies moved to BRIGADE CAMP, A.26.b.2.6. Bn. H.Q. closed at RAILWAY CUTTING, H.14.a.0.7., and re-opened at BRIGADE CAMP, A.26.b.2.6. Companies cleaning up.	
	4.	10.00	Warning Order received from Division; 51st (H) Division to relieve 3rd Canadian Division on the night 10th/11th Oct. in the sector W. of CAMBRAI.	
	5.		Church Parades.	
	6.	07.00	Transport moves by march route via ARRAS - GUEMAPPE - CHERISY - HENDICOURT - CAGNICOURT to Canadian Corps "D" Area, arriving about 20.00 hours.	See O.O.74.
	7.	16.50	Battalion leaves BRIGADE CAMP, A.26.b.2.6. at 18.30 hours and arrives at INCHY-en-ARTOIS at 01.30 hours, 8th.	
	8.		Battalion occupies billets in dugouts, trench shelters, etc. in HINDENBURG SUPPORT LINE, D.5.d.3.8.	
			Transport at G.12.b.5.5.	
		15.00	Transport moves to D.5.d.3.8.	
	9.	21.00	Divisional Order received stating that the 51st Division will move tomorrow, 10/10/18, to the area around BOURLON WOOD, taking the place of the 3rd Canadian Division. Companies allotted to Brigades as follows :-	

			"A" Coy. ::: 152nd Inf. Bde.
			    "D" " ::: 153rd " "
			    "C" " ::: 154th " "
			    "B" " ::: In Divisional Reserve with Bn. H.Q.	

	10.	08.00	Moves to take place under orders of Brigades. "C" Coy. moves by march route via LOEUVRES to CAMBRAI - BAPAUME Road, E.28.a.0.2. to 154th Inf. Bde. Sub-Area.	

Army Form C. 2118.

WAR DIARY
or
INTELLIGENCE SUMMARY.
(Erase heading not required.)

Instructions regarding War Diaries and Intelligence Summaries are contained in F. S. Regs., Part II. and the Staff Manual respectively. Title pages will be prepared in manuscript.

Place	Date	Hour	Summary of Events and Information	Remarks and references to Appendices
	10.	11.00	"A" Coy. moves by march route (as above) to 152nd Inf. Bde. Sub-Area.	
		13.00	Bn. H.Q. closes at D.5.d.3.8.	
		14.00	"D" Coy. moves by march route (as above) to 153rd Inf. Bde. Sub-Area.	
		18.30	Bn. H.Q. opens at E.11.c.5.5.	
			Dispositions of Coys. in Bde. Sub-Areas as follows :-	
			"A" Coy. ... F.9.a.8.2. "B" Coy. ... E.18.a.9.5. "C" Coy. ... A.8.b.4.3. (57.B.N.W.)	
			"D" Coy. ... F.7.d.3.4.	
	11.	01.00	Battalion to be prepared to move at 10.00 hours.	
		07.30	Divl. Order received that 51st (H) Division is to be prepared to move forward at ZERO hour, with a view to relieving the 2nd Canadian Division on night 11th October.	
		12.30	ZERO hour fixed at 12.30 hours.	
			Bn. H.Q. to move at ZERO plus 3 hrs. 20 mins., i.e. 15.50.	
		15.50	"B" Coy. and Bn. H.Q. proceed by march route from cross roads, F.7.b.1.4., to 153rd Bde. Area.	
		23.15	Whilst Battalion is on the march orders received that 152nd and 154th Bdes. will relieve 2nd Canadian Division in the line tonight, 11/10/18.	
			Bn. H.Q. and "B" Coy. to remain in NEUVILLE-ST.-REMY.	
		24.00	Battalion arrived at and is billeted in NEUVILLE-ST.-REMY.	
			"A" "C" & "D" Coys. proceeded under orders of respective Brigades.	
	12.	09.00	"B" Coy. & Bn. H.Q. proceed by march route from NEUVILLE-ST-REMY to CHATEAU D'ESWARS area, arriving at 09.40 hours.	
		12.00	152nd and 154th Inf. Bdes. carry out an attack, the objective being the line VILLERS-en-CAUCHIE - AVESNES-le-SEC (both inclusive), thence along the road through 0.15.c. to 0.8.d.0.0. and thence along the spur to the railway in N.12.c.	
			After capture of objective, 154th Inf. Bde. is to exploit success with a view to securing the line from 0.8.c.7.1. - LIEU ST. AMAND (inclusive) to the Station in N.6.b.	
		14.00	Bn. H.Q. established at S.30.d.6.0.	
		15.00	Bn. H.Q. moves by march route to NAVES, T.23.a.9.1. "B" Coy. remains at ESCAUDOEUVRES.	
			Orders received for attack to be continued.	

Army Form C. 2118.

WAR DIARY
or
INTELLIGENCE SUMMARY.
(Erase heading not required.)

Instructions regarding War Diaries and Intelligence Summaries are contained in F.S. Regs., Part II. and the Staff Manual respectively. Title pages will be prepared in manuscript.

Place	Date	Hour	Summary of Events and Information	Remarks and references to Appendices
	13.		8 guns of "B" Coy. attached to "A" Coy. for operation. These two Sections occupied rear positions. The attack on LIEU ST. AMAND and high ground to the S.E. was held up owing to strong resistance by machine guns in the wood in 0.9.c. and the village.	
	14.	Night.	Relief of "A" Coy. in line by "B" Coy. "A" Coy. moves to the vicinity of THUN ST. MARTIN and come into Divisional Reserve.	
	15-16.		Relief of "C" Coy. in line by "D" Coy. "C" Coy. moves to the vicinity of THUN ST. MARTIN and come into Divisional Reserve. No material change.	
	17.	19.40	Divisional Order received. Division to attack, in conjunction with 4th Division, to take the system of woods on the high ground E. of LIEU ST. AMAND. ZERO hour probably at midnight 19th/20th. "C" & "D" Coys. 102nd Bn. M.G.C. attached for operations.	
	18.	23.00	Operation Order for the attack issued. "B" Coy. attached to the 154th Inf. Bde. } "D" " " " 153rd " " " } For consolidation of ground captured. "A" & "C" Coys. 51st (H) Bn. M.G.C. } "C" & "D" Coys. 102nd Bn. M.G.C. } To carry out barrage.	
	19.	~~HRS.~~ 15.30	Completion of preparations for barrage. Operation Order cancelled. Enemy reported retiring. SEC. "A" Coy. 51st (H) Bn. M.G.C. to concentrate in AVESNES-le-SEC. "C" Coy. 51st (H) Bn. M.G.C. in THUN ST. MARTIN, "C" & "D" Coys. 102nd Bn. M.G.C. in IWUY.	
	20.	07.50 09.00 16.00	"C" Coy. 51st (H) Bn. M.G.C. moved to LIEU ST. AMAND. Advance continues. Line runs - DOUCHY-NOYELLES-FLEURY (all inclusive) - HASPRES (exclusive). Bn. H.Q. closed at NAVES and opened at AVESNES-le-SEC 16.00 hours.	
	21.		Advance continues. Line runs - MONCHAUX-sur-ECAILLON (exclusive) - THIANT (inclusive) - PROUVY (inclusive).	
		10.00	"A" Coy. 51st (H) Bn. M.G.C. moves to NOYELLES. "C" Coy. 51st (H) Bn. M.G.C. moves with 152nd Inf. Bde. to DOUCHY. "C" & "D" Coys. 102nd Bn. M.G.C. move to DOUCHY.	
		Night.	"D" Coy. 51st (H) Bn. M.G.C. withdrawn from the line with 153rd Inf. Bde. and take up billets in DOUCHY.	
	22.	Night.	"B" Coy. 51st (H) Bn. M.G.C. relieved by "A" Coy. 51st (H) Bn. M.G.C. in the line. Relief complete 20.30 hours. "B" Coy. take over billets vacated by "A" Coy. in NOYELLES.	

Army Form C. 2118.

WAR DIARY
or
INTELLIGENCE SUMMARY.
(Erase heading not required.)

Instructions regarding War Diaries and Intelligence Summaries are contained in F.S. Regs., Part II. and the Staff Manual respectively. Title pages will be prepared in manuscript.

Place	Date	Hour	Summary of Events and Information	Remarks and references to Appendices
	23.	15.30	Operation order issued for the attack or the 24th to gain the high ground E. of the EGAILLON River.	See O.O.80.
			"C" & "D" Coys. 102nd Bn. M.G.C. take up barrage positions for operations on the 24th.	
			"A" Coy. 51st (H) Bn. M.G.C. attached to 153rd Inf. Bde. to consolidate ground captured.	
	24.	04.00	Attack carried out by 153rd Inf. Bde. Line reached - village of MAING (inclusive).	
		Night.	152nd Inf. Bde. (with "C" Coy. 51st (H) Bn. M.G.C.) relieved 153rd Inf. Bde. in the Right Subsector.	
			"C" Coy. 102nd Bn. M.G.C. concentrate in DOUCHY.	
			"D" Coy. 102nd Bn. M.G.C. take up positions on line from J.17.c.0.5. to J.29.c.0.3.	
	25.	07.00	Attack continued by 152nd and 153rd Inf. Bdes. (with "A" & "C" Coys. 51st (H) Bn. M.G.C. respectively). Line reached - railway E. of MAING.	See O.O.81.
			"D" Coy. 102nd Bn. M.G.C. moving forward, took up positions on line running from J.30.d.7.7. to J.24.a.6.3.	
		Night.	Battery of EIGHT guns of "D" Coy. 51st (H) Bn. M.G.C. take up barrage positions at TRITH ST. LEGER for operations on the 26th.	
	26.	10.00	Attack carried out by 152nd and 153rd Inf. Bdes. "C" Coy. 51st (H) Bn. M.G.C. attached 152nd Inf. Bde. and "A" Coy. 51st (H) Bn. M.G.C. attached 153rd Inf. Bde. Line reached - MONT HOUY (exclusive) - FAMARS (inclusive).	See O.O.82.
			"D" Coy. 102nd Bn. M.G.C. moved forward and took up positions on line K.7.d. - ROUGEMONT, K.14.d. - CAUMONT FME.	
		Night.	"B" Coy. 51st (H) Bn. M.G.C. relieve "A" Coy. 51st (H) Bn. M.G.C. on Inter-Brigade relief of 153rd Inf. Bde. by 154th Inf. Bde. Relief complete 10.50 hrs. 27th.	See O.O.83.
			On completion of relief "A" Coy. take up billets in HAULCHIN.	
	27.		"C" Coy. 102nd Bn. M.G.C. relieved "D" Coy. 102nd Bn. M.G.C. Relief complete 19.30 hours.	
			"D" Coy. take up billets in DOUCHY.	
			Remaining EIGHT guns of "B" Coy. 51st (H) Bn. M.G.C. take up barrage positions at ST. LEGER, J.6.d.3.7. for the operations on the 28th.	See O.O.84.
		21.00	Order received. 51st (H) Division to be relieved in the line by the 49th Division. Cancelled 08.00 hours, 28th.	
	28.	05.15	154th Inf. Bde. (with "B" Coy. 51st (H) Bn. M.G.C.) carry out attack to capture MONT HOUY. Line reached - MONT HOUY.	
		08.45	Order received. 51st (H) Division will be relieved in the line by two Brigades of 49th	

Army Form C. 2118.

WAR DIARY
or
INTELLIGENCE SUMMARY.
(Erase heading not required.)

Instructions regarding War Diaries and Intelligence Summaries are contained in F. S. Regs., Part II. and the Staff Manual respectively. Title pages will be prepared in manuscript.

Place	Date	Hour	Summary of Events and Information	Remarks and references to Appendices
	28.	12.00	"A" Coy. 51st (H) Bn. M.G.C. moved to BASSEVILLE.	
		17.30	"D" Coy. 102nd Bn. M.G.C. at tactical disposal of 154th Inf. Bde., move into the line in support of Brigade.	
		Night.	152nd Inf. Bde. and "C" Coy. 51st (H) Bn. M.G.C. relieved in the line by 146th Inf. Bde. and "D" Coy. 49th Bn. M.G.C. respectively.	
		20.20	"C" Coy. 51st (H) Bn. M.G.C. take over billets at NOYELLES. Order that relief of 154th Inf. Bde. by one Bde. of 4th Canadian Division postponed for 24 hours received.	
	29.	10.00	H.Q. close at AVESNES-le-SEC and re-open at BASSEVILLE on relief by 49th Division.	
		20.00	"D" Coy. 51st (H) Bn. M.G.C. withdraw from line and move to DOUCHY. "B" Coy. 51st (H) Bn. M.G.C. relieved in the line by one Coy. of 4th Canadian M.G. Battn. "B" Coy. moved on relief to NOYELLES.	
	30.		"D" Coy. 51st (H) Bn. M.G.C. moved to BASSEVILLE.	
	31.	08.30	H.Q., "A" & "D" Coys. move via ESTRUN to PAILLENCOURT.	See O.O.87.
		07.15	"B" & "C" Coys. 51st (H) Bn. M.G.C. move via LIEU ST. AMAND and ESTRUN to PAILLENCOURT.	

Lieut. Colonel,
Comdg. 51st (H) Bn. M.G. Corps.

SECRET.   51st (H) BATTALION, M.G.CORPS.   Copy No...9..

WARNING ORDER.

1st October, 19

Reference Map:
FRANCE, 51b. N.W., 1/20,000.

1. The 8th Division is to take over the front at present held by the 51st (H) Division, which will move on relief into Army Reserve in the ECURIE - MONT ST. ELOY - FREVIN CAPELLE area, with Headquarters at Chateau D'ACQ (W.30.b.2.5.).

2. The 51st (H) Battalion M.G.C. will be relieved in the line as follows:-

1st October:-

"B" Coy. 51st (H) Bn. M.G.C. will be relieved by 1 Coy. 103rd Bn. M.G.C.

2nd October:

"D" Coy. 51st (H) Batt. M.G.C. "   "   "   " 1 Coy. 8th Bn. M.G.C.

3. On relief, Coys. will move to billets in the vicinity of ECURIE.

4. 103rd M.G. Battalion will remain in the line.

5. A C K N O W L E D G E.

Issued at 11 a.m.

Lieut. & Adjt.,
51st (H) Battalion, M.G.Corps.

Issued to Copy 1-4 - Coys. 51st Bn.
             5-6 - "B" & "D" Coys. 103rd Bn.
             7 - 103rd Bn. M.G.C.
             8 - Q.M. & T.O.
             9 - War Diary.
             10 - File.

SECRET.   51st (H) BATTALION, M.G.CORPS.   Copy No....9

                         WARNING ORDER.   1st October, 19

Reference Map:
FRANCE, Sh. 4.B., 1/20,000.

1.   The 8th Division is to take over the front at present held by
the 51st (H) Division, which will move on relief into Army Reserve in
the BOURIN - MONT S*. ELOI - PREVIN CAPELLE area, with Headquarters
at Chateau D'AUQ (W.30.b.2.5.).

2.   The 51st (H) Battalion M.G.C. will be relieved in the line as
follows:-

1st October:-

"B" Coy. 51st (H) Bn. M.G.C. will be relieved by 1 Coy. 103rd Bn.M.G.C.

2nd October:

"D" Coy. 51st (H) Batt.M.G.C. "   "   "   "   " 1 Coy. 5th Bn. M.G.C.

3.   On relief, Coys. will move to billets in the vicinity of BOURIN.

4.   103rd M.G.Battalion will remain in the line.

5.   A C K N O W L E D G E.

                                                        [signature]

                                                        Lieut. & Adjt.,
Issued at 11 a.m.   51st (H) Battalion, M.G.Corps.

Issued to Copy 1-4 - Coys. 51st Bn.
               5-6 - "B" & "D" Coys. 103rd Bn.
                 7 - 103rd Bn. M.G.C.
                 8 - O.M. & T.O.
                 9 - War Diary.
                10 - File.

SECRET.

51st (H) BATTALION, M.G. CORPS.

ADDENDUM TO OPERATION ORDER No. 73.

2.10.18.

Reference Para. 4.

The 51st (H) Bn. M.G.C. will be relieved in the line as follows :-

2nd October.

(a). "C" Coy. 103rd Bn. M.G.C. will relieve:-

    2 guns of "B" Coy. 51st (H) Bn. M.G.C. at I.14.b.9.5.
    2 " " "B" " " " " " " I.13.b.4.9.
    2 " " "D" " " " " " " I. 8.d.4.3.
    2 " " "D" " " " " " " I. 8.d.1.4.
    2 " " "D" " " " " " " I. 8.a.7.3.
    2 " " "D" " " " " " " I. 7.b.1.2.
    2 " " "D" " " " " " " I. 7.b.0.8.
    2 " " "D" " " " " " " I. 1.c.8.6.

(b). "B" Coy. 103rd Bn. M.G.C. will relieve 4 guns of "B" Coy. 51st (H) Bn. M.G.C. as follows :-

    2 guns of "B" Coy. 103rd M.G. Bn. from I.19.c.6.9. will relieve
    2 " " "B" " 51st (H) Bn. M.G.C. at I.14.b.1.1.

    2 guns of "B" Coy. 103rd M.G. Bn. from E.13.d.0.1. will relieve
    2 " " "B" " 51st (H) Bn. M.G.C. at I.14.b.1.1.

(c). Guns at the following positions will be withdrawn without relief, withdrawal to commence at 19.00 hours 2nd October, 1918.

    2 guns of "B" Coy. 51st (H) Bn. M.G.C. at I.17.c.1.2.
    4 " " "B" " " " " " " I.18.d.45.50.
    2 " " "B" " " " " " " I. 8.d. 8. 0.
    2 " " "D" " " " " " " H. 6.d. 0. 1.
    2 " " "D" " " " " " " H.12.a. 1. 7.

W.A.Pasley
Lieut. & Adjt.,
51st (H) Bn. M. G. Corps.

Issued at 13.00 hours.
Addressed all recipients of O.O.73.

51st (H) BATTALION MACHINE GUN CORPS.

WARNING ORDER.

5/10/18.

1. The 51st (H) Bn. M.G.C. will move from present area on 7th/8th instant and will relieve in the line 10th/11th instant.

2. Move will be by bus.

3. Transport will probably move a day earlier by road.

4. ACKNOWLEDGE.

Wallprasby
Lieut. & Adjt.,
51st (H) Bn. M.G.C.

Issued at 11.00 hours.

Copies 1 - 4 - Companies.
       5 - Q.M.
       6 - T.O.
       7 - S.O.
       8 - War Diary.
       9 - File.

SECRET.

Copy No. 12

51st (H) BATTALION, M. G. CORPS.

OPERATION ORDER No. 74.

5/10/18.

1. The 51st (Highland) Division is to relieve the 3rd Canadian Division on the front from S.27.d. to A.9.d. (Sheet 57.B., 1/40,000), in the Sector east of CAMBRAI.

2. The relief of machine guns in the line will take place on the night 10th/11th October. Detailed arrangements will be issued later.

3. On arrival in the Canadian Corps area, units will come under the tactical command of the Canadian Corps and of the G.O.C. 3rd Canadian Division until the command passes.

   The 51st (H) Bn. M. G. Corps (less Transport) will move by bus on the night 7th/8th October to Reserve Area, 3rd Canadian Division.
   Details of embussing will be notified later.

4. Transport of 51st (H) Bn. M. G. Corps will move under Battalion Transport Officer under orders of 152nd Infantry Brigade by march route on 6th October via ARRAS - GUEMAPPE - CHERISY - HENDICOURT - CAGNICOURT, to Canadian Corps "D" Area and on the 7th October to Reserve Area, 3rd Canadian Division.

5. During move Transport will move in groups of not more than 4 waggons, at 300 yards intervals. Tracks are to be used where available.
   The essential is to avoid appearance of columns on the march, so these intervals must be preserved during halts.
   Owing to the long march it is most important that Transport be not overloaded.

6. Time Table for Transport moves will be issued later.

7. The supply wagons will march with Transport. Rations for Transport Details will be carried for the 7th October. Rations for the Battalion on the 8th October will be drawn by supply wagons from No. 4 Company Divisional Train in "D" Area, 3rd Canadian Corps.
   Personnel moving by bus will draw rations for the 8th October on the morning of the 8th in the Reserve Area, 3rd Canadian Division.

8. A C K N O W L E D G E.

Lieut. & Adjt.,
51st (H) Bn. M. G. Corps.

Issued at 20,00 hours.
                19

Copies 1 - 4 - Companies.
       5   - 51st (H) Division, "G." v "Q"
       6 - 8 - Brigades.
       9   - T.O.
       10   - Q.M.
       11   - S.O.
       12   - War Diary.
       13   - File.

War Diary

SECRET.   Copy No 12.

51st (H) BATTALION MACHINE GUN CORPS.

ADDENDUM No. 2 TO OPERATION ORDER No. 74.   7/10/18.

1. The 51st (H) Bn. M.G.C. will ~~be kxxd~~ ombus at 16.30 hours to-day. Head of the column will be on the SOUCHEZ – ARRAS Road at MADAGASCAR CORNER facing ARRAS.

2. BUSSES ARE ALLOTTED as under, numbering from head of the column :-

1 – 3.	...	Battalion H.Q.
4 – 10.	...	"A" Company.
11 – 17.	...	"B" "
18 – 24.	...	"C" "
25 – 30.	...	"D" "

3. Companies will ombus under Company arrangements.

4. An Officer will be detailed to be i/c of each bus. No men will leave the busses without permission.

                                                        [signature]
                                                        Lieut. & Adjt.,
                                                        51st (H) Bn. M. G. Corps.

Addressed to all
recipients of O.O.74.

SECRET.   51st (H) BATTALION MACHINE GUN CORPS.

ADMINISTRATIVE INSTRUCTIONS TO ACCOMPANY OPERATION ORDER No. 75.

Sheet 2.

6. Companies will take ONE each tent to the new area.

7. Train Coys. (except No.1) and Refilling Point will not move tomorrow.

8. The S.A.A. Section will take over the S.A.A. Dump of the 3rd Canadian Division at F.1.c.8.6. at 15 hours.

9. Divisional Canteen will remain at QUEANT.

10. Water Points and wells are given in Appendix "A". The D.A.P.M. will detail one M.M.P. and 3 Traffic Control men for the water points at BOURLON.

APPENDIX "A".

HORSE TROUGHS.
D.12.a.2.0.   E.3.c.7.7.   E.14.a.8.9.   E.6.d.4.3.   F.7.a.7.4.
F.7.a.3.7.   E.12.a.9.6.   E.12.b.7.8.
NOTE:- As no watering points for horses are between BOURLON and ST.OLLE horses in forward area water at present at FONTAINE NOTRE DAME and RAILLENCOURT Pumping Stations.

PUMPING STATIONS:
V.13.b.7.4.   E.12.b.4.5.   E.12.b.7.7.   E.12.d.2.6.
           (W.C. & W.B. filling pt.)   F.7.a.5.7.

WELLS:
E.9.b.8.3.   E.4.a.4.6.   E.5.c.6.3.   E.12.c.0.3.   E.11.b.9.8.
E.12.a.1.8.   E.12.a.4.7.   E.12.a.7.7.   E.12.a.8.2.   E.12.a.7.3.
E.12.a.8.3.   E.12.b.0.6.   E.12.b.0.8.   E.12.b.6.9.   E.12.b.3.8.
E.12.d.6.2.   F.1.c.0.4.   F.1.d.0.4.   F.7.b.1.2.   F.13.a.3.4.
D.6.d.3.2.   D.12.a.3.1.   X.20.c.6.4.   F.5.b.4.4.   F.5.b.6.3.
F.5.b.8.2.   F.6.c.5.8.   A.1.c.3.6.   A.1.c.4.5.   A.1.c.6.4.
A.2.c.2.4.   A.2.c.3.3.   A.8.c.5.6.   A.8.c.2.7.   A.8.c.4.6.
A.8.d.8.8.   (Reservoir)

PONDS:
E.12.a.8.6.   E.12.b.3.8.   F.7.a.0.2.   F.7.a.4.7.   F.7.a.7.4.
E.1.d.4.6.

TANKS:
E.13.a.3.1.   E.17.a.4.9.   E.12.c.2.9.   X.25.d.2.3.   E.2.a.6.0.

Lieut.& Adjt.,
51st (H) Battalion M.G.Corps.

SECRET.   Copy No ...13

51st (H) BATTALION MACHINE GUN CORPS.

OPERATION ORDER No. 75.

9/10/18.

Ref: map :-
FRANCE 57C. 1/40,000.

1. The 51st (H) Division will move tomorrow to the area around BOURLON WOOD, taking the place of the 3rd Canadian Division, which is to move back to the area vacated by the 51st (H) Division.

2. Companies are allotted to Brigades as under :-

"A" Coy.   ....   152nd Inf. Bde. (moves 11.00 hours.)
"D" Coy.   ....   153rd Inf. Bde. (moves 14.00 hours.)
"C" Coy.   ....   154th Inf. Bde. (moves 08.00 hours.)

"B" Coy. Divisional Reserve with Battalion H.Q.

3. "A" "D" & "C" Coys. will move under orders to be issued by Brigades for moves to Brigade Sub-Areas. Coys. will notify Battalion H.Q., as early as possible, of the location of their new Headquarters.

4. Battalion H.Q. and "B" Coy. will parade at 12.45 hours to move to 153rd Inf. Bde. Sub-Area.

5. On the line of march, 100 yards intervals will be maintained between Companies and their transports; march route will be :-

S. of INCHY - MOEUVRES - ANNEUX CHAPELLE - CAMBRAI ROAD.

6. Battalion H.Q. will close at D.5.d.3.8. at 13.00 hours; location of new Battalion H.Q. will be notified later.
   Divisional H.Q. will open at E.11.c.0.0. at 16.00 hours.

7. All billets will be left in a clean and sanitary condition and usual certificates rendered to Battalion Orderly Room.

8. A C K N O W L E D G E.

                                                Lieut. & Adjt.,
                                                51st (H) Bn. M.G.C.

Issued at 23.30 hours.

Copy 1-4 - Coys.
     5-7 - Brigades.
     8-9 - Division "G" & "Q."
      10 - T.O.
      11 - Q.M.
      12 - S.O.
      13 - War Diary.
      14 - File.

SECRET.   Copy No. 13

                    51st (H) BATTALION M. G. CORPS.

                AMENDMENT to OPERATION ORDER No.75. dated 9/10/18.
                ✳✳✳✳✳✳✳✳✳✳✳✳✳✳✳✳✳✳✳✳✳✳✳✳✳✳✳✳✳✳

1. Delete paragraph 5 and substitute the following:-

    "On the line of march 200 yards intervals will be maintained between
    "Coys. and their transports. March route will be Via MOEUVRES to
    "CAMBRAI-BAPAUME Road, E.28.a.0.2.

                                                    [signature]
                                                    Lt. & Adjt.,
                                                    51st (H) Battalion M.G.C.

10/10/18.
03.00.
        Issued to all recipients of O.O.75.

SECRET.   Copy No. 13.

51st (W) BATTALION MACHINE GUN CORPS.

ADDENDUM No. 2 to OPERATION ORDER No. 75.   10/10/18.

1.   Reference para. 6 :-

     Battalion H.Q. will be at E.11.c.0.0.

                                         [signature]
Issued to all   Lieut. & Adjt.,
recipients of O.O.75.   51st (M) Bn. M.G.C.

O.C. A Company

Reference attached. These guns are being placed at your disposal to free your furthest back guns so that you may have 16 guns available if necessary to cover the advance or to specially deal with any ground or deal with any point holding up the advance. The ground in this operation is equally adapted for opposition and covering fire.

12/10/18

[signature]
31st Bn M.G.C.

22.50

O.C.,
"B" Company, 51st (H) Bn. M.G.C.

12/10/18.

1. Two Sections of your Company will be placed at the disposal of 152nd Infantry Brigade for operation tomorrow 13th instant, and will move from ESCAUDOEUVRES at 02.00 hours, to reach Brigade H.Q. at IWUY, N.36.c.05.06., 03.00 hours.

2. These guns will come under the orders of O. C. "A" Company, 51st (H) Bn. M.G.C. and an Officer will proceed in advance to report to O. C. "A" Company at N.36.c.05.06.

3. The remaining Sections of your Company will remain at present location until further orders.

4. A C K N O W L E D G E.

Lieut. & Adjt.,
51st (H) Bn. M.G. Corps.

Distribution :-
O. C. "A" Coy.
Division "Q."
152nd Inf. Bde.

DRAFT.

51st (H) BATTALION M. G. CORPS.

Copy No. 13

OPERATION ORDER No. 78.

14/10/18.

1. "B" Coy. will relieve "A" Coy. in the line night 14th/15th instant, and will come under the orders of 152nd Infantry Brigade.

2. Details of relief will be arranged between Company Commanders concerned.

3. On completion of relief, "A" Coy. will come into Divisional Reserve and will move to vicinity of THUN ST. MARTIN.

4. A C K N O W L E D G E.

Issued at 14.30 hours.

Lieut. & Adjt.,
51st (H) Bn. M.G. Corps.

Copy 1 - 4 - Companies.
      5 - 7 - Brigades.
         8 - Division "G."
         9 - Rear H.Q.
    10 - 12 - M.O., C.N.; S.C.
       13 - War Diary.
       14 - File.

SECRET.   ~~Cancelled~~ see OO 78   Copy No. 13

51st (H) BATTALION MACHINE GUN CORPS.

Ref: map :-
FRANCE 51A. S.W.

OPERATION ORDER No. 77.

17/10/18.

1. The 4th Division is to carry out an attack to gain an objective running through P.23.central, P.22.central, P.15.c.0.0., and thence South and West of HASPRES to O.17.c.1.3.

2. In order to protect the left flank of the 4th Division the 51st Division will, at the same time, attack the following objective :-
From O.17.c.1.3., to include the wood at O.10.d.2.8., thence through O.9.a.0.0. to our present front line at Mon. BLANCHE FME.

3. The dividing line between the 51st and 4th Divisions will be from the railway crossing at O.22.c.9.9. - white ruin at O.22.b.9.9., both inclusive to 51st Division, thence to O.12.central.

4. The attack will be carried out by the 154th Inf. Brigade on the right and the 153rd Inf. Brigade on the left, the dividing line between Brigades running from the Chapel at O.14.d.1.9. (1/20,000 map) along the hedge which runs through O.14.b., O.15.a. and O.9.c. to the road at O.9.c.5.8.
    The inter-Brigade boundary will be adjusted prior to the attack by mutual arrangement between the two Brigades concerned.

5. The attack will be made under a creeping barrage which will open at Zero hour.

6. **Action of Machine Guns.**

    (a). Objectives, Boundaries, Barrage Positions and Lines are shown on map to be issued later to all concerned.

    (b). "B" Company is attached to the 154th Inf. Brigade and "D" Company to the 153rd Inf. Brigade for consolidation of ground captured and defence of Brigade areas.

    (c). "A" & "C" Companies 51st (H) Bn. M.G.C. and "C" & "D" Companies 102nd Bn. M.G.C. will carry out barrage in accordance with map and Fire Organisation Orders and detailed instructions.

    (d). When barrage is completed, batteries will remain laid on "S.O.S." Further orders will be issued for return of Companies to Reserve Areas.

    (e). O.C. Barrage Groups are responsible that preparation of Barrage Positions, S.A.A., Water Supply, etc. are complete and in readiness on Y/Z night.
    Os. C, "C" & "D" Companies 102nd Bn. M.G.C. will arrange for use of limbers from "A" & "C" Companies 51st (H) Bn. M.G.C. to get up their supplies.

    (F). Completion of preparations and assembly of barrage batteries will be reported by Group Commanders to O.C. 51st (H) Bn. M.G.C. by code "O.R.25 RECEIVED."

    (g). Watches will be synchronised with Brigade on Y/Z night. Exact time of opening of barrage will be taken from opening of Artillery 18-pdr. barrage.

(h). Headquarters of Companies will be as follows :-

"A" Coy. 51st Bn. & "D" Coy. 102nd Bn. M.G.C. at "B" Coy. 51st Bn.
M.G.C. Headquarters.
"C" " " " & "C" " " " " at "D" Coy. 51st Bn.
M.G.C. Headquarters.

(j). Headquarters 51st (H) Bn. M.G.C. will be at Divisional Headquarters.

7. Zero hour will be at midnight, probably on the night 19th/20th instant, when the moon will be full.

8. The objective named will be consolidated and outposts will be pushed forward.

9. After capture of their objective, the 4th Division will be pushing forward patrols in the HASPRES, which will be occupied, if found to be clear of the enemy.
If HASPRES is occupied by the 4th Division, the 154th Inf. Brigade will push forward to connect with the 4th Division at about O.17.central.

10. A C K N O W L E D G E.

Issued at ..2130....

W. A. Gnawby
Lieut. & Adjt.,
51st (H) Bn. M. G. Corps.

Copy No. 1 - 4 - All Coys. 51st Bn.
5 - 6 - "C" & "D" Coys. 102nd Bn.
7 - 9 - Brigades.
10 -11 - 51st (H) Division "G" & "Q."
12 - 102nd Bn. M.G.C.
13 - War Diary.
14 - File.

INSTRUCTIONS FOR BARRAGE GROUPS TO ACCOMPANY 51st (H) BN. M.G.C. O.O.77.

1. The Barrage Group will be divided into a Forward and a Rear Battery of EIGHT guns each.

2. The position of the Forward Battery will be such that fire can be continued until completion of barrage.

3. The Forward Battery may not be able to open on first barrage lines.

4. If the Forward Battery cannot open on first barrage lines, it will open at ZERO (provided para. 5 is complied with) on the nearest line with safety clearance and will remain on this line until the lift of the barrage from this line.

5. Special precautions will be taken for clearance by the Forward Batteries over all troops formed up for the attack.

6. The exact location of Barrage Batteries will be reported to Battalion Headquarters early on the 18th instant.

7. All arrangements for laying out ~~barrage~~ lines of fire will be completed by daylight on the 19th instant.

8. The barrage will be a creeping barrage with lifts of 200 yards and a protective "S.O.S." Barrage during consolidation.

SECRET.

51st (HIGHLAND) BATTALION MACHINE GUN CORPS.

OPERATION ORDER No. 76.

18/10/18.

1. 51st (H) Bn. M.G.C. Order No. 75 of 17/10/18 is cancelled.

2. The 4th Division is to carry out an attack to gain an objective running through P.23.a. and b. - P.22.central - P.15.d.0.0. - P.15.a.0.0. - P.8.c.8.0. - P.8.a.0.2. - O.12.b.3.4.

3. In order to protect the left flank of the 4th Division, the 51st Division will, at the same time, attack with the objective shown on the attached sketch.

4. The attack will be carried out by the 154th Brigade on the right and the 153rd Brigade on the left, with inter-Brigade boundary as shewn on attached map.

5. The attack will be made under a creeping barrage which will open at zero hour, at which time the attacking troops will be ready to advance from the forming up line.

6. The barrage will begin to creep forward at zero plus six minutes, the pace being about 100 yds. in 2 minutes on the right, and 100 yds. in 4 minutes on the left. There will be a short pause when the Infantry are on the line of the first objective.

7. The C.R.E. will arrange to throw a light bridge across the River SELLE as soon as the barrage allows our troops to reach that river.

8. The Artillery will fire a protective barrage for 30 mins. after the Infantry have reached their objective. After this time, in case the S.O.S. Signal is sent up, the barrage will be put down for 15 mins. and will then cease unless the S.O.S. Signal is put up again, in which case the procedure will be repeated.

9. Action of Machine Guns.

   (a). Objectives, Boundaries, Barrage Positions and Barrage are shown on tracing issued to Companies concerned.

   (b). Tracing will be issued later showing Barrage Lines and times of lifts.

   (c). "B" Company is attached to the 154th Inf. Brigade and "D" Company to the 153rd Inf. Brigade for consolidation of ground captured and defence of Brigade Areas.

   (d). "A" & "C" Companies 51st (H) Bn. M.G.C. and "C" & "D" Companies 102nd Bn. M.G.C. will carry out barrage in accordance with tracing and Fire Organisation Orders and detailed instructions.

   (e). Orders for assembly of Barrage Groups will be issued later.

   (f). When barrage is completed, batteries will remain laid on "S.O.S." Further orders will be issued for return of Companies to Reserve Areas.

   (g). O.C. Barrage Groups are responsible that preparation of Barrage Positions, S.A.A., Water Supply, etc. are complete and in readiness on Y/Z night.
      Os. C. "C" & "D" Companies 102nd Bn. M.G.C. will arrange for use of limbers from "A" & "C" Companies 51st (H) Bn. M.G.C. to get up their supplies.

   (h). Completion of preparations and assembly of barrage will be reported by Group Commanders to O.C. 51st (H) Bn. code "O.R.25 RECEIVED." on Y/Z night.

- 2 -

(i). Watches will be synchronised with Brigade on Y/Z night. Exact time of opening of barrage will be taken from opening of Artillery 18-pdr. barrage.

(j). Headquarters of Companies will be as follows :-

"A" Coy. 51st Bn. & "D" Coy. 102nd Bn. M.G.C. at "B" Coy. 51st Bn. M.G.C. Headquarters.
"C" " " " & "C" " " " " at "D" Coy. 51st Bn. M.G.C. Headquarters.

(k). Headquarters 51st (H) Bn. M.G.C. will be at Divisional Headquarters.

10. The date and zero hour will be notified later.

11. The 154th Brigade will establish a Battle Headquarters in AVESNES LE SEC at O.27.b.5.8.
The 153rd Brigade Headquarters will remain at IWUY.

12. Contact Aeroplanes will call for flares at the following hours :-
Zero plus 5 hrs., zero plus 7 hrs. and zero plus 9 hrs.
A counter-attack plane will be in the air from dawn onwards.

13. A C K N O W L E D G E.

Issued at 2330.

W.A.Grasby
Lieut. & Adjt.,
51st (H) Bn. M. G. Corps.

Copy No. 1 - 4 - All Coys. 51st Bn. M.G.C.
5 - 6 - "C" & "D" Coys. 102nd Bn. M.G.C.
7 - 9 - Brigades.
10 - 11 - 51st (H) Division "G" & "Q."
12 - 102nd Bn. M.G.C.
13 - War Diary.
14 - File.

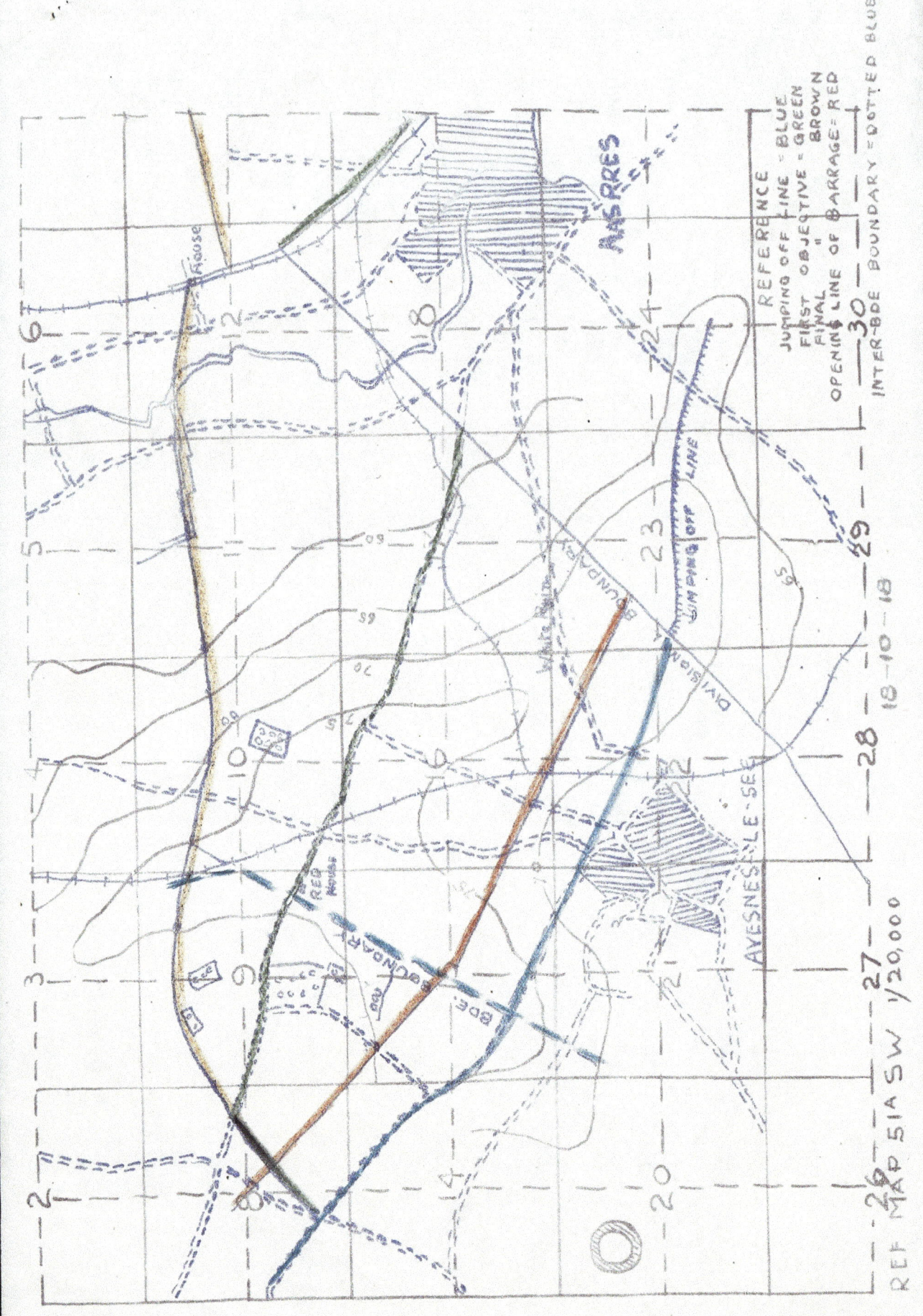

INSTRUCTIONS FOR BARRAGE GROUPS TO ACCOMPANY
51st (H) BN. M.G.C. O.O.78.

1. The ~~Battery~~ Barrage Group will be divided into a Forward and a Rear Battery of EIGHT guns each.

2. The Forward Battery may not be able to open on first barrage lines.

3. If the Forward Battery cannot open on first barrage lines, it will open at ZERO (provided para. 4 is complied with) on the nearest line with safety clearance and will remain on this line until the lift of the barrage from this line.

4. Special precautions will be taken for clearance by the Forward Batteries over all troops formed up for the attack.

5. Location of Batteries is shown on Fire Organisation Orders.

6. All arrangements for laying out lines of fire will be completed by daylight on the 19th instant.

7. The barrage will be a creeping barrage with lifts of 200 yds. and a protective "S.O.S." barrage during consolidation.

8. The barrage lines are 400 yds. in front of advancing Infantry. Clearance calculations will be based on this. "D" Group is an enfilade barrage in area N.W. of barrage lines.

9. The barrage will be clear of areas at times as shewn on barrage tracing.

FIRE ORGANISATION ORDERS TO ACCOMPANY OPERATION ORDER No. 78.

Group.	Battery.	Location. Approximate.	Composition.	Commander.	R E M A R K S.
A.	1.	O.28.a.9.9.	8 guns of "A" Coy. 51st (H) Bn. M.G.C.	Major J. PYLE.	Targets are shewn on Barrage Tracing to be issued later. Rate of fire will be one belt per 4 minutes.
	2.	O.28.c.9.4.	8 guns of "A" Coy. 51st (H) Bn. M.G.C.		
B.	3.	O.20.b.2.7.	8 guns of "D" Coy. 102nd Bn. M.G.C.	Major WHITE.	
	4.	O.20.d.3.6.	8 guns of "D" Coy. 102nd Bn. M.G.C.		
C.	5.	O.19.b.4.3.	8 guns of "C" Coy. 51st (H) Bn. M.G.C.	Capt. J. BLACK.	
	6.	O.14.c.6.0.	8 guns of "C" Coy. 51st (H) Bn. M.G.C.		
D.	7.	O.13.c.8.7.	8 guns of "C" Coy. 102nd Bn. M.G.C.	Capt. PEARSON.	
	8.	N.18.d.4.8.	8 guns of "C" Coy. 102nd Bn. M.G.C.		

ORDERS FOR ASSEMBLY OF BARRAGE GROUPS
TO ACCOMPANY O.O No. 78.

1. "A" & "C" Companies 51st (H) Bn. M.G.C. and "C" & "D" Companies 102nd Bn. M.G.C. will assemble in Barrage Positions on Y/Z night to carry out barrage in accordance with Operation Order No. 78.

2. "C" & "D" Companies 102nd Bn. M.G.C. will debus on ESCAUDOEUVRES - IWUY Road, T.10.a. at 15.00 hours on Y day.

3. Companies will move into the line as follows :-

"A" Coy. 51st Bn. M.G.C. to pass cross roads, N.36.d.0.0. at 16.45 hrs.
"D" "   102nd "   "   "   "   "   "   " 17.00 "
"C" Coy. 51st   "   "   "   "   Railway and Road Junction, N.30.a.1.3
                                                           at 16.45 hours.
"C" "   102nd "   "   "   "   "   "   "   at 17.00 hours.

4. A C K N O W L E D G E.

W. A. Grasby
Lieut. & Adjt.,
51st (H) Bn. M. G. Corps.

Issued 23.30.

Distribution as for O.O.78.

MACHINE GUN BARRAGE TRACING.

To accompany O.O.78.

Z+25 to Z+32
Z+18 to Z+25
Z+12 to Z+18
Z+8 to Z+12
Z+4 to Z+8
Z to Z+4

SHEET 51A S.W. 1:20,000
19-10-18

S.O.S.
"C" Coy. 51 Bn.
"D" Coy. 102 Bn.
"C" Coy. 102 Bn.

JUMPING OFF LINE

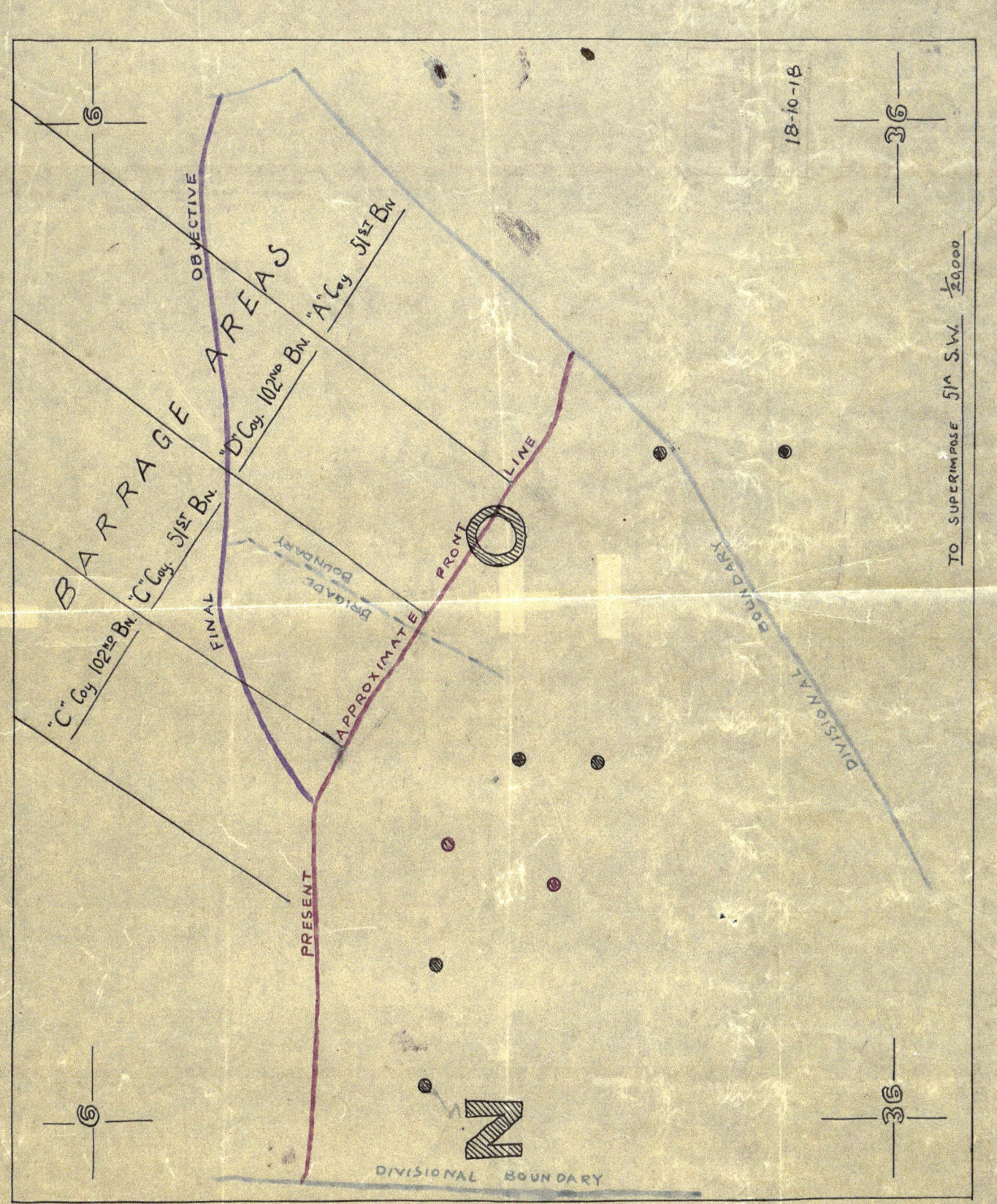

S E C R E T. Copy No. 13.

00 78/1

19/10/18

1.   Reference 51st (Highland) Battalion Machine Gun Corps Operation Order No. 78, para. 10, ZERO HOUR will be at 02.00, October 20th.

2.   A synchronised watch will be sent to all concerned between 14.00 and 17.00 on the 19th instant.

3.   A C K N O W L E D G E.

W A Grasby
Lieut. & Adjt.,
51st (H) Bn. M. G. Corps.

Issued 12.00.

Distribution as per O.O.78.

SECRET.   51st (H) BATTALION, M.G. CORPS.   Ref.O.O.82
                 ****
                                                             19/10/18.

To All Recipients of O.O.78.

1.   Operation Order No.78, dated 18/10/18, is cancelled.

2.   "A" Coy. 51st (H) Battalion, M.G.Corps, will remain in AVESNES-le-SEC; location of new Company Headquarters to be reported to Battalion Headquarters. "A" Coy. transport will not move until further orders.

3.   "C" Coy., 51st (H) Battalion, M.G.Corps, will remain in present location until further orders.
     O.C., "C" Coy. will report forthwith to B.G.C., 152nd Infantry Brigade.

4.   "C" and "D" Coys, 102nd Bn. M.G.C. will concentrate in IWUY and report location of Company Headquarters.

5.   Further orders will be issued later.

6.   ACKNOWLEDGE.

                                                  W A Grasby
                                                  Lieut. & Adjt.,
                                              51st. (H) Battalion M.G.Corps.

Issued at 15-30.

SECRET.

51st (H) BATTALION, MACHINE GUN CORPS.
No. C.2
Date......

O. C.,
"C" Company, 102nd Bn. M.G.C.
"D" Company,   "   "   "

1.   "C" & "D" Companies, 102nd Bn. M.G.C. may be called upon to fire a barrage to cover the advance of our troops from the SCAILLAN River to HADE.

2.   Boundaries of the attack will probably be :-

     Right Divisional Boundary and the line from J.16.c.8.5. to J.18.c.8.5.

3.   The suitable area for barrage batteries is :-

J.14.d., 15.c. a b 4., 20.b. and d., 21.a.

4.   If both Companies are called upon to fire the barrage, "D" Coy. will be on the right and "C" Coy. on the left.
     If one Company only is required "D" Coy. will be employed.

5.   Os. C, "C" & "D" Coys. will reconnoitre area for suitable barrage positions tomorrow and forward report as soon as completed.

6.   Operations will probably take place night 23rd/24th.

7.   ACKNOWLEDGE.

                                              [signature]
                                              Lieut. & Adjt.,
21/10/18.   51st (H) Bn. M. G. Corps.

SECRET.
51st (H) Battalion, M.G.Corps.

Copy No. 15

22/10/18.

OPERATION ORDER No. 79.

Reference Map:
FRANCE, Sheet 51A.S.W., 1/20,000.

1. The 153rd Infantry Brigade will relieve the 154th Infantry Brigade in the line tonight, 22/23rd October, 1918.

2. "A" Coy. 51st (H) Bn. M.G.C. will relieve "B" Coy. 51st (H) Bn. M.G.C. in the line tonight, 22/23rd October, 1918.

3. All arrangements will be made between Os.C. Companies concerned.

4. Completion of relief will be notified by code word "PILE".

5. On completion of relief, "B" Coy. will be withdrawn into Divisional Reserve, and will take over billets vacated by "A" Coy.

6. "D" Coy. 51st (H) Bn. M.G.C. will remain in present location and will be attached to 154th Infantry Brigade. O.C. "D" Coy. will report to B.G,C., 154th Infantry Brigade on completion of Inter-Brigade relief.

7. A C K N O W L E D G E.

Lieut. & Adjt.,
Issued at 15-15. 51st H) Battalion, M.G.Corps.

Copies 1-4 - Coys.
     5-6 - "C" & "D" Coys., 102nd Bn. M.G.C.
     7 - 102nd Bn. M.G.C.
     8-9 - 51st (H) Division, "G" & "Q".
  10-12 - Brigades.
    13 - Rear H.Q.
    14 - Q.M.
    15 - War Diary.
    16 - File.

SECRET.

O. C.,
 "C" Coy.,
  102nd Bn. M.G.C.

G.7.A.

22/10/18.
21.00

"C" Coy., 102nd Bn. M.G.C. will take up positions tomorrow, 23/10/18, as follows :-

1. (a). Battery of EIGHT guns in RAILWAY EMBANKMENT in J.15.a. & b. to be in position by 10.00 hours. Positions for these guns are being constructed tonight, 22/23rd October, 1918.

   (b). O. C. "C" Coy., 102nd Bn. M.G.C. will arrange for the necessary horse transport direct with O.C. "D" Coy., 51st (H) Bn. M.G.C. H.Q. "D" Coy., 51st (H) Bn. M.G.C. are at I.18.d.1.7.

   (c). Battery Commander will keep in touch with O.C. LEFT Battalion 153rd Infantry Brigade, whose H.Q. are at J.15.c.7.3.

   (d). Lines of Fire will be laid out so that fire can be brought to bear on the area J.16., 17., 22. and 23.

2. (a). A battery of EIGHT guns in the vicinity of J.11.a. and b.

   (b). Lines of Fire for these guns will be laid out during daylight so that fire can be brought to bear on area, J.18. & 24. and K.13. & 19.

   (c). Routes and transport to be used will be as detailed in Special Instructions already given to O.C. "C" Coy.

3. Further instructions and fire orders for these batteries will be issued later.

4. Completion of move will be reported to this Office by code word "PEARSON."

W Algrastry
Lieut. & Adjt.,
51st (H) Bn. M. G. Corps.

Copy to :- "D" Coy., 102nd Bn. M.G.C.
           102nd Bn. M.G.C.
           153rd Inf. Bde.
           51st (H) Division "G."
           "D" Coy. 51st (H) Bn. M.G.
           "A" "   "   "   "   "
           4th Canadian M. G. Bn.
           War Diary.
           File.

S E C R E T.　　　　　　　　　　　　　　　　　　　　　　Copy No. 17.

51st (H) BATTALION MACHINE GUN CORPS.

Ref: map :-　　　　OPERATION ORDER No. 80.　　　　　　23/10/18.
MAING,
1/40,000.

1. The XXII Corps in conjunction with the Third Army is to renew the attack tomorrow with a view to securing the high ground N.E. of the ECAILLON River.
   The 4th Division is attacking in the Right Sector of the XXII Corps with an objective running from L'EPINE in Q.2.b. through K.31.a. to J.30.d.7.7. They are to be prepared to capture the village of QUERENAING by a secondary deliberate operation either tomorrow or on the following day.

2. The 51st Division is to attack in the Left Sector of the XXII Corps with objectives as shown on the attached sketch.

3. The 153rd Infantry Brigade will carry out the attack and will secure and consolidate the third objective (BROWN LINE) shown on the attached map as the Main Line of Resistance with outposts pushed in advance.

4. The attack will be carried out under a creeping barrage.

5. The C.R.E. will arrange to throw two bridges capable of carrying field guns across the ECAILLON River at THIANT as soon as situation renders work possible. One bridge will be in the neighbourhood of the main road and the other will be further South near the Southern outskirts of the village.

6. As soon as the final protective barrage has ceased the 153rd Infantry Brigade will exploit up to the line of the Railway from K.20.a.5.8. to E.26.a.0.0.; the final line gained being held as an Outpost Line.

7. ACTION OF MACHINE GUNS.

　　(a). Objectives, Boundaries, Barrage Positions and Barrage Areas are shewn on map issued to Companies concerned.

　　(b). Tracing attached shows barrage lines and times of lifts.

　　(c). "A" Coy. is attached to 153rd Inf. Bde. for consolidation of ground captured and defence of Brigade Area.

　　(d). "C" & "D" Coys. 102nd Bn. M.G.C. will carry out barrage in accordance with tracing and Fire Organisation Orders and detailed instructions.

　　(e). O. C. Barrage Groups are responsible that preparations for Barrage Positions, S.A.A., Water Supply, etc. are complete and in readiness on Y/Z night.
　　　　Os. C. "C" & "D" Coys. 102nd Bn. M.G.C. will arrange for use of limbers from "D" & "C" Coys., 51st (H) Bn. M.G.C. to get up their supplies.

　　(f). Completion of preparations and assembly of Barrage Batteries will be reported by Commanders of A & B Groups to O.C. 51st (H) Bn. M.G.C. by code words "WHITE" and "PEARSON" respectively.

　　(g). A synchronised watch will be sent to Companies concerned on Y/Z day. The exact time of opening of barrage will be taken from the opening of the 18-pdr. barrage.

- 2 -

(h). Battery Commanders will keep in touch with O. C. LEFT Battalion of 153rd Inf. Bde., whose H.Q. are at J.15.c.7.3.

(i). H.Q. of Barrage Companies will remain in present locations.

8. Contact planes will call for flares at :-

$$\text{ZERO plus } 3\tfrac{1}{2} \text{ hours.}$$
$$\text{"} \quad \text{"} \quad 5\tfrac{1}{2} \quad \text{"}$$
$$\text{"} \quad \text{"} \quad 7\tfrac{1}{2} \quad \text{"}$$

9. ZERO hour will be 04.00 hours 24th October, 1918.

10. A C K N O W L E D G E.

W A Grasby
Lieut. & Adjt.,
51st (H) Bn. M. G. Corps.

Issued at 15.30.

Copies 1 - 4 - All Coys. 51st (H) Bn. M.G.C.
        5 - 6 - "C" & "D" Coys. 102nd Bn. M.G.C.
        7 - 8 - 51st (H) Divsion "G" & "Q."
        9 - 11 - All Brigades.
           12 - 102nd Bn. M.G.C.
           13 - 2nd Canadian Bn. M.G.C.
           14 - 4th Bn. M.G.C.
           15 - C.M.G.O.
       17 - 18 - War Diary and File.
           19. - Artillery.

A Coy   Map & Tracing
B C & D   Map.
C & D. 102   Map & Tracing.
Div. G & Q   "
153 Bdes.   Map & Tracing.
15,29,754   "
102.   Map & Tracing.
2nd Can.   " "
4 Bn   " "
C M G O   " "
W D   " "
F   "
Artillery

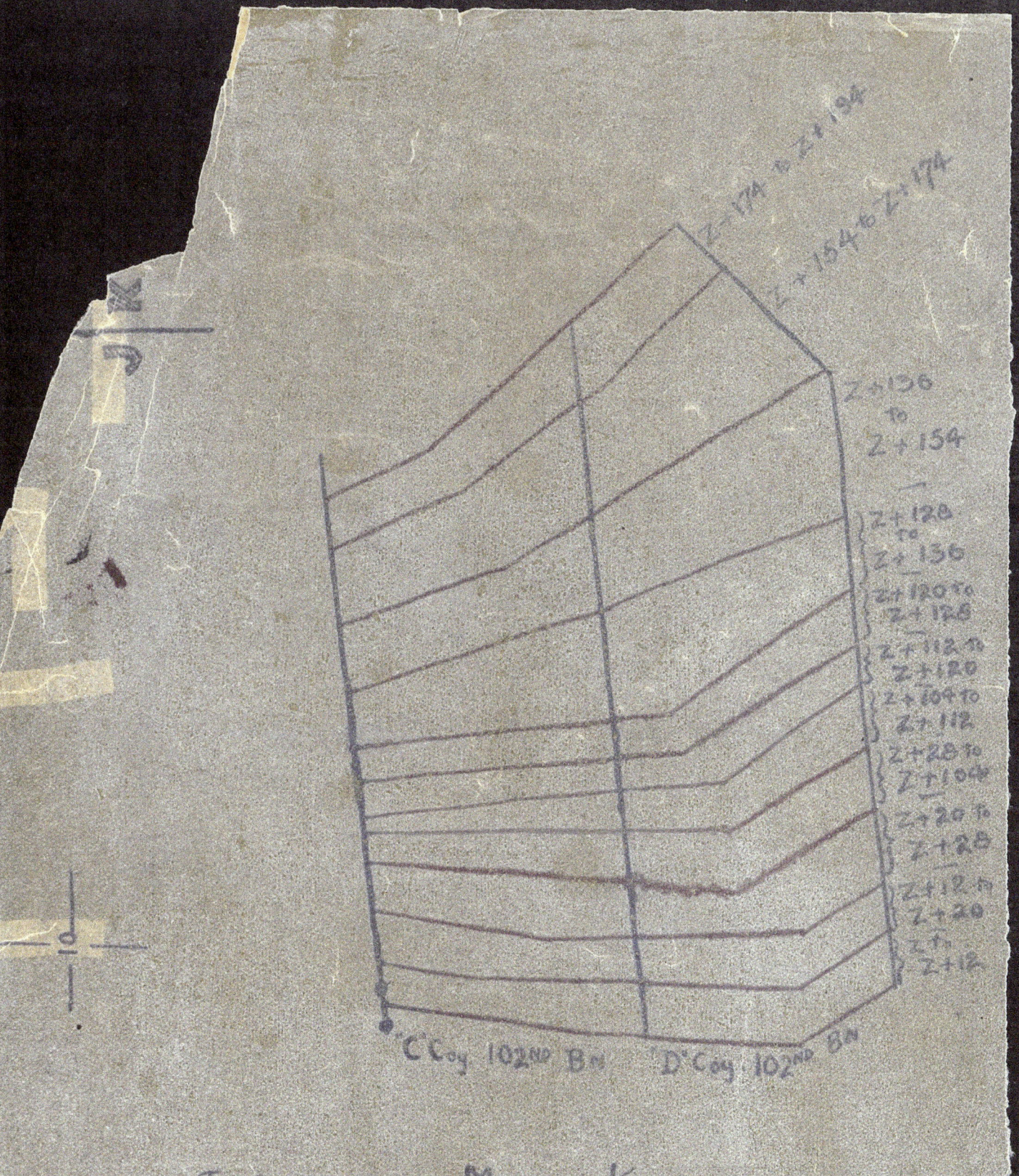

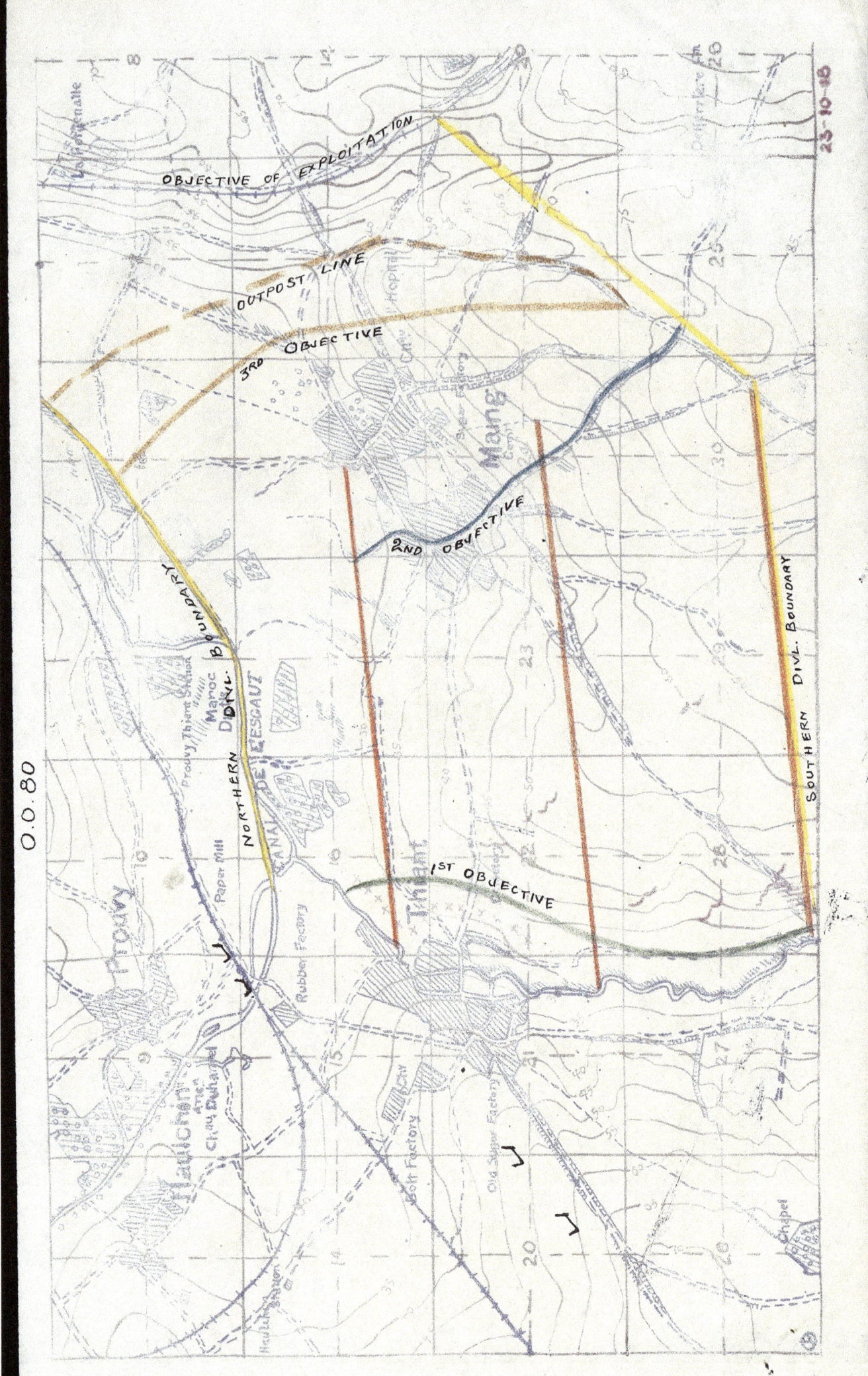

SECRET.

51st (H) BATTALION MACHINE GUN CORPS.

INSTRUCTIONS FOR BARRAGE GROUPS TO ACCOMPANY O.O. 80.

1. Location of batteries is shown on Fire Organisation Orders.

2. All arrangements for laying out Lines of Fire will be completed by daylight on the 23rd instant.

3. The barrage will be a creeping barrage with lifts of 200 yds. ~~and a protective "S.O.S." barrage during consolidation.~~

4. The barrage lines are 400 yds. in front of advancing Infantry. Clearance calculations will be based on this.

5. The barrage will be clear of areas *at times* shown on barrage tracing.

6. Special precautions will be taken for clearance by the forward batteries over all troops formed up for the attack.

23/10/18.

SECRET.

FIRE ORGANISATION ORDERS TO ACCOMPANY OPERATION ORDER No.80.

Group.	Battery.	Location Approximate.	Composition.	Commander.	R E M A R K S.
A.	1.	J.20.d.3.6.	8 Guns of "D" Coy. 102nd Bn. M.G.C.	Major WHITE.	Targets are shewn on Barrage Tracing to be issued later. Rate of fire will be ONE belt per 4 minutes. from ZERO to ZERO plus 42.
	2.	J.21.a.0.1.	8 Guns of "D" Coy. 102nd Bn. M.G.C.		ONE belt per 15 mins. from ZERO plus 42 to ZERO plus 100.
B.	3.	J.15.b.1.5.	8 Guns of "C" Coy. 102nd Bn. M.G.C.	Captain PEARSON.	ONE belt per 6 mins. from ZERO plus 100 to ZERO plus 194.mins.
	4.	J.15.b.5.5. /5.a.8.2.	8 Guns of "C" Coy. 102nd Bn. M.G.C.		

SECRET.

War Diary 23/10/18

51st (H) BATTALION MACHINE GUN CORPS.

ADDENDUM TO OPERATION ORDER No. 80, DATED 23/10/18.
****

Reference last sentence of para. 1, the 4th Division will take QUERENAING tomorrow either by exploitation, or, if this fails, by a separate operation. Left flank of their Main Line of Resistance will then rest at K.25.a.3.3. 153rd Inf. Brigade's right flank will conform. Exploitation will be continued if possible to include high ground at K.14.central and K.13.b.

ACKNOWLEDGE.

Lieut. & Adjt.,
51st (H) Bn. M. G. Corps.

Issued 22.30.
To all recipients of O.O. No. 80.

SECRET.   Copy No ... 16

51st (H) BATTALION MACHINE GUN CORPS.

Ref: map :-   OPERATION ORDER No. 81.
MAING,   *********************
1/20,000.   24/10/18.

1. The 4th and 51st Divisions are to attack tomorrow to capture an Objective which includes the Village of QUERENAING, CAUMONT FM., LA BATTERAVE FM., ROUGE MONT, and thence to K.7.c.5.3.

2. The dividing line between Divisions runs from J.30.d.7.7. to Crossing over Railway at N.20.d.8.1., to cross Roads K.21.d.3.4., to K.10.c.5.3. and thence N.E. along Road.

3. The attack on the 51st (H) Division front will be carried out by the 152nd Inf.Bde. on the RIGHT and the 153rd Inf.Bde. on the LEFT., the Inter-Brigade boundary being the THIANT - MAING - FAMARS Road, inclusive to the LEFT Brigade.

4. "A" and "C" Coys. 51st (H) Battalion M.G.C. will be attached to 153rd and 152nd Infantry Brigades respectively for consolidation of ground captured and defence of Brigade areas.

5. "D" Coy. 102nd Bn. M.G.C. will remain in present defensive positions.

6. The Jumping Off line for the Infantry will run as shewn on the attached sketch. All troops to the East of this line will be withdrawn before ZERO hour.

7. The attack will be carried out under an Artillery Barrage which will fall at ZERO 200 yards in advance of the Jumping Off line. The barrage will begin to creep at Z. plus 15 mins., the pace will be about 100 yds. to 4 mins. There will be no pause until the barrage reaches the line of the Railway where it will pause for 10 mins. At the conclusion of this pause, the barrage will again begin to creep at 100 yds. in 4 mins. until it stops at 300 yds. beyond the final objective.

8. The magnetic bearing of the Right Divisional Boundary is 82°. This is the general direction of the attack.

9. The final objective will be consolidated and also a line through K.19.central, as shewn on the attached sketch.

10. As soon as the Protective Barrage has ceased, Brigades will exploit with a view to occupying FAMAR. and MONT HOUY.

11. ZERO hour will be 07.00 hours. 25/10 18.

12. A C K N O W L E D G E.

                                              Walgrasby
                                              Lieut.& Adjt.,
Issued at 21.15.   51st (H) Battalion, M.G.C.
Copies 1-4 - Coys. 51st (H) Bn. M.G.C.,
       5-6 - "C" & "D" Coys. 102nd Bn. M.G.C.
         7 - 102nd Bn. M.G.C.
       8-9 - 51st (H) Division "G" & "Q".
     10-12 - Brigades.
        13 - 2nd Canadian Bn. M.G.C.
        14 - 4th Bn. M.G.C.
        15 - C.M.G.O. XXII Corps.
     16-17 - War Diary & File.

SECRET.   Ref: C.17.

INSTRUCTIONS FOR THE ASSEMBLY OF GUNS IN ACCORDANCE WITH

51st (H) BN. M. G. C. LETTER DATED 25/10/18.

1. The two Sections will move as soon as possible. Route will be via :- Bridge at DENAIN, I.6.d.1.2., thence by ROUVIGNIES, PROUVY, TRITH ST. LEGER.

   (a). The route from DENAIN is uncertain, as some bridges and cross roads are blown up and it is not certain that those are repaired yet.

   (b). Bridge at J.1.b.5.9. was not repaired two days ago, but if not repaired route can be taken from D.25.c.7.1. to D.25.d.1.9., thence over the open back to the ROUVIGNIES Road.

   (c). There is an Infantry foot bridge at ROUVIGNIES, J.2.d.1.2., A runner relay post might be established here, but the bridge at J.7.b.9.5. is destroyed and runners would require to proceed to level crossing at J.7.b.9.9. and back to road.

2. Two Officers should proceed ahead reconnoitring routes.

3. Great care must be taken in choosing positions and digging-in tonight, if positions chosen are not in houses. Some of the houses in J.6.d. might be suitable positions for the guns, but if possible, the guns should be kept in groups of four. Fire will be directed by an Officer.

****

25/10/18.

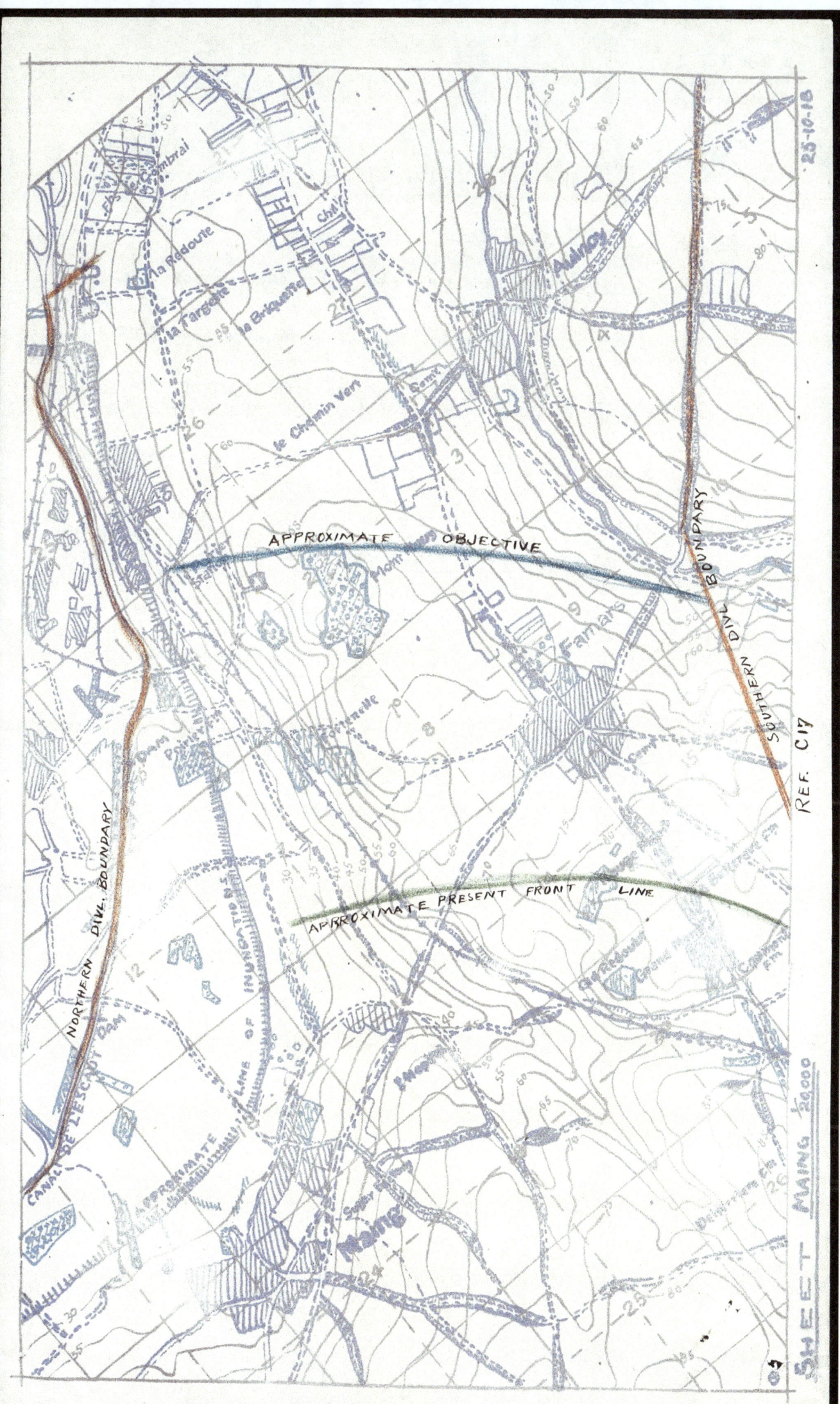

SECRET.

O. C., "D" Coy.,
         51st (H) Bn. M.G.C.

No. O.17.

Reference map MAING, 1/20,000.

You will move two Sections tonight to take up positions at TRITH ST. LEGER in J.6.c. or d.

These guns will be in position by 08.00 hours tomorrow, 26th October, 1918.

Guns will be prepared to cover the advance of our Infantry from the present line to the objective shewn approximately on attached map.

Sections will move in accordance with detailed instructions issued.

Further detailed orders for the attack will be issued tonight, but in case there is not sufficient time for these orders to reach the guns, all arrangements will be made for opening fire by direct observation.

Fire will be opened and kept 400 yards ahead of Artillery creeping barrage.

Zero hour will be after 08.00 hours tomorrow and will be taken from the opening of the Artillery barrage.

On completion of task guns will be laid on a "S.O.S.", but as the Infantry may be exploiting success no fire will be opened beyond objective after completion of barrage, except by direct observation of the enemy, in the event of a hostile counter-attack.

Locations of guns will be reported.

ACKNOWLEDGE.

Lieut. & Adjt.,
51st (H) Bn. M. G. Corps.

25/10/18.
21.00

Copies to :-   51st (H) Division "G."
               152nd Inf. Bde.
               153rd Inf. Bde.
               154th Inf. Bde.
               War Diary.
               File.

SECRET.   51st (H) BATTALION, M.G.CORPS.   Copy No... 13 ...

OPERATION ORDER No. 82.   25/10/18.

Ref.Map:
MAING. 1/20,000.

1. The 4th and 51st Divisions are to attack tomorrow to capture the Villages of ARTRES and FAMARS, and MONT HOUY.

2. The boundary between the 4th and 51st Divisions is altered to read as follows:-
   From the point where the Road crosses the Railway at K.20.d.9.1. to the Cross Roads at K.10.c.1.7.

3. The attack on the 51st Divisional front will be carried out by the 152nd Infantry Brigade on the RIGHT and the 153rd Infantry Brigade on the LEFT.
   The Inter-Brigade boundary runs from the Railway Crossing at K.13.b.7.3. to the Church at AULNOY, the magnetic bearing being 55°.

4. The Infantry will jump off from the line of the Railway between the crossings at K.20.d.9.1. and K.13.b.7.3. and any troops which may be EAST of that line will be withdrawn before ZERO hour.

5. The attack will be carried out under a creeping barrage which will fall at ZERO hour 250 yards in advance of the jumping off line. The Barrage will begin to creep:-
   On the front of the 152nd Inf.Bde. at Z. plus 10 mins.,
   and   "   "   "   "   " 153rd Inf.Bde. at Z. plus 22 mins.

and will creep at the rate of about 100 yards in 4 mins.

6. There will be a pause of 10 mins. when the Infantry are on the line of the first Objective.

7. "C" and "A" Coys. 51st. (H) Bn. M.G.C. will be attached to 152nd and 153rd Inf.Bdes. respectively for consolidation of ground captured and defence of Brigade areas.

8. "D" Coy. 102nd Bn. M.G.C. will remain in present positions but will be prepared on receipt of orders to move forward to take up positions in depth for the defence of the Jumping Off line shewn on attached map.

9. "D" Coy. 51st (H) Bn. M.G.C. will cover the advance of the Infantry with a battery of EIGHT guns sited in area J.6.c.& d.
   Barrage tracing will be issued later to Company concerned.

10. The general line of the final objective will be consolidated and outposts will be pushed forward.
    The following line will also be consolidated:- From the RIGHT Divisional Boundary near LA BETTERAVE FM., West of FAMARS to join the first Objective on the Inter-Brigade boundary, and thence along the line of the first objective.

11. The attached sketch shews boundaries and objectives.

12. As soon as the protective barrage has ceased the 152nd Inf.Bde. will exploit to secure Bridgeheads in K.10. and at AULNOY, and the 153rd Inf.Bde. will exploit towards VALENCIENNES.

13. ZERO hour will be 10.00 hrs. 26th. Oct. 1918.

14. A C K N O W L E D G E.

                                              W A Grasby
                                              Lieut.& Adjt.,
Issued at 23.00.   51st (H) Battalion, M.G.Corps.
Distribution overleaf.

DISTRIBUTION:-

Copies 1-4 - All Coys. 51st (H) Bn. M.G.C.
      5-6 - "C" & "D" Coys. 102nd Bn. M.G.C.
        7. - 102nd Bn. M.G.C.
     8-10 - Brigades.
   11-12 - 51st (H) Division, "G" & "Q".
      13 - War Diary.
      14 - File.

SECRET.   Copy No ..17..

51st (H) BATTALION MACHINE GUN CORPS.

of: map :-   OPERATION ORDER NO. 83.
\ING,   ************************
/20,000.   26/10/18.

1. The 154th Infantry Brigade will relieve the 152nd Infantry Brigade and 153rd Infantry Brigade in the line today, 26th October, 1918.

2. "B" Coy. 51st (H) Bn. M.G.C. will relieve "A" Coy. 51st (H) Bn. M.G.C. in the line 26th October, 1918.

3. All arrangements for relief will be made direct between Os. C. Coys. concerned.

4. Completion of relief will be notified by code word "ROSE."

5. On completion of relief "B" Coy. 51st (H) Bn. M.G.C., "C" Coy. 51st (H) Bn. M.G.C., two Sections of "D" Coy. 51st (H) Bn. M.G.C. in position on the North of the CANAL and "D" Coy. 102nd Bn. M.G.C. will come under orders of the 154th Infantry Brigade.

6. On completion of relief "A" Coy. 51st (H) Bn. M.G.C. will move to billets in the THIANT - HAULCHIN area. Accommodation will be allotted by 153rd Infantry Brigade.

7. Companies will report location of new H.Q. and dispositions of guns as early as possible.

8. A C K N O W L E D G E.

                                           Walgrasby
                                           Lieut. & Adjt.,
Issued at 10.50   51st (H) Bn. M. G. Corps.

Copy 1 - 4 - Coys. 51st (H) Bn. M.G.C.
     5 - 6 - "C" & "D" Coys. 102nd Bn. M.G.C.
     7 - 9 - Brigades.
    10 - 11 - 51st (H) Division "G" & "Q."
         12 - 102nd Bn. M.G.C.
         13 - T.O.
         14 - Q.M.
         15 - S.O.
    16 - 17 - War Diary and File.

SECRET.   Copy No ..16..

51st (H) BATTALION MACHINE GUN CORPS.

OPERATION ORDER No. 84.

Ref: map :-   26/10/18.
MAING,
1/20,000.

1. "C" Company, 102nd Bn. M.G.C. will relieve "D" Company, 102nd Bn. M.G.C. in the line 27th October, 1918.

2. O. C. "C" Coy., 102nd Bn. M.G.C. will obtain necessary horse transport from "D" Coy., 51st (H) Bn. M.G.C. Arrangements will be made direct with O. C. "D" Coy., 51st (H) Bn. M.G.C.

3. Limbers supplied will be used to carry in the guns of "C" Coy., 102nd Bn. M.G.C. and to carry out the guns of "D" Coy., 102nd Bn. M.G.C. after relief.

4. All further details will be arranged between Os. C. Coys. concerned.

5. Completion of relief will be notified by code word "SYKES."

6. On completion of relief "C" Coy., 102nd Bn. M.G.C. will come under the orders of the 154th Infantry Brigade and will maintain close liaison with that Brigade.

7. On completion of relief "D" Coy., 102nd Bn. M.G.C. will take over billets vacated by "C" Coy., 102nd Bn. M.G.C.

8. A C K N O W L E D G E.

                                                    Lieut. & Adjt.,
                                                    51st (H) Bn. M. G. Corps.

Issued at 18.20

            Copies 1 - 4 - Coys. 51st (H) Bn. M.G.C.
                   5 - 6 - "C" & "D" Coys. 102nd Bn. M.G.C.
                   7 - 9 - Brigades.
                  10 - 11 - 51st (H) Division "G" & "Q."
                  12   - 102nd Bn. M.G.C.
                  13   - T.O.
                  14   - Q.M.
                  15   - S.O.
                  16 - 17 - War Diary & File.

SECRET.   Copy No 17.

51st (H) BATTALION MACHINE GUN CORPS.

OPERATION ORDER No. 85.
                                                                   27/10/18.

1. The 154th Infantry Brigade will carry out an attack tomorrow to capture MONT HUOY.

2. The objectives are shewn on the attached sketch.

3. The attack will be carried out under a barrage which will fall at Zero hour 250 yards beyond the jumping off line, and will begin to creep at Zero plus 3 minutes.
   There will be a pause of 10 minutes when the infantry are on the First Objective.

4. Both objectives will be consolidated.

5. As soon as the protective barrage has ceased, the 154th Inf. Brigade will exploit towards AULNOY and VALENCIENNES.

6. ACTION OF MACHINE GUNS.

   (a). Objectives, Boundaries, Barrage Positions, Barrage Areas and times of lifts are shown on map and tracing attached.

   (b). "B" Coy., 51st (H) Bn. M.G.C. is attached to the 153rd Inf. Brigade for consolidation of ground captured and defence of Brigade Area.

   (c). "D" Coy., 51st (H) Bn. M.G.C. will cover the advance of our infantry in accordance with barrage tracing attached from battery position North of Canal l'ESCAUT as shewn on map.

   (d). On completion of barrage guns will be laid on "S.O.S." and will not fire except by direct observation of the enemy in the event of a hostile counter-attack.

   (e). Eight guns of "C" Coy. 102nd Bn. M.G.C., at present in position on railway in K.13. and 14., will bring concentrated fire to bear on the wood at MONT HUOY in accordance with barrage tracing.

   (f). Barrage lines shown on tracing are 400 yards in advance of our infantry and all safety clearances will be calculated on this basis.

   (g). Rate of fire will be ONE belt per FOUR minutes.

7. A Contact Plane will call for flares at Zero plus 2 hrs.

8. ZERO hour will be 05.15 hours on 28th October, 1918. Opening of machine gun barrage will be taken from opening of 18-pdr. barrage.

9. A C K N O W L E D G E.

                                                          W Agnasby
                                                          Lieut. & Adjt.,
                                                          51st (H) Bn. M. G. Corps.

Issued at 19.30.
                  normal
Distribution overleaf.

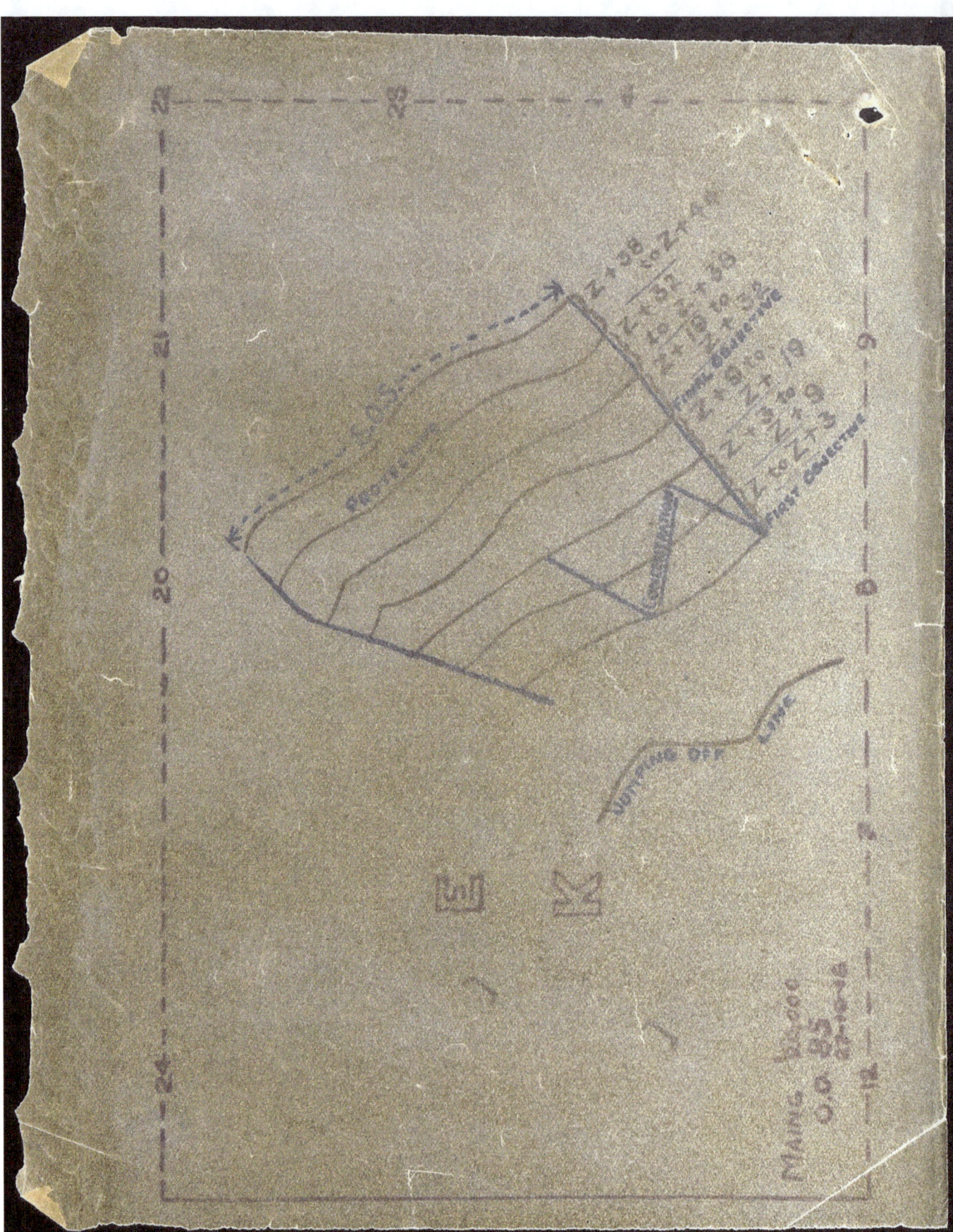

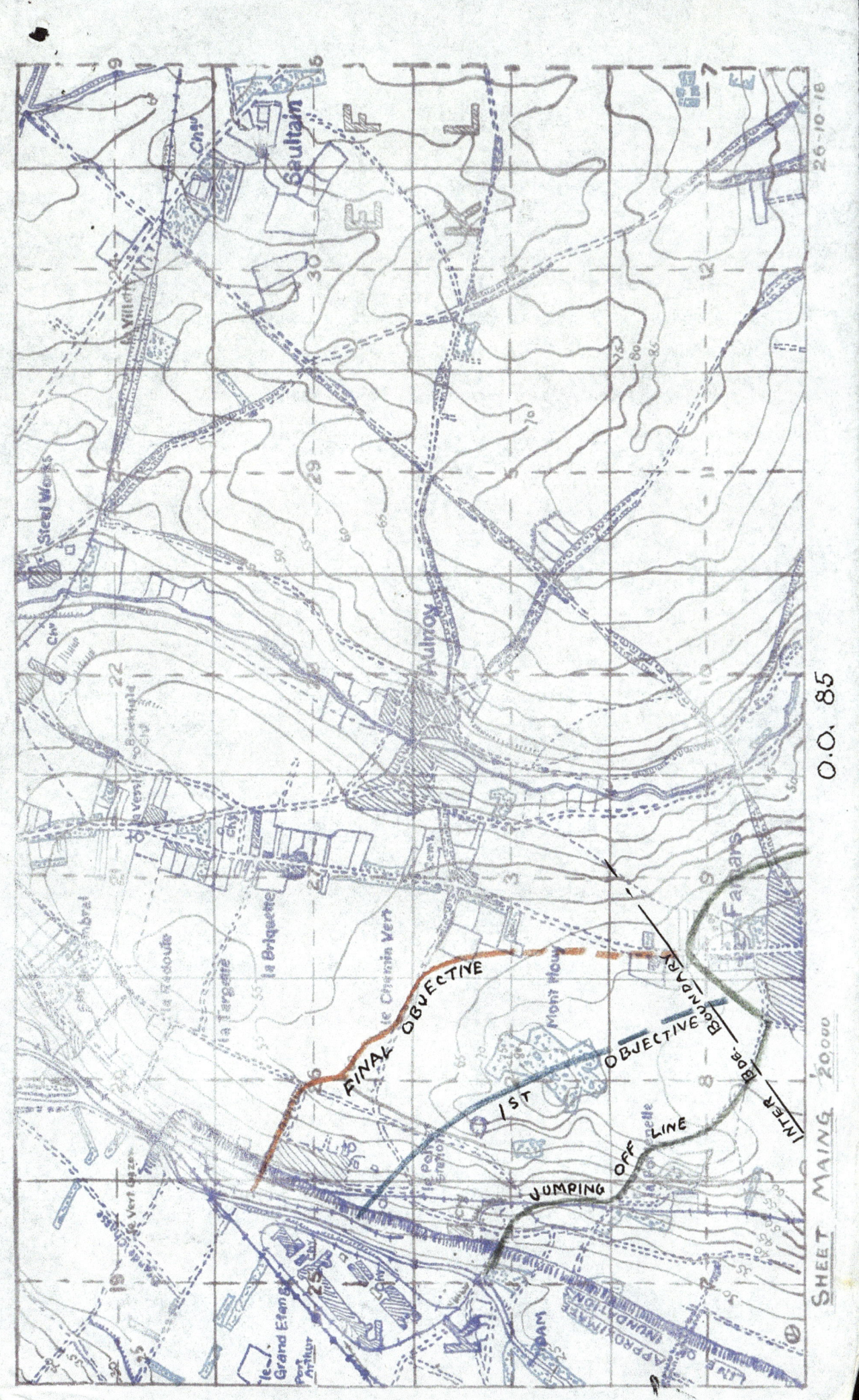

SECRET.   Copy No ..18..

51st (H) BATTALION MACHINE GUN CORPS.

OPERATION ORDER No. 86.   28/10/18.

Ref: map :-
Sheet 51.A.
1/40,000.

1. The 51st (Highland) Division will be relieved in the line by 2 Brigades of the 49th Division and one Brigade of the 4th Can. Div., and will move on relief to the BASSEVILLE – NEUVILLE – DOUCHY – FOYELLES Area, with Divisional Headquarters at BASSEVILLE.

2. "A" "B" & "C" Coys. 51st (H) Bn. M.G.C. attached to the 153rd, 154th and 152nd Inf. Brigades respectively will be relieved and will move to billets under orders of their respective Brigades.

3. "D" Coy. 51st (H) Bn. M.G.C. will be withdrawn, without relief, at --- hours and will move to billets in BASSEVILLE. (Hour will be notified later).

4. "B" Coy. 49th Bn. M.G.C. will come under the orders of the O.C. 51st (H) Bn. M.G.C. and will be held in Divisional Reserve until the command of the Divisional Front passes. "B" Coy. 49th Bn. M.G.C. will move today to billets in THIANT.

5. "C" & "D" Coys. 102nd Bn. M.G.C. will come under the command of the G.O.C. 49th Division when the command passes.

6. Completion of relief will be reported by Companies concerned by code phrase "M.G.94. RECEIVED."

7. All 1/20,000 maps, except sufficient for reports, etc., will be handed over on relief.
    All 1/40,000 Sheets 44, 45 and 51, and 25% of 1/40,000 Sheet 51.A. will be handed over if required by incoming units.

8. (a). Intervals will be maintained on the march in accordance with S.S.724, para. 19.
    There will be no movement East of MAING in parties larger than one platoon.
    (b). All troops and transport will move off the roads as far as possible and will avoid using heavy traffic bridges.
    (c). On the line of march troops will move in threes.

9. On arrival in billets Coys. will forward location of H.Q. to this Office.

10. Headquarters, 51st (H) Bn. M.G.C. will close at AVESNES-le-SEC at 10.00 hours 29th instant and open at BASSEVILLE.

11. Command of the Right SubSector of the Divisional Front will pass to the G.O.C. 49th Division and of the Left SubSector to the G.O.C. 4th Canadian Division, at 10.00 hours, 29th inst., at which hour Divisional Headquarters will close at AVESNES-le-SEC and open at BASSEVILLE.
    "A" and "Q" Office and Administrative Departments will move to BASSEVILLE on 28th Oct., closing at AVESNES-le-SEC at 14.30 hours, and opening at BASSEVILLE at the same hour.

12. A C K N O W L E D G E.

Issued at 1600
                                                    Lieut. & Adjt.,
                                                 51st (H) Bn. M.G. Corps.

Distribution overleaf.

Copies 1 - 4 - Coys. 51st (H) Bn. M.G.C.
       5 - 6 - "C" & "D" Coys. 102nd Bn. M.G.C.
       7   - 102nd Bn. M.G.C.
       8   - "B" Coy. 49th Bn. M.G.C.
       9   - 49th Bn. M.G.C.
      10   - 4th Canadian Bn. M.G.C.
     11 - 13 - Brigades.
      14   - 51st (H) Division, "G."
     15 - 16 - T.O. & Q.M.
      17   - S.O.
     18 - 19 - War Diary and File.

SECRET.   Copy No. 12

51st (HIGHLAND) BATTALION MACHINE GUN CORPS.

OPERATION ORDER No. 87.   30/10/18.

1. The Division is placed in First Army Reserve from the 31st October, inclusive, and will move to the IWUY, ESCAUDOEUVRES and ESWARS Areas today and tomorrow.

2. The 51st (H) Bn. M.G.C. will move tomorrow, Companies moving independently, in accordance with attached Table.

3. Troops will move across country wherever possible; the regulation distances will be maintained. When marching on roads, troops will move in file.

4. One lorry may be available for "B" & "C" Coys. to move Blankets, Surplus Kit, etc. This will be confirmed later.

5. Billetting parties will be at the Church in PAILLENCOURT, N.26.a.4.7. at 08.00 hours tomorrow.

6. A C K N O W L E D G E.

                                              [signature]
                                              Lieut. & Adjt.,
Issued at 18.00.   51st (H) Bn. M. G. Corps.

Copies 1 - 4 - Coys. 51st (H) Bn. M.G.C.
        5 - 7 - Brigades.
        8 - 9 - 51st (H) Division "G" & "Q."
        10   - T.O.
        11   - Q.M.
        12 - 13 - War Diary and File.

TABLE TO ACCOMPANY 51st (II) BN. M.G.C. OPERATION ORDER No. 87.

Serial No.	Unit.	From.	To.	Time.	Route.
1.	"C" Coy.	NOYELLES.	PAILLENCOURT.	0715.	Track to LIEU ST. AMAND and via ESTRUN.
2.	"B" "	"	"	0725.	"
3.	"A" "	BASSEVILLE.	"	0830.	Via ESTRUN.
4.	"D" "	"	"	0840.	"
5.	H.Q.	"	"	0850.	"

SECRET.   51st (H) BATTALION, M. G. CORPS.

REPORT on OPERATIONS, N.E., of CAMBRAI.

11th to 29th OCT., 1918.

Reference Maps:-
Sheet 51A., 1/40,000.
HAING, 1/20,000.

11th: Companies moved to RAMILLIES, MORENCHIES area with their Brigade Groups.

Battalion Headquarters at NEUVILLE ST. REMY.

152nd and 154th Infantry Brigades relieved 2nd CANADIAN DIVISION in line in front of IWUY night of the 11/12th.

"A" Coy. with the 152nd Infantry Brigade on the RIGHT and "C" Coy. with 154th Infantry Brigade on LEFT.

Orders issued by Division for an attack at 12.00 hours on 12th by Brigades already in the line with a view to gaining line AVESNES-le-SEC (inclusive) LIEU ST. AMAND (exclusive).

12th: The attack was carried out by 152nd Inf.Bde. employing 5th SEAFORTH HIGHRS. and 6/7th GORDON HIGHRS. with 6th SEAFORTH HIGHLANDERS in reserve and 154th Inf.Bde. employing 4th SEAFORTH HIGHRS. and 7th A.& S.HRS. with 4th GORDON HRS. in reserve.

The guns of "A" Coy. were employed as follows:-
One section attached to each attacking Battalion, the Two remaining Sections were held in reserve until objectives were taken, when they moved to high ground in O.25. & 26.

Two Sections of "C" Coy. were attached to Two Battalions of 154th Inf.Bde., remaining 8 guns were moved in Reserve on to Ridge in O.19. as soon as the situation permitted.

The attack was very successful and AVESNES-le-SEC was taken, but it was impossible for the 154th Inf.Bde. to exploit their success and take LIEU ST. AMAND as this was strongly held.

The four sections attached to the attacking Battalion consolidated good positions on line approximately 500 yards

-1-

behind AVESNES le SEC - LIEU ST. AMAND Road.

About 14.00 hours, the H.Q. of 152nd and 154th Inf.Bdes. together with co-operating Machine Gun Coys. moved to IWUY.

"D" Coy. 51st (H) Bn. M.G.C. with 153rd Inf.Bde. moved to THUN ST. MARTIN area.

"B" Coy. and Battalion H.Q. moved to ESCAUDOEUVRES.

During the afternoon, Battalion H.Qrs. moved with Divisional H.Qrs. to NAVES.

Orders were received from Division that advance would be continued on the 15th in conjunction with 49th Division with the object of securing FLEURY and NOYELLES-sur-SELLE line, and if this was taken to exploit the success by taking the high ground and woods in J.32.

13th: Eight guns of "B" Coy. were ordered to report to 152nd Inf. Bde. Headquarters by 08.00 hours to take the place of Two Sections of "A" Coy. in reserve, so that the whole of "A" Coy. could be employed in the forward area for consolidation.

The attack commenced at 09.00 hours. All the forward sections advanced close behind the attacking Battalions.

From the beginning, heavy hostile Machine Gun fire was encountered, and Infantry made little progress. Guns were pushed forward in an effort to beat down hostile fire but owing to the extremely open nature of the ground, heavy casualties were suffered amongst the gun teams. The two sections with 6/7th GORDON HIGHRS. on Left managed to gain position in O.15.a.& d. with the forward Infantry.

Both sections Officers were casualties and three of the eight guns were knocked out. Two sections with the 5th SEAFORTHS on right also had three guns put out of action and had the Section Officer killed.

Owing to the unfavourable situation, the line was brought back to AVESNES-le-SEC - LIEU ST. AMAND Road, and all four Sections reorganised and distributed as far as possible in depth so as to secure the following positions.

North edge of AVESNES-le-SEC.   M. de PIERRE,
MAISON BLANCHE.   S.W. Outskirts of LIEU ST. AMAND.

14th: During the day, pressure on the enemy was continued by strong fighting patrols supported by the Artillery.

At night, the 153rd Infantry Brigade relieved the 154th Inf.Bde. in the Left Sub-sector, and "D" Coy. relieved "C" Coy. which withdrew to THUN ST. MARTIN.

The remaining 8 guns of "B" Coy. in ESCAUDOEUVRES moved up to IWUY, and by midnight "A" Coy. was relieved by 16 guns of "B" Coy. "A" Coy. then withdrew to THUN ST. MARTIN.

15th: The following was position of guns in line on the 15th:-

"D" Coy: (153rd Inf.Bde.) 2 guns at O.21.b.7.8. O.14.b.5.7. O.32.a.3.1., O.21.a.6.8. O.27.a.1.7. O.25.c.5.5. O.32.a.6.5., O.25.d.0.8.

"B" Coy: (152nd Inf.Bde.) 2 guns at O.21.b.8.8., O.14.b.1.5., O.21.a.3.9., O.26.b.9.6., 8 on Ridge O.25.& 26.

16th: Two Coys. of Army Machine Gun Battalion (102nd Battalion) were attached to the Division.

154th Inf.Bde. relieved 152nd Inf.Bde. in Right Sub-sector. "B" Coy. remaining in the line.

Vigorous harassing fire was carried out during the night by Coys. in the line.

17th: Situation was unchanged. Vigorous harassing fire was again carried out.

Orders were received in the evening for an attack to be carried out by the 4th Division with object of seizing line running through P.23.c., P.22.c., and P.15.c. then S. by W. of HASPRES, and the 51st (H) Division would attack at the same time in order to protect left flank of the 4th Division, the objective being to seize the woods in O.10.d. and O.9.

"B" Coy. was attached to 154th Inf.Bde., and "D" Coy. to 153rd Inf.Bde. for consolidation of ground.

"A" and "C" Coys. 51st (H) Bn. M.G.C. and "C" and "D" Coys. 102nd Bn. M.G.C. to carry out barrage for the attack.

and to remain laid on "S.O.S." when barrage was completed. It was intended that ZERO should be midnight 19th/20th, ~~20th~~

19th: All barrage positions were duly completed but this operation was cancelled owing to the retirement of the enemy.

"A" Coy. moved to AVESNES-le-SEC complete with Transport.

"C" Coy. remained in THUN ST. MARTIN and came under orders of 152nd Inf.Bde.

"C" and "D" Coys. 102nd Bn. concentrated in IWUY.

Enemy commenced to withdraw on the afternoon of the 19th and was followed by 153rd and 154th Inf.Bdes. on the left and right respectively.

Bridges were thrown over the SELLE River during the night 19th.

20th: The high ground West of the ECAILLON River and the Village of THIANT were captured.

Two sections of "B" Coy. were attached to the attacking Battalion of the 154th Inf.Bde. One section was attached to the 4th SEAFORTH Hrs. and the remaining section in reserve.

The section with the 7th A.& S.Hrs. took up its first position in I.35.a. The section with the 4th GORDON Hrs. about 500 yards S.W. of FLEURY.

The 152nd Inf.Bde. and "C" Coy. moved to LIEU ST. AMAND. "A" Coy. remained at AVESNES-le-SEC in Divisional Reserve. Battalion H.Qrs. moved to AVESNES-le-SEC with Divisional Headquarters.

Reserve Battalion of 154th Inf.Bde. with section attached moved at 00.01 hours 21st to occupy LE GRAND BOIS and BOIS l'ENTREE where this section provided Right flank defence.

The 8 guns of "D" Coy. attached to the attacking Battalion of the 153rd Inf.Bde. on left moved forward by stages behind the Infantry and finally took up positions on the Railway Embankment in J.14.d. and J.15.c. in order to protect Right flank of the 6th A.& S.Hrs. as touch had not been gained with the Battalion on its right.

On reaching the Canal d'ESCAUT, the 153rd Inf.Bde. with "D" Coy. was squeezed out and withdrawn to billets in DOUCHY.

21st: The Guns of "B" Coy. were finally disposed as follows:-
        2 at J.15.c.4.8.,   4 at J.26.a.8.8.,   2 at J.27.d.2.6.,
        2 at J.21.b.8.8.,   4 at P.1.d.5.9.,   2 at J.31.b.1.7.

The 152nd Inf.Bde. moved to NOYELLES - DOUCHY area, with "C" Coy. at DOUCHY.

At 09.30 hours, "A" Coy. was ordered to NOYELLES, and "C" and "D" Coys. of 102nd Bn. to DOUCHY.

Orders received (issued) that "C" and "D" Coys. 102nd Bn. may be called upon to fire barrage to cover advance of our troops from the River ECAILLON to MAING.

22nd: The 153rd Inf.Bde. relieved the 154th Inf.Bde. in the line.

"A" Coy. at NOYELLES relieved "B" Coy. in the line.

"C" and "D" Coys. 51st (H) Bn. remained at DOUCHY, the latter being attached to the 154th Inf.Bde.

Orders were issued to "C" Coy. 102nd Bn. to take up barrage positions in Railway Embankment in J.15.a. and b., and to be in position by 10.00 hours 23rd.

23rd: "C" Coy. 102nd Bn. and 3 guns of "A" Coy. co-operated with the Artillery which fired practice barrages between River ECAILLON and MAING at 15.00 and 15.45 hours.

"D" Coy. 102nd Bn. assembled in positions in J.20.d. and J.21.a.

Orders were received that Division would attack on the 24th. The 153rd Inf.Bde. would carry out attack with two Battalions, the objective being the high ground in J.30. and Village of MAING and to exploit up to the line of Railway in E.20.a.5.8. to E.26.a.0.0.

"A" Coy. attached to the 153rd Inf.Bde. for this operation. "C" and "D" Coys. 102nd Bn. fired barrage to cover the attack from their previously prepared positions.

24th: ZERO was at 04.00 hours. The 6th BLACK WATCH on Right, and 7th BLACK WATCH on Left.

Two Sections of "A" Coy. were attached to attacking Battalions for forward consolidation. The two remaining Sections were held in reserve until BROWN line was taken.

Attacking Sections moved forward with the Infantry across the ECAILLON River and on several occasions during the advance successfully beat down hostile machine gun fire.

One section finally reached positions in HAING - neighbourhood of Cross Roads in J.24.a.2.0., and a Section with 6th B.W. reached position in J.24.c.5.7.

The reserve sections moved with Limbers to J.27.b.2.2. Owing to casualties of Left Battalion, one of these reserve Sections was sent to reinforce their front and the remaining section in reserve moved to consolidate high ground in J.29.central.

"D" Coy. 102nd Bn. on completion of their barrage also took up consolidation positions during the evening from J.18.central along high ground to vicinity of J.29.central.

Evening 24th: "C" Coy. 102nd Bn. withdrew from its barrage positions to billets in DOUCHY, ~~the~~

The 152nd Inf.Bde. relieved the 153rd Inf.Bde. in right Sub-Sector of Divisional front. 8th A.& S.Hrs. relieved 7th B.W. in Left Sub-Sector, dispositions of Infantry now being:-

153rd Inf.Bde. on Left with 8th A.& S.Hrs.
152nd Inf.Bde. on Right with 6/7th Gordon Hrs. on Right and 6th
    Seaforth Highlanders on left.

Eight guns of "A" Coy. in Right Sub-sector were relieved by 8 guns of "C" Coy. and on relief withdrew to reserve in THIANT.

Orders issued that the attack will be continued on morning of 25th with the object of seizing line running from K.7.c.5.3. to ROUGE MONT and with the 4th Division attacking on Right.

"A" and "C" Coys. were attached to the 153rd and 152nd Inf. Bdes. respectively for consolidation of ground captured. "D" Coy. 102nd Bn. was ordered to remain in present defensive positions.

25th: ZERO was 07.00 hours. Guns of "C" Coy. were used as follows:-

One section moved forward with attacking Infantry, and by 11.00 hours was in position about K.19.d.7.9. Two more sections were sent up in close reserve near HAING in readiness to support any enterprise by Right Brigade.

By 15.00 hours objectives reported held and one of the close reserve sections was sent to a position near Railway, K.14.c.2.4. and two more guns of the fourth section, as yet unused, were attached and sent up with a view to occupying ROUGE MONT. The Officer in charge of these 6 guns on reaching the line of Railway found an enemy counter-attack in progress, and in view of the situation placed two of his guns about K.19.a.9.3. and placed his four remaining guns in position at K.14.c.2.4. The section in position at K.19.d.7.2. obtained good targets during the enemy counter-attack and wiped out parties of the enemy coming over crest in K.14.central.

Guns of "A" Coy. were used as follows:-

The two sections in resting positions near BOLT FACTORY were attached to the 6th A.& S.Hrs. (153rd Inf.Bde.).

One section for consolidation of GREEN line, neighbourhood of Railway K.13.b., and afterwards to consolidate RED dotted line if it was taken. In the latter case the second section would move up to occupy GREEN line in positions vacated by first section.

The other sections of "A" Coy. to remain in HAING on the BLUE line.

The first section advancing behind the Infantry used top-storeys of houses in HAING to give direct overhead covering fire and eventually reached line of Railway K.13.b.9.9. As the

(*) The enemy counter attacked at 16.00 hours and the Section at J.13.b.9.9. had some excellent targets which assisted materially in breaking up the counter attack.

take up positions in depth on LImpCross Roads, J.30.d.7.7. along Sunken Road to Cross Roads, J.31.a.7.7.

Two sections of "D" Coy. 51st (H) Bn. moved evening 25th to TRIER SE. LEGER in J.6. to be in position by 03.00 hours 26th.

were sent up in close reserve near HAING in readiness to support any enterprise by Right Brigade.

By 15.00 hours objectives reported held and one of the close reserve sections was sent to a position near Railway, K.14.c.2.4. and two more guns of the fourth section, as yet unused, were attached and sent up with a view to occupying ROUGE MONT. The Officer in charge of these 6 guns on reaching the line of Railway found an enemy counter-attack in progress, and in view of the situation placed two of his guns about K.19.a.9.8. and placed his four remaining guns in position at K.14.c.2.4. The section in position at K.19.d.7.8. obtained good targets during the enemy counter-attack and wiped out parties of the enemy coming over crest in K.14.central.

Guns of "A" Coy. were used as follows:-

The two sections in resting positions near BOLT FACTORY were attached to the 6th A.& S.Hrs. (153rd Inf.Bde.).

One section for consolidation of GREEN line, neighbourhood of Railway K.13.b., and afterwards to consolidate RED dotted line if it was taken. In the latter case the second section would move up to occupy GREEN line in positions vacated by first section.

The other sections of "A" Coy. to remain in HAING on the BLUE line.

The first section advancing behind the Infantry used top-storeys of houses in HAING to give direct overhead covering fire and eventually reached line of Railway K.13.b.9.9. As the Infantry were held on this line, the second section was moved up to the West end of HAING.

"A" Coy. H.Q. moved to J.31.b.34.80. at 15.00 hours.

Orders issued to "D" Coy. 102nd Bn. to move forward to take up positions in depth on line from Cross Roads, J.30.d.7.7. along Sunken Road to Cross Roads, J.31.a.6.5.

Two sections of "D" Coy. 51st (H) Bn. moved evening 25th to TRITH ST. LEGER in J.6. to be in position by 03.00 hours 26th.

-8-

These guns to be prepared to cover advance of Infantry from the line gained on 25th to a final objective in front of MONT HOUY and FAHARS.

Orders received during evening that Division would continue the attack on 26th to capture FAHARS-MONT HOUY line. 152nd Inf.Bde. on right, 153rd Inf.Bde. on left.

26th: ZERO 10.00 hours. For this operation 6th B.W. relieved 6th A.& S.Hrs. and attacked with the 4th Gordon Hrs. and 152nd Inf. Bde. on right.

One Section of "A" Coy. attached to 6th B.W. for this operation and one section remained in reserve with 6th A.& S.Hrs.

Section with 6th B.W. advanced with them to K.3.d., then moved to K.8.a.3.5. as this gave a better field of fire.

Two sections of "C" Coy. on right were detailed to work with attacking Battalions of 152nd Inf.Bde. One section endeavoured to get into position N.E. of FAHARS but as the enemy still held part of the village, this was impossible and positions were taken up in K.14.d.5.8.

Two guns in Reserve were moved to close reserve at J.24.a.3.1. in order to release the section going forward.

These two guns eventually followed the second section going forward on the right which had taken up positions behind GRAND MONT and ROUGE MONT and itself took up positions near OLD REDOUBT, K.20.a.3.9.

The fourth section moved from South of HAING to Railway, K.14.c.2.4.

"D" Coy. 51st (H) Bn. M.G.C. covered the advance by direct fire from HAUTE ST. LEGER and obtained some good targets of the enemy retiring. Some excellent targets presented themselves during the afternoon and were effectively engaged. An enemy machine gun was located in a shallow dip near POIRIER FM. which was holding up a party of infantry taking cover 300 yards from gun. Concentrated fire was opened and the gun team scattered enabling the Infantry to take the gun and afterwards the surviving members of the team.

-9-

<u>Evening 26th</u>: "B" Coy. was sent up to relieve "A" Coy. on Left Brigade Front. The two sections of in HAING were relieved, but owing to the uncertain situation in front, the two forward sections were not relieved until dawn 27th.

During afternoon, 26th, "D" Coy. 102nd Bn. moved forward from positions S. of HAING to observation line CAUROIE FM. through high ground to K.14.central. This Company was relieved by "C" Coy. 102nd Bn. on morning of 27th.

<u>27th</u>: By the morning of 27th, 154th Inf.Bde. had taken over line from 153rd Inf.Bde. Coys. now in the line were "B" Coy. on the left, "C" Coy. on the right, two sections of "D" Coy. in J.c.d. and :C: Coy. 102nd Bn. in positions in K.14. and K.21.

153rd Inf.Bde. and "A" Coy. move to HAULCHIN.

<u>Evening 27th</u>: Orders received that 154th Inf.Bde. would carry out an attack on 28th to capture MONT HOUY. "B" Coy. 51st (H) Bn. attached for consolidation of ground.

<u>28th</u>: This attack was covered by "D" Coy. 51st (H) Bn. from barrage positions North of the Canal d'ESCAUT and by 8 guns of "C" Coy. 102nd Bn. in position on Railway in K.15. and K.14.

Guns of "B" Coy. co-operated with 154th Inf.Bde. as follows:-

Two sections were attached to attacking Battalion and jumped off with them at ZERO 05.15.

One section reached position in K.8.c.a.4. and one section K.8.b.7.5., but were unable to move further forward owing to an enemy counter-attack.

The third section took up a position in K.8.c.1.5. and a defensive position established there in co-operation with reserve Infantry Coy. The position evacuated by this section was occupied by the fourth section. About noon on the 28th, enemy reported to be in Wood at MONT HOUY. Two guns at K.2.c.4.4. opened fire and forced the enemy to retire to Northern edges.

-10-

A counter-attack by the enemy at 15.00 hours was stopped on the line 200 yards N. of QUARRY in K.26.c.e.k. The enemy again attempted to advance through the wood but was unable to get past the West edge where he was held up by M.G. and L.G. fire from K.2.c.6.7. and K.9.a.3.8.

"C" Coy. was relieved night 28/29th by "C" and "D" Coys. 49th Battalion M.G.C.

"D" Coy. were to be relieved by No.1 Coy. of 4th Canadian M.G. Battalion, but it was delayed for 24 hours owing to situation on the left front.

"D" Coy. 102nd Bn. M.G.C. were placed at tactical disposal of 154th Inf.Bde. and took up position in support along the line of the Railway.

The 8th A.&.S.Hrs. relieved the 4th Seaforth and 7th A.&.S.Hrs. in the forward positions.

29th: The enemy attacked again on 29th at 15.45 hours but were driven off with heavy casualties by Lewis, Machine Gun and Rifle fire. The Infantry firing rapid fire with rifles with great effect.

The 154th Inf.Bde. with "D" Coy. were relieved by a Brigade of the 4th Canadian Division and "D" Coy. was withdrawn to DOUCHY.

Lieut.Colonel.,
Commanding 51st (H) Bn. M.G.C.

7/11/18.

LESSONS LEARNT.

1. Co-ordination required of methods in employment of Machine Guns under Brigades and under Battalion Commanders.

2. The following general principles should be laid down :-

   (1). The Section of four guns is the unit and will not be split up out of control of the Section Commander.

   (2). Guns will be in depth at commencement of operations and this depth will be maintained throughout operations.

   (3). Machine Gun Sections will advance by bounds.
   The forward Section maintaining normally 400 to 600 yards behind the leading Infantry.
   The rear Section maintaining normally 800 to 1000 yards behind forward Sections.

   (4). Vickers Guns will not be put into the Outpost Line except in exceptional circumstances.

   (5). The Machine Gun Strong Points will form the rallying points for the Infantry, if driven in.

   (6). The thin Machine Gun System for defence of the Artillery gun line will normally be supplied from the Divisional Company by attaching a Section or more to each Company attached to Brigades.

   (7). The guns of this system will be moved forward by corresponding bounds to the Forward and Rear Guns.

3. The importance of having a Sub-Group Commander at each attacking Infantry Battalion H.Q. was brought out. Companies have now been organised with two Sub-Group Commanders, one of which, will be attached to each Attacking Infantry Battalion.

4. Some Companies did not make full use of Transport. It must be impressed on Infantry Commanders that a Section man-handling equipment and S.A.A. when fully loaded can only get forward 2000 rounds per gun and with their loads cannot keep up with an Infantry advance. Transport should, therefore, be used wherever possible. The assembly positions and routes of advance must, therefore, be left to the Machine Gun Officer and in some cases it may be necessary to deviate from the area to get a route to objective.

5. In an advance the fighting Section Transport will be under the control of the Sub-Group Commander and will be kept well forward.

6. Full use was made in some Companies of mounted Orderlies, but more use could have been made of this method of communication.

7. The choice of final objectives for guns and their tasks requires more consideration. The use of buildings in or out of villages, both for defensive and offensive purposes, requires more consideration. In this type of warfare a village is not the death-trap it was in trench warfare.

Lieut. Colonel,
Comdg. 51st (H) Bn. M. G. Corps.

7/11/18.

Confidential

War Diary
of
51st (H) Bn. M.G. Corps

from 1st to 30th November, 1918

Army Form C. 2118.

WAR DIARY
— of —
INTELLIGENCE SUMMARY.
(Erase heading not required.)

Instructions regarding War Diaries and Intelligence Summaries are contained in F.S. Regs., Part II. and the Staff Manual respectively. Title pages will be prepared in manuscript.

Place	Date	Hour	Summary of Events and Information	Remarks and references to Appendices
	1918. Nov.		Reference map :- Sheet 51A.	
	1		Battalion H.Q. and Companies at PAILLENCOURT.	
	2		Cleaning up billets and roads in vicinity.	
	3		Baths at IWUY.	
	4		Cleaning up, Inspections and Deficiencies.	
	5		Church Parades.	
	6		Cleaning up, Company Inspections and Training.	
	7		Commanding Officer's Inspection of Companies.	
	8		Training.	
	9		"	
	10		Church Parades.	
	11	1100	Armistice declared. General holiday.	
	12		Training.	
	13		General holiday - celebration of BEAUMONT HAMEL.	
	14		Training.	
	15		Inspection by G.O.C. 51st (Highland) Division.	
	16		Training - Battalion Route March.	
	17		Church Parades.	
	18		Training.	
	19		"	
	20		" Baths at HORDAIN.	
	21		"	
	22		" - Battalion Route March.	
	23		Church Parades.	
	24		Training.	
	25		" - Battalion Route March.	
	26		"	
	27		"	
	28		" - Preliminary Day for Divisional Sports.	
	29		"	
	30		Divisional Sports.	

[signature]
Lieut. Colonel,
Comdg. 51st (H) Bn. M.G. Corps.

M 10

Confidential

War Diary
of
51st Bn. M.G. Corps
for December, 1918.

Army Form C. 2118.

WAR DIARY
or
INTELLIGENCE SUMMARY.
(Erase heading not required.)

Instructions regarding War Diaries and Intelligence Summaries are contained in F. S. Regs., Part II. and the Staff Manual respectively. Title pages will be prepared in manuscript.

Place	Date	Hour	Summary of Events and Information	Remarks and references to Appendices
Field.	1918. Dec.			
	1.		Battalion at PAILLENCOURT.	
	2.		Training.	
	3.		Battalion Route March.	
	4.		Training.	
	5.		Salvage of S.A.A., R.E. Material, etc. in neighbourhood of village.	
	6.		Salvage continued.	
	7.		Battalion Route March.	
	8.		Training.	
	9.		Church Parades.	
	10.		Baths & Salvage.	
	11.		Salving. "A" Coy. on Range.	
	12.		Battalion Route March.	
	13.		Salving.	
	14.		Battalion Route March.	
	15.		Training.	
	16.		Church Parades.	
	17.		Baths & Salving.	
	18.		Training.	
	19.		Training.	
	20.		Battalion Route March.	
	21.		Training.	
	22.		Training.	
	23.		Training.	
	24.		Church Parades and Kit Inspections.	
	25.		Holiday.	
	26.		Training.	
	27-29.		Training.	
	30.		Baths and Training.	
	31.		General holiday.	

Lieut. Colonel,
Comdg. 51st (H) Bn. M. G. Corps.

1182

Confidential

War Diary

of

51st (H) Bn M.G. Corps

for January 1919

Army Form C. 2118.

WAR DIARY
or
INTELLIGENCE SUMMARY.

(Erase heading not required.)

Instructions regarding War Diaries and Intelligence
Summaries are contained in F.S. Regs., Part II.
and the Staff Manual respectively. Title pages
will be prepared in manuscript.

Place	Date 1919.	Hour	Summary of Events and Information	Remarks and references to Appendices
FIELD,	Jan. 1.		General Holiday.	
"	" 2.		Training.	
"	" 3.		Training.	
"	" 4.		Holiday.	
"	" 5th.		Baths & Church Parade.	
"	" 6.		Training.	
"	" 7.		Training.	
"	" 8.		Training.	
"	" 9.		Training.	
"	" 10.		Training.	
"	" 11.		Holiday.	
"	" 12.		Church Parade. Transport move to Famars. 09.00 hours.	
"	" 13.	8.30.	Transport move to Jemappes. B.H.Q. & Coys. march to Pave d'Hordain. Dismounted Personnel embus at Pave d'Hordain, 09.45 hours. Debus at Godarville, 16.00 hours.	
"	" 14.		Transport move to Godarville. Arrive Godarville 18.00 hours. Coys. Training.	
"	" 15.		Training & Baths.	
"	" 16.		Training.	
"	" 17.		Training.	
"	" 18.		Holiday.	
"	" 19.		Church Parade.	
"	" 20.		Training.	
"	" 21.		Training.	
"	" 22.		Training & Baths.	
"	" 23.		Training.	
"	" 24.		Training.	
"	" 25.		Holiday.	
"	" 26.		Church Parade.	
"	" 27.		Training.	
"	" 28.		Training.	
"	" 29.		Training & Baths.	
"	" 30.		Training.	
"	" 31.		Training.	

Comdg. 51st (H) Bn. M.G. Corps.

S E C R E T.　　　　　　　　　　　　　　　　　　　　Copy No ....

51st (H) BATTALION M. G. CORPS.

OPERATION ORDER No. 88.

Ref: maps:-　　　　　　　　　　　　　　　　　　　　　　　　　　10/1/19.
FRANCE. Sheets 45 & 46.
　"　　Sheet 51.A.

1. The 51st (H) Bn. M.G.C. will move to billets in THIEU-VILLE-SUR-HAINE Area, as follows :-

    (a). Dismounted personnel by bus on 13th Jan. 1919.
    (b). Transport by Road under orders of 1/8th Royal Scots, staging as under :-

        12/13th Jan.　　　...　　　FAMARS.
        13/14th　"　　　...　　　JEMAPPES.

2. Transport will march in the order "A", "B", "C", "D" Coys., Bn. H.Q., and will pass Main Bridge between ESTRUN and HORDAIN at 06.30 hours 12th inst.

3. Baggage wagons will be allotted on the scale of ONE per COMPANY and ONE for BATTALION H.Q. As much baggage as possible will be sent by Transport.

4. Transport will be rationed up to and including 14th inst.

5. Sufficient cooking utensils will be retained by Companies for the period they are detached from their Transport.

6. Personnel embussing on 13th inst. will carry two blankets per man.

7. Lorries will be allotted on the scale of ONE lorry or bus per TWENTY-FIVE men.

8. Officers will be distributed throughout the Convoy.

9. Baggage lorries will be allotted on the scale of ONE lorry for "A" & "C" Coys., ONE lorry for "B" & "D" Coys., ONE lorry for Battalion H.Q. and Q.M. Stores.

10. TWO men per COMPANY and FOUR men from BATTALION H.Q. will travel with the baggage lorries.

11. No baggage will be carried on the bus convoy.

12. Cycles will be distributed as under :-

        Per Company.　　　　　　　...　　　...　　SIX.
        No. 5 Sig. Section.　...　　　　　...　　　TWO.
        Battalion H.Q. Runners.　　　　　...　　　FOUR.
        Post Corporal.　　　...　　　　　...　　　ONE.
        Canteen.　　　　　　...　　　　　...　　　ONE.
        Q.M. Stores.　　　　...　　　　　...　　　ONE.

    and Companies, etc. will be responsible for cycles until further orders.

13. Personnel proceeding by lorry will carry rations for 13th inst. Rations for 14th inst. will be carried on baggage lorries.

14. Embussing will take place about 09.00 hours 13th inst. on the PAILLENCOURT - ESTRUN Road. Further orders will be issued later.

- 1 -

- 2 -

15. Lieut. M.G. TODD and 2/Lieut. J.C. McDERMOTT, MC. will act as embussing Officers.

16. Order of embussing will be :- Bn. H.Q., "D", "B", "C", "A" Coys.

17. Convoy will halt for 15 minutes, 1½ hours after starting and after every subsequent 2½ hours.

18. Approximate duration of journey - 7 hours.

19. "A" & "C" Coys. will debus at VILLE-SUR-HAINE.

    Bn. H.Q., "B" & "D" Coys. will debus at THIEU.

20. All Billets will be left clean and tidy. Certificates to this effect will be rendered to this Office before embussing.

21. In the new area Divisional H.Q. will be at CHATEAU BOCH, LA LOUVIERE, Sheet 4C, H.26.a.8.8.

22. A K N O W L E D G E.

                                            Capt. & Adjt.,
Issued at 10.45 hours.   51st (H) Bn. M. G. C.

Copies 1 - 4.   ...   Companies.
       5 - 6.   ...   51st (H) Div. "G" & "Q."
           7.   ...   1/8th R. Scots.
           8.   ...   Q.M.
           9.   ...   R.T.O.
          10.   ...   S.O.
          11.   ...   War Diary.
          12.   ...   File.

SECRET.   Copy No .....

51st (H) BATTN. M. G. CORPS.

AMENDMENT TO OPERATION ORDER No. 88.

The first two lines of para. 1 and paras. 18 & 19 are cancelled.

The Battalion will now move to billets in GODARVILLE.

A C K N O W L E D G E.

[signature]

Capt. & Adjt.,
51st (H) Bn. M. G. C.

Issued at 20.00 hours.
To all recipients of O.O.88.

SECRET.   Copy No......

51st (H) BN. M. G. CORPS.

AMENDMENT No.2 to OPERATION ORDER No.88.   12/1/19.

1. Paragraph 9 is cancelled.
   Baggage lorries will be allotted at the scale of ONE Lorry for "A" & "B" Coys. and Q.M. Stores & Battalion Orderly Room, "C" & "D" Coys.

2. Paragraph 14 is cancelled.
   Embussing will take place at 09.45 hours 13th inst. at PAVE D'HORDAIN.

3. Paragraph 16 is cancelled.
   Order of embussing will be, Bn. H.Q., "D", "C", "B", "A".

4. Baggage lorries will report as under:-
   "A" Coy., "B" Coy. & Q.M. Stores,
   ONE lorry each at ... 07.30 hrs.

   afterwards reporting to

   "B" Coy., "D" Coy. & Bn. Orderly Room. ... 07.45 "

5. Companies will have all baggage collected at a convenient spot to expedite loading.

   "B" Coy., "D" Coy., & Bn. Orderly Room will arrange for guides to conduct lorries to their respective baggage dumps.

6. Companies will parade ready to move off at 08.30 hrs.
   Order of March - Bn. H.Q., "D", "C", "B", "A".
   Head of Column at "D" Company's Q.M. Stores, facing East.
   Dress - Full Marching Order, with blankets.

7. A C K N O W L E D G E.

                                        Capt. & Adjt.,
                                        51st (H) Bn. M. G. C.

Issued at 15.15hrs.

Army Form C. 2118.

WAR DIARY
or
INTELLIGENCE SUMMARY.
(*Erase heading not required.*)

Instructions regarding War Diaries and Intelligence Summaries are contained in F. S. Regs., Part II and the Staff Manual respectively. Title pages will be prepared in manuscript.

Place	Date 1919	Hour	Summary of Events and Information	Remarks and references to Appendices
FIELD	Feb. 1.		Holiday.	
	" 2.		Church Parade.	
	" 3.		Training.	
	" 4.		Training.	
	" 5.		Baths & Training.	
	" 6.		Training.	
	" 7.		Training.	
	" 8.		Holiday.	
	" 9.		Church Parade.	
	" 10.		Training.	
	" 11.		Training.	
	" 12.		Baths & Training.	
	" 13.		Training.	
	" 14.		Training.	
	" 15.		Holiday.	
	" 16.		Church Parade.	
	" 17.		Training.	
	" 18.		Training.	
	" 19.		Baths & Training.	
	" 20.		Training.	
	" 21.		Training.	
	" 22.		Holiday.	
	" 23.		Church Parade.	
	" 24.		Training.	
	" 25.		Training.	
	" 26.		Baths & Training.	
	" 27.		Training.	
	" 28.		Training.	

Lieut. Colonel,
Comdg. 51st. (H) Bn. M.G. Corps.

D.A.D.V.S.
51st (H) Division

Herewith war diary for month of
March 1917.

E. J. Angler. Captain.
O.C.

1/1st HIGHLAND
MOBILE VET. SECTN.,
51st DIVISION.

No.............
Date... 3/4/19

www.ingramcontent.com/pod-product-compliance
Lightning Source LLC
Chambersburg PA
CBHW080847230426
43662CB00013B/2041